DRUG POLICY AND THE DECLINE OF AMERICAN CITIES

DRUG POLICY
AND THE DECLINE
OF AMERICAN CITIES

Sam Staley

Foreword by
Kurt L. Schmoke

Transaction Publishers
New Brunswick (U.S.A.) and London (U.K.)

Second printing 1993
Copyright © 1992 by Transaction Publishers,
New Brunswick, New Jersey 08903.

Library of Congress Catalog Number: 91-32570
ISBN: 1-56000-039-2 (cloth); 1-56000-718-4 (paper)
Printed in the United States of America

Library of Congress Cataloging-in-Publication Data

Staley, Sam, 1961–
Drug policy and the decline of American cities / Sam Staley.
    p. cm.
Includes bibliographical references.
ISBN 1-56000-039-2
1. Narcotics, Control of—Economic aspects—United States. 2.
Inner cities—United States. 3. Urban economics. 4. Drug traffic—
Economic aspects—United States. I. Title.
HV5825.S65   1992
363.4'5'0973091732—dc20
                                                            91-32570
                                                            CIP

To my parents, who taught me principles matter in public policy as well as in life.

To my great-granddaughter Lucia, who was to come later

J. B. Black

Contents

Figures and Tables

Figures

Tables

Foreword

In August 1991, the National Commission on AIDS released a report whose findings were both extraordinary and self-evident. The report acknowledged the strong link between intravenous (IV) drug use and the spread of AIDS. That was not new. What was new was the report's endorsement of needle exchange programs as a way of slowing the transmission of AIDS, both among drug users and from drug users to their sexual partners and children. Never before had a commission of such stature so boldly chosen public health over the criminal law in fighting a drug-related disease. AIDS does that. This devastating disease, for which, as of now there is no cure, has led many people to rethink their assumptions about national drug policy. It led me to rethink mine.

In 1988, I was on a panel of the U.S. Conference of Mayors. By then I had already served as Baltimore City State's Attorney, the City's chief prosecutor. In that role, I prosecuted thousands of drug offenders, including the murderer of a police officer on an undercover drug assignment. The officer was a friend of mine. His death, and the obvious futility of trying to prosecute our way out of addiction and drug-related crime, was the beginning of my search for a more rational and effective national drug policy. Then came the panel of the U.S. Conference of Mayors.

The panel was looking into the spread of AIDS in urban communities. The cities were (and still are) being especially hard hit by AIDS, with most of the victims being poor and minorities. (That trend has continued. In Baltimore, as of August 1990, 77 percent of the adult AIDS cases were African-American, 21 percent were white, and 1 percent were Hispanic.) The principal cause of transmission of AIDS in cities was needle sharing among IV drug users. I drew the conclusion that our nation could no longer ignore the connection between AIDS and drugs. AIDS had become a national health crisis, and at least in cities, IV drug use was its primary agent.

Since AIDS is a public health problem, it makes sense to treat drug abuse as a public health problem too. That may include, as the Commission suggests, carefully controlled and thoroughly evaluated needle exchange programs. It certainly includes recognition that committing endless resources to catch and incarcerate drug addicts is not going to slow the spread of AIDS. The only effective way to do that is to (1) arrest the practice of sharing dirty needles, and (2) give substance abusers the treatment they need to control and preferably end their addiction.

Unfortunately, our current national drug policy remains heavily oriented toward the criminal law and mired in failure. That has been the story of the War on Drugs for seventy six years. It is also why following my participation on the AIDS panel for the U.S. Conference of Mayors, I publicly declared that it was time for a national debate on decriminalizing drugs. I put the question this way: Should we continue to pursue a policy that has not worked for almost three quarters of a century or should we look for both a new strategy and new generals?

In the four years since I called for this debate, there have been some moves toward treating substance abuse as a public health problem. Many states are putting more money into prevention and treatment. And the federal government also is paying more attention to the need for treatment.

But those changes, while visible and newsworthy, are less important than what is going on in universities, think tanks, and conferences and quiet discussions among policy makers and writers. That is where the core of the debate on national drug policy is taking place. And it is from this careful, rational, and analytical work that changes in national drug policy will come.

This book is an excellent example of the kind of thoughtful analysis that is needed if we are to come up with a better policy for dealing with substance abuse and its attendant problems, such as AIDS. *Drug Policy and the Decline of American Cities* analyzes the devastating cost American cities are paying because of the War on Drugs.

The spread of AIDS is one such cost, but not the only one. The criminal justice system in many cities is breaking down under the strain of drug arrests and incarcerations. In 1989, the Baltimore Police Department arrested over nineteen thousand people for drug violations, a 100 percent increase over 1984. This enormous volume of arrests has kept the Baltimore City Jail under federal court supervision for years. I was only one of several mayors required to keep the city jail's population under a court imposed cap. It was not easy.

In 1991, the state of Maryland finally agreed to take over the city jail. That means better control and management of the prison population; but the underlying problems of overcrowded jails; overcrowded court dockets; a shortage of prosecutors, public defenders, and judges; and a lack of substance abuse treatment are bound to linger until drugs are made the responsibility of the surgeon general and not the attorney general.

The criminal justice system is but one of many urban institutions being crushed under the weight of the War on Drugs. Almost every local government service, including schools, health care, juvenile services, and neighborhood development and job training, is underfunded because billions of dollars are being syphoned off to pay for a failed national drug strategy. That money would be much better spent if it were invested in public education, Head Start, prenatal care, and other services designed to help children grow up healthy, smart, and full of self-esteem. Such an investment would also be a giant step toward fairness and justice. There are now more African-American men under the control of the criminal justice system than there are in college. There is something profoundly wrong with a policy that leads to such an unjust outcome. The fact of the matter is, those with the least hope, the least education, and the least chance of achieving economic opportunity are bearing most of the burden of drug addiction, incarceration, and drug-related crime. That might change, however, with a national drug policy that emphasizes public health.

Advocates of treating drugs as a public health problem are frequently criticized for not explaining how such a policy would work. The criticism is unfounded. There are already many articles and books offering new ideas and strategies for controlling substance abuse.

I have supported a national commission to study how all drugs—legal and illegal—should be regulated. Generally, drugs would be regulated on the basis of "harm reduction." That means drugs that have been shown to have few dangerous side effects would be lightly regulated. Drugs known to cause death or injury would be more heavily regulated. A policy of harm reduction would include allowing public health professionals to give drugs to addicts as part of an overall treatment program. This policy is already being used successfully in the Netherlands.

The Dutch take a balanced approach to drug abuse that emphasizes treatment and minimizes risk to both the community and the drug user. The essential components of the program are (1) providing a network of medical and social services, (2) ensuring accessibility to these programs for drug abusers, (3) promoting social rehabilitation of addicts, and (4) implementing a comprehensive program of health education. Under this program, marijuana use has declined and overall drug use also appears to be declining. Cocaine use is thought to be up, but only slightly.

Why did the Dutch opt for a public health approach to drug abuse? Because they discovered what many of our national leaders choose to ignore: drug prohibition leads to huge profits and the creation of criminal enterprises determined to maintain those profits. The result, as you will discover in *Drug Policy and the Decline of American Cities*, is chaos and tragedy in our urban communities.

Today's policy makers would do well to heed the advice of August Vollmer, a one-time police chief and president of the International Association of Chiefs of Police, who said:

> Drug addiction ... never has and never can be solved by policemen. It is first and last a medical problem, and if there is a solution it will be discovered not by policemen, but by scientific and competently trained medical experts whose sole objective will be the reduction of this devastating appetite.

Those words are as true today as they were in 1936 when Vollmer wrote them. Unfortunately, they are not yet national policy. But that day must eventually come, and this book will help its readers understand why.

KURT L. SCHMOKE
Mayor, City of Baltimore

Preface

My interest and concern in public policy and urban development dates back many years even though my foray into an analysis of the drug problem did not begin until I began the research for this book. Although the manuscript itself was put together in a relatively short period of time, pulling together bits and pieces of research spanning several years, the ideas, themes, and arguments that underlie the analysis can be traced to an experience in the mid-1980s.

Crack was coming into widespread use and AIDS was in the forefront of public health concerns in 1985. Inner cities were reeling from the rapid outmigration of businesses and people, competing fiercely with suburban cities and villages with more undeveloped land and hospitable business climates. The economic future of inner-city neighborhoods seemed bleak and the future uncertain. Poverty, unemployment, homelessness, and an economic recession seemed to define the times and choices facing urban youth of the early and mid-1980s.

During this period, I also had the opportunity to work with a group of young inner-city high school students who were working to avoid becoming another statistic in a faltering central city economy and community. This group, the top of their class in the local public school system, was by all measures successful. These students stayed in school, performed well, and were active in school as well as in their neighborhood. They were articulate, ambitious, and hardworking. They knew the odds, accepted them, and put their energies into moving forward. These students were a far cry from the inner-city youth making front-page headlines as the drug war invaded their communities, neighborhoods, and schools.

For me, the images and statistics that are such an important part of a policy analyst's education now had names, experiences, feelings, and aspirations. Why did they choose this route rather than the seemingly more lucrative career in the drug trade and crime? How did public policy influence these decisions? What were the consequences for the future of central cities given the decisions made by these youth? This book attempts to answer these questions and fully explore the implications for central cities and urban development.

The final message in a complex analysis is simple: The drug war is ravaging our inner cities and compromising their ability to rebound economically and socially. More important, public policy has a profound impact on the pace, pattern, and content of urban development. Unfortunately, policies currently being pursued on the national, state, and local levels are significantly undermining the ability of the central city to regroup and become an integral part of metropolitan-wide economic development. This book, in effect, chronicles the steps leading to this conclusion and the reasoning that inevitably leads to its final recommendations.

In the course of writing a book, many debts accumulate. The most important in this project belong to the people who went to great lengths to review portions of the manuscript at varying stages of development. These people served as an important sounding board for the ideas and arguments that evolved into the final product. Although they clearly cannot be held responsible for any errors that may remain, the book is infinitely better because of their attention and interest.

Thus, I owe substantial debts to Fletcher Mangum, Cal McKenzie, James Ostrowski, Richard Wagner, John Blair, Ola Oyefusi, David Boaz, Sheldon Richman, Nicole Verrier, Dave Gallaher, and Bernard Baltic. These credits are not meant to ignore the valuable insights I received from dozens of discussions with family, friends, and colleagues over the years that have contributed to the final manuscript.

Many of the ideas evolved while I was a graduate student in the Center for Study of Public Choice at George Mason University. The analytical framework linking property rights, public policy, and economic growth was directly tied to the support, encouragement, and disciplined direction I received from faculty in the center and in the Department of Economics, most notably Richard Wagner, Robert Tollison, Mark Crain, Jack High, Don Lavoie, and from the writings of James Buchanan, F.A. Hayek, and Ludwig Von Mises. Richard Dennis should be singled out as instrumental in the evolution of this project. In many ways, this book would not have been written without his interest, concern, and support. I owe similar debts to Father Robert Sirico, Kris Mauren, Alex Chafuen, and John Blundell whose interest in the project at an early stage were extremely important in its initiation.

I also would like to thank the editors at Transaction Publishers who decided this book's message was worth publishing and improved its readability. Finally, but by no means least, I want to thank my wife who had to endure the seemingly endless hours spent compiling, writing, and rewriting the manuscript.

PART I

INSTITUTIONS, ECONOMIC GROWTH, AND THE MODERN CITY

1

Setting the Stage:
Central City Decline and the Rise of the
Drug Economy

On a warm August night, a five-month-old baby boy was sleeping contentedly in a Manhattan apartment. At about 12:30 A.M., a loud noise woke the child's grandmother. Another loud noise prompted an exodus of people from the apartment next door. Gunshots in this building on 109th Street are a common event. This time, however, a small child lay covered with blood in his bed, the victim of a "stray" bullet crashing through the wall from the adjacent apartment. The family, which had intended to move to an apartment in Queens at the end of the month, now plans to move back to their native Haiti. Once again, the American dream was shattered by violence.

In New York, six children ranging from nine years old to only five months were shot by "stray" bullets during a two-week period in the summer of 1990. Four died. In each case, the bullets were intended for someone else and details of the shootings remained "vague." During the last week of July, 1990, an average of two hundred shots per day were reported to the New York Police Department.

Few causes for this increase in violence can be pinpointed precisely. James Q. Wilson, a leading criminologist, observed that "the best we can do is speculate," but suggested that most of the violence is drug-related.[1] Instrumental in this rise in violence appears to be the role of organized

3

gangs. Drug-driven people, heavily armed, translate into "gang warfare" that "has ceased being 'West Side Story' and has become instead Beirut."[2]

Moreover, throughout the country, reports of violence and murder are on the rise. In almost all cases, the rise is being attributed to drug-related violence. As a result, the illicit drug industry has risen to the forefront of contemporary public policy debate. Few, however, have attempted to thoroughly analyze the role of the illicit drug industry in urban economies and explain the intricate interdependence between contemporary, im-poverished inner cities and the rising importance of a drug-industry culture.

Virtually every corner of the American society is influenced by illicit drugs in one way or another. In October 1990, one of the nation's leading political figures, Washington, D.C. Mayor Marion S. Barry was sentenced to six months in prison for cocaine possession. Barry was a prominent crusader in the drug war as America's national capital became the central battleground for the "hearts and minds" of inner-city residents. In the end, "the enemy" was so strong that even the highest ranked "generals" were corrupted. As Barry was sentenced in federal court, the mayor lamented the "American injustice system," claiming he was the victim of a racist conspiracy against black leaders.[3]

In Kentucky, Gatewood Galbraith, an attorney turned gubernatorial candidate, electioneered on a platform of legalizing the sale and produc-tion of marijuana. In some counties, 40 percent of local farmers grow marijuana to stave off unemployment and poverty.[4] Indeed, Galbraith sees the marijuana industry as a potential tool to revitalize Kentucky's sagging rural economy. Given that marijuana is Kentucky's largest cashcrop, valued at over $1 billion, Galbraith's position does not seem that distant from political acceptability.

Public concern over drug abuse in the United States is clearly reflected in the results of recent public opinion polls. The George Gallup organi-zation found that the percentage of people indicating that drug abuse was "the most important problem facing the country" soared from only 2 percent in 1985 to 38 percent in 1989.[5] In contrast, while it was the second largest category, only 10 percent of the respondents believed poverty was the most important problem. In an independent Media General/Associ-ated Press poll, 61 percent of the respondents indicated "drugs" were "the most important problem facing this country today" compared to the federal deficit, the economy, the environment, and homelessness.[6]

The rising importance of the drug problem in the eyes of the American public may well be connected to its link to children and education. In fact, public opinion polls reveal that the American public believes drug use tops the list of the "biggest problems" public schools must deal with.[7]

Drug use and trafficking are widespread in the United States. The prevalence of drug use during the twentieth century even resulted in titling a widely regarded history of U.S. narcotic control *The American Disease*.[8] Indeed, of a population of about two hundred and forty million people, at least twenty million Americans currently admit using marijuana regularly, another six million are estimated to use cocaine periodically, and between eight hundred thousand and nine hundred thousand use or have used heroin. This contrasts with over one hundred million alcohol drinkers and another fifty million smokers. In many social circles, drugs as disparate as alcohol and cocaine are used routinely.

The prevalence of drug use, illegal, legal, or prescription, has generated a large subeconomy earning hundreds of billions of dollars per year. The retail value of illicit drug sales alone exceeds $100 billion and is by most accounts a growing market.[9] Cocaine profits may have exceeded $80 billion already.[10] Technical innovations such as "crack," or rock cocaine, have reached even further into our social fabric by making mind-altering substances even more accessible to children and the poor in urban areas.

Moreover, marijuana is America's largest cash crop. In 1986, the National Organization for the Reform of Marijuana Laws (NORML) calculated that the estimated value of marijuana crops totaled $26.7 billion.[11] In contrast, the estimated value of corn for grain was $10.8 billion, hay $9 billion, soybeans $9 billion, and wheat $4.8 billion. California, Hawaii, Oregon, Kentucky, and North Carolina each produced over a billion dollars worth of marijuana. The Drug Enforcement Administration (DEA) calculates that the annual value of the domestic marijuana harvest exceeds the NORML estimates, reaching $41 billion.[12]

In the midst of the widespread use (and abuse) of drugs in American society, and the huge underground economy it generates, twentieth-century public policy has consistently attempted to thwart its development. Indeed, the current Reagan-Bush "War on Drugs"—a policy of complete prohibition (except for highly restrictive medical uses)—represents a well-financed attempt to use criminal law to destroy the illegal drug economy via the principle of law and order. The combined direct cost of the "Drug War" on local, state and federal levels is expected to exceed $12 billion in 1990.[13]

The focus of this book is the strategic use of drug prohibition to control drug use and the implications for economic development in urban areas. These two issues are so thoroughly intertwined that, from an economist's viewpoint, their separation is incomprehensible. Indeed, many of the ill effects of the drug trade are linked directly to attempts to eliminate the market for illicit drugs. Through attempts to restrict the supply of drugs, governments on all levels have created the avenues for elaborate, sophisticated, and often violent black markets that support and promote their use. Thus, despite the tendency to relegate drug abuse and drug use problems to physiological research and health care specialists, a surprising amount of economic analysis can be used to better understand the contemporary drug problem.

This book will further argue that drug prohibition undermines the process of economic development in America's cities. The social costs of maintaining the underground drug economy through prohibition far outweigh the potential social costs of deregulation as an alternative. In effect, the unintended consequences of the drug war are so pervasive that the economic and cultural future of American cities is jeopardized.

The Social Costs of the Drug Economy

The social costs of drug abuse and the drug war can be measured in several ways. The most prominent are the costs to economic productivity, public health, and civil liberties. The most common, of course, are attempts to count the number of drug addicts and calculate their lost productivity. Indicators of the ill effects of drugs are also evident in the emergency rooms of hospitals as drug users overdose on their drug of choice, experience complex chemical and physical reactions from multiple drug use, or suffer physical reactions to poor quality street drugs. Still others include in their calculus the loss of civil liberties resulting from a wholesale war on drugs that sacrifices rights to privacy, property, and freedom of expression to ensure some obedience to "law and order."

Most observers are discovering that the consequences of the drug war move beyond the traditional "body count" of overdose deaths or emergency room visits. The costs of drug abuse and the drug war must include crimes committed to generate enough income to sustain drug use and the costs of "enforcing" contracts on the street, usually through violence. The rise of gang-related violence in many major cities, the spread of gangs to new markets in smaller cities, and the rising prominence of drug-related murders in cities (sometimes as high as 80 percent of all murders) are all costs of the drug war.

Yet, as disparate as these indicators appear, they are related. They all provide a glimpse of the wrenching social and economic transformations experienced by central cities in recent years. The malaise of America's cities is at least a partial reflection of how urban economies have adapted to several decades of economic decline. The drug economy represents a stilted, perverse attempt at economic rejuvenation.

More important, the rising prominence of the drug economy in central cities reflects the destruction of the institutional framework necessary to encourage and promote sustained economic development. Ironically, the policies that form the core of the Drug War strategy are hastening the destruction of central city economies by abrogating the institutions that are most likely to lead to economic rejuvenation: private property, respect for civil liberties, and smoothly operating markets.

An important theme running through this book is that the drug war is unwinnable. This observation is not new or unique. In fact, as the following chapters will detail, several observers and critics of the drug war have already reached this conclusion. The argument in the following pages differs from earlier critiques by moving beyond the cost-benefit analysis to explore the interrelationships between public policy and economic development. Social and economic progress depends on a crucial set of institutions that are being systematically destroyed by our current drug war strategy and contemporary economic development policy in American cities. The implications of this critique of drug policy are that the Drug War is not just unwinnable, but economically and socially counterproductive.

The ways in which public policy undermines the processes necessary for encouraging productive economic and social development requires an understanding of the changing economic environment of central cities. Central city decline is a necessary (but not sufficient) condition for the expansion and growth of the drug economy. As later chapters will detail, the decline of the central cities and the inability of urban areas to adapt to the complexities of the late twentieth century urban economy are import- ant for understanding the supply-side aspects of drug trafficking.

Indeed, without the complex transportation and communications sys- tems available through many of America's largest central cities (such as

New York, Los Angeles, or Miami), drug trafficking would be far more cumbersome and expensive. Drug trafficking, in fact, is extremely well suited to the "new city" transformed from a traditional manufacturing to a high-technology, advanced services economic base.

Two elements make up the current drug problem in the United States. The first is the most talked about: the demand side. Americans enjoy and want to use drugs of all kinds. This demand encourages drug producers to supply illicit drugs to drug users through a black market if the price is high enough. Unfortunately, an approach that emphasizes only the demand side of the problem is extremely narrow, ignoring many more important and salient consequences of the drug economy. Indeed, many of the costs of the drug economy stem directly from the growth and development of the supply side, or drug trafficking.

The problems often associated with drug trafficking and the drug economy are largely urban in character. Drug traffickers tend to recruit in densely populated urban areas. Major cities serve as principal distribution centers for a myriad of drug trafficking organizations, from small street-level retailers to mid-level wholesalers to large organizations operating as cartels. While the user population tends to be more decentralized, drug trafficking tends to be centralized, and retailing tends to be very hierarchical. Central cities provide a variety of natural defenses against detection by law enforcement authorities.

Unfortunately, lost in the anecdotal news stories about individual dealers, drug abusers, law enforcement personnel, and other victims, is the story of how central cities have provided a lucrative supply of labor to black marketeers. Public policies have created a vast underground economy that fuels a perverse form of economic development in many inner-city neighborhoods, undermining a wide range of social and cultural institutions that are necessary to sustain productive communities. The true consequences of the drug economy and the startlingly persistent attempts to destroy it through an "all out war" on drugs are destroying the processes most likely to lift the central city out of its depressed state.

Public policy plays a preeminent role in defining what activities will be permitted or encouraged. Yet, if policy is inconsistent with the will of large segments of the population, the results can be catastrophic, leading to the degeneration of entire societies. The remainder of this chapter will set the stage for a more thorough and comprehensive analysis of the link between the drug economy, inner-city economic development, and public policy in later chapters. In fact, an important element in understanding the growth and importance of the drug economy is understanding the recent economic and social transformations that most of America's central cities have undergone over the past three decades.

The Decline of Central Cities

The drug economy is directly tied to the fortunes of central cities. Indeed, a recent report by the U.S. attorney general observes that the drug distribution network in the United States centers around a few specific major cities that serve as primary importation nodes. Heroin traffickers, for example, use New York as a primary port of entry; Los Angeles dominates marijuana trafficking; and Miami serves as a primary port for cocaine. These preferences for cities shift with the relative safety of trafficking and contacts with local populations.[14]

The drug economy flows far beyond a few, large cities that serve as ports of entry. Every major city in the United States reports major increases in drug trafficking and drug abuse during the 1980s. Since the drug trade is service oriented, cities are uniquely suited for supporting retail, wholesale, finance, and distribution activities. Ironically, as this section will detail, the very changes that have forced cities to adapt to a technologically advanced economy and educated labor market provide an ideal climate to promote drug trafficking in the hardest hit areas of the inner cities.

Understanding the interconnection between illegal drugs and the changing fortunes of American cities provides a unique perspective on public policy in urban areas. The recent decline and tentative resurgence of traditional central cities provides an important, if not essential, context for understanding the growth and persistence of the drug economy. In particular, recent trends in demographics and economic development have created large urban labor markets characterized by fewer and lower-paying jobs.

Decentralization of Population and Employment

The 1950s and 1960s witnessed a startling out-migration of the urban middle-class population to suburban communities. Although central cities have always experienced a degree of out-migration as wealthier classes moved beyond the congestion and dense residential areas of cities, the post-World War II era significantly increased its pace. Several reasons for this out-migration have been isolated by urban scholars.

The most important may have been the steady emergence of a wealthy middle class.[15] The manufacturing boom resulting from post-World War II "pent-up demand" and the worldwide rebuilding of war-ravaged economies created demand for U.S. manufacturing goods on an unprecedented scale. The pillars of industry during the 1950s and 1960s were traditional manufacturing economic sectors such as steel, automobiles, textiles, rubber, and plastics. A high degree of unionization ensured that as long as demand for American products in these industries continued, wages would steadily increase.

The result was the emergence of a substantial middle class that chose to exercise its new economic power by moving to less dense suburban areas. Wealthy and middle income households increasingly looked toward rural areas to provide an "escape" from the congested, noisy city. The demand for more spacious and "orderly" neighborhoods resulted in the emergence of predominantly residential suburban communities. As these communities flourished, they quickly established rules and regulations over land use to ensure that more traditional citylike features would not encroach upon the upstart bedroom residential neighborhoods.

Equally important in this demographic shift was federal policy designed to stimulate home ownership. The Federal Housing Authority began guaranteeing private home mortgages in 1934, eventually reducing minimum down payments for a single-family home from almost one third to less than 10 percent.[16] The creation of several mortgage guarantee associations for veterans and farmers also helped reduce the lending rate for new home owners.

A final contribution to the out-migration of families and, eventually, businesses, was the development of the interstate highway system.[17] Most users of interstate highways are local residents commuting into the city for work, shopping, or entertainment. Indeed, the ability to commute from a central city office to a suburban home has become a prominent feature of recent attempts to measure the importance of suburban "amenities" in explaining residential location decisions.[18]

Accompanying the out-migration of residential populations has been the emigration of businesses. New firms are more likely to start up in outlying suburban and rural areas than in central cities. To some extent, this is a natural outgrowth of the out-of-the city movement. As increas-

ingly large portions of central city residents moved out, retail and conve-
nience businesses followed. Indeed, the growth of suburban malls can be
seen as an attempt to recapture the shopping density necessary for small
shops to thrive in the more decentralized and inherently hostile suburban
areas. Businesses, particularly personal service and retail, tend to move
closer to their natural market: the broad-based, middleclass.

Suburbs, then, are increasingly taking up citylike characteristics. Office space is in high demand in suburban areas, while many central cities
market empty office buildings.[19] Poverty, homelessness, crime, and unemployment are also becoming important features of suburban cities as
they mature.[20] Ring cities have sprouted around the beltways of many
major metropolitan areas, competing for new residential development as
well as new business development. Suburbs are thus major competitors
with central cities for people and jobs.

More disturbing, however, has been the willingness of firms that do not
depend on a local base to locate or start up in suburban areas. In some cases,
these location decisions reflect the requirements of modern industry. High-
technology manufacturing facilities, for example, desire large single story
buildings that are difficult to find and expensive to build in central cities.

High-technology firms are also driven by qualitative aspects of plant sites.
Environmental conditions and "quality of life" characteristics of a particular
site may figure prominently in a high-tech executive's decision matrix when
he searches for a new site.[21] More important, high-technology firms have
formed the core of recent job creation. From 1972 to 1981, for example, high
technology firms accounted for 87 percent of the growth in the manufacturing sector in the United States.[22] By 1981, hi-tech firms claimed 27 percent
of all manufacturing employment in the United States.

Many of these new high-technology firms are small businesses.[23] Overall,
the average employment size of firms has decreased since the early 1970s.
Firm decisions are thus much more closely tied to the subjective valuations
of the owners or CEO. Many times, a new firm or branch will be established
according to the personal preferences of the executive in charge rather than
the calculus of a larger firm's accounting department.

The Changing Role of the City

Three decades of steady suburbanization and the growth of suburban
businesses have created a system of "ring cities." These cities are often

substantial, exceeding one hundred thousand residents at times, and exist as separate entities largely independent of the central city.

The full effect of the decentralization of population and employment was not fully discernible until research on suburbanization and the problems of central-city stagnation began to detail and measure the extent of urban decline. One of the first comprehensive examinations of urban growth and decline was published in the early 1980s using data from the early to mid-1970s.[24] Katherine Bradbury, Anthony Downs, and Kenneth Small analyzed over one hundred of the country's largest metropolitan areas and attempted to isolate the causes of decline and stagnation. By developing several indicators of distress and decline, they were able to develop a typology of metropolitan areas and differentiate between trends occurring in the central city and trends on a metropolitan level.

The authors found that of the 121 metropolitan areas in their survey, only 36 percent could be characterized as having a growing city and growing metropolitan areas. Thus, almost two-thirds of the central cities in the largest U.S. metropolitan areas were in a state of decline or stagnation. Moreover, the second largest group of metropolitan areas consisted of stagnant cities within growing metropolitan areas or severely declining cities in growing metropolitan areas (42 percent). Another 26 metropolitan areas (21 percent) could be characterized by declining or stagnant central cities in declining metropolitan areas.

Katherine Bradbury later extended the group's analysis to include 1980 census data.[25] Unfortunately, the trends were just as discouraging. The revised analysis focused on 153 cities with populations over 100,000 in 1980. Only 63, or 41 percent, gained population over the decade, while 90 lost population.

The declines in population, however, also reflect declines in employment. In fact, the shifts in employment and population can be rather dramatic. For example, from 1953 to 1980, employment increased and then decreased in the major cities of New York, Philadelphia, and Boston (table 1.1). Employment in New York climbed from almost 3 million in 1953 to 3.3 million in 1970, only to fall to below the levels of the 1950s by 1980. The same trends in employment growth and decline are evident in Philadelphia and Boston, although Boston did not appear to have declined as significantly.

General trends in employment, however, mask significant changes in the composition of employment. During the post-World War II period, dramatic shifts in employment occurred within the national economy.[26] In 1948, service-producing industries employed 58 percent of all nonfarm workers while manufacturing industries employed 35 percent. By 1987, service industries employed more than 75 percent of the nation's work force, while manufacturing's share declined to under 20 percent.[27] Manufacturing as a proportion of total employment—the traditional mainstay of low-skilled workers that was the primary drawing card for cities in the late nineteenth century—declined precipitously in all three cities from 1953 to 1980. The largest decline occurred in Philadelphia, where manufacturing employment as a proportion of total employment fell from 50 percent in 1953 to 27 percent in 1980.

Yet, the proportion of information-processing jobs as a percentage of total employment increased significantly. These jobs—which require more education and skills than traditional manufacturing jobs—began to dominate urban economies during the 1980s. Indeed, these jobs accounted for over half of employment in Boston and Suffolk County, Massachusetts. Even with New York City's historical dominance as a center of international finance and personal services, information-processing jobs increased to 45 percent of the total work force from only 22 percent in 1953.

TABLE 1.1
Employment Changes in New York, Philadelphia, and Boston, 1953 to 1980

City	1953	1970	1980
Employment (in thousands)			
New York	2,977	3,350	2,866
Philadelphia	788	772	628
Boston (Suffolk Cty)	402	465	437
Percent in Manufacturing			
New York	40%	29%	23%
Philadelphia	50	38	27
Boston (Suffolk Cty)	32	22	17
Percent in information Processing			
New York	22%	35%	45%
Philadelphia	12	28	43
Boston (Suffolk Cty)	22	42	53

Source: U.S. Bureau of the Census, Current Population Survey, March 1982 and County Business Patterns, 1970, 1980. Reported in John D. Kasarda, "Urban Change and Minority Opportunities," in The New Urban Reality, ed. Paul E. Peterson (Washington, D.C.: Brookings Institution, 1985), 48, table 3.

These trends in the composition of jobs were not restricted to a few large cities. Indeed, they were generalized across cities in different regions of the country. Although some cities experienced a general growth in jobs (at least one third in the analysis mentioned earlier), in almost every case, knowledge-intensive jobs increased at a faster rate. John D. Kasarda calculated the growth of entry-level jobs and knowledge-intensive jobs in several cities from census data (table 1.2). The results demonstrate that entry-level jobs declined precipitously in most large cities and knowledge-intensive job growth increased at a faster rate in every city.

The largest declines in entry-level jobs were reported in cities located in the Midwest and Northeast,[28] but the rate of job creation in the "new" service economy was significantly more rapid in all cases. Thus, even though Houston posted a net gain in entry-level jobs of 73 percent, the number of knowledge-based jobs increased by 119 percent.

The problems of central cities are not narrowly structural. Although the transformation of the national economy into a services and high-technology manufacturing economy placed many central cities at a comparative disadvantage, many sectors have chosen to move out of the central city altogether. For example, in his examination of cyclical variations in urban economies, George E. Peterson analyzed 53,929 establishments from Dun and Bradstreet data files in three sectors of the economy: machine tools, electronic components, and motor vehicles.[29] An analysis of the average annual growth rates of employment revealed that, in the machine tool industry, employment declined by 2.4 percent per year from 1972 to 1982 in central cities but increased by 4 percent per year in the suburbs. While employment declined in the motor vehicles industry, the decline was only 3.7 percent per year in the suburbs, while central cities experienced a decline of 6.5 percent per year.

The electronic components industry, in contrast, increased employment in central cities by 2.2 percent over the same time period, while suburbs registered only a 0.5 percent increase. These jobs, however, require more skills and education than the more traditional manufacturing sectors, particularly motor vehicles, which experienced the most dramatic declines.

A slightly broader application of this same principle is found in table 1.3. Taking ten metropolitan areas, David Birch estimated the job loss and gain rates for the period 1972 through 1975. As the table illustrates, job losses are relatively stable between central cities and suburbs. The key difference appears to be the gain rates for central cities and suburbs.

TABLE 1.2
Job Growth in Selected Cities, 1970 to 1980

| City | Percent Employment Growth, 1970-1980 | |
	Entry Level	Knowledge Intensive
New York	-38.2	24.9
Philadelphia	-32.9	37.8
Baltimore	-32.4	20.6
Boston (Suffolk Cty)	-22.6	33.3
St. Louis	-18.2	-26.3
Atlanta (Fulton Cty)	-12.1	35.6
Houston (Harris Cty)	73.8	119.4
Denver	14.5	91.4
San Francisco	-10.2	46.8

Source: Census data reported in Kasarda, "Urban Change," 50, table 4.

Suburban Hartford, Baltimore, Charlotte, Dayton, and Houston each registered double-digit increases in jobs during this time period. In addition, Boston, Worcester, and Rochester experienced net gains of at least 9 percent. In contrast, only the central cities of Charlotte and Houston experienced double-digit increases in jobs. Moreover, none of the other central cities could boast at least a 9 percent increase in jobs. Thus, while every suburb experienced a net gain of jobs (comparing loss rates and gain rates), every central city except Houston experienced a net decline from 1972 to 1976. Birch notes that, given these job loss and gain rates, a pattern of employment dispersal to "lower-density settings" appears with "an apparent lack of interest in the traditional business areas."[30] Moreover, declining cities tend to become more dependent on services and small businesses, suggesting that larger employers are more willing to locate in more prosperous communities than in declining ones.[31] Small businesses, in contrast, tend to be more locally oriented. Thus, "larger, frequently manufacturing-oriented businesses are expanding their employment base in economically prosperous, growing areas and are, at the margin, abandoning the older areas as sites to do business."[32] These results further confirm Peterson's earlier analysis concerning employment changes in specific industries. Motor vehicle and machine tools, for example, tend to be older manufacturing-oriented firms.

This migration of employment outside the central city can be seen in more recent data for selected cities collected by the U.S. Department of

Labor (table 1.4). Aggregating employment data in services, wholesale trade, retail trade, finance, insurance, and real estate provides a rough estimate of how dominant the service industry has become in many cities and metropolitan areas. These data, however, exclude construction, government, transportation, communications, and public utilities. Nevertheless, the other sectors clearly dominate employment in the central cities. In fact, central cities consistently have lower concentrations of employment in manufacturing jobs when compared to their metropolitan areas. Moreover, cities that have experienced a great deal of recent growth (e.g., those in the South and West) tend to have the lowest concentrations of manufacturing employment. These data further confirm the trends and shifts emphasized in the earlier sections.

Thus, the wrenching transformation of the American economy to the high-tech, globalized economy combined with growing suburban communities has radically altered the function of the central city. The central city has not been replaced but has been challenged by the prospect of adapting to a new role within the metropolitan hierarchy. As John Kasarda notes, cities have always had a valuable social and economic function,

> but changing technological and industrial conditions . . . alter these functions over time. In this regard, it must be remembered that blue-collar job opportunities expanded most rapidly in the largest and oldest cities during a transportation and industrial era that no longer exists. . . . Modern advances in transportation and communication technologies, the spread of population and public services, and changing modes of production organization have virtually wiped out the comparative advantages of major metropolitan cities as locations for large-scale manufacturing and warehousing facilities.[33]

In many cases, the central city is no longer the dominant force driving economic growth and development within the metropolitan area. These changes and shifts have had a dramatic impact on the employment prospects for central city residents. More important, the economic and social transformation of the central city has important implications for understanding the rise of the underground economy and, more specifically, the drug economy.

Drugs and the Central City

The bottom line for central cities has been reduced competitiveness and dramatically altered internal structure of urban labor markets. Moreover, traditional manufacturing cities have had a difficult time adjusting to these new realities. Economic growth continues to be sluggish and central city populations have become increasingly poor relative to the more affluent suburbs. Indeed, the fastest growing component of central city populations is the underclass.[34]

TABLE 1.3
Job Gain and Loss Rates for Central Cities and Suburbs
1972-1976

Area	Job Loss Rate (in percent) Cemtral		Job Gain Rate (in percent) Central	
	City	Suburb	City	Suburb
Hartford	9.3	7.9	5.7	10.7
New Haven	7.3	6.7	5.6	6.9
Baltimore	7.7	7.9	6.0	13.3
Boston	9.7	7.3	8.3	9.1
Worcester	6.0	6.1	4.7	9.0
Rochester	6.9	6.9	6.5	9.4
Charlotte	9.1	8.3	10.9	13.0
Dayton	8.4	6.6	6.8	11.0
Greeneville	10.2	7.2	6.5	6.5
Houston	8.1	10.7	14.4	19.7

Source: David L. Birch, *Job Creation in Cities* (Cambridge, Mass: M.I.T. Program on Neighborhood and Regional Change, 1980), 11, table 3-2.

One of the most important urban phenomena that has emerged over the past several decades has been the growth of the underground or informal economy. With the significant out-migration of population and jobs since the late 1950s, central city residents have been faced with declining opportunities and many with increasing isolation. Recently, social scientists have begun to concentrate on the problems of minority communities that appear increasingly isolated from job opportunities. As sociologist William J. Wilson notes in his most recent book on the underclass, these communities are often socially isolated from the mainstream metropolitan society.[35]

TABLE 1.4
Distribution of Employment in Selected
Metropolitan Areas and Cities: 1988
(percent)

| Area | Metropolitan Area | | Central City | |
	Manufac-turing	Trade and Service	Manufac-turing	Trade and Service
Baltimore	15.0	48.0	11.9	56.4
Chicago	19.5	52.7	18.8	52.5
Cleveland	20.9	49.6	22.7	43.0
Dallas	19.4	50.2	14.9	58.7
Detroit	26.8	47.3	23.3	48.4
D.C.	4.5	48.5	3.0	47.6
Houston	11.6	51.8	10.0	56.4
Indianapolis	19.6	48.3	18.7	48.2
Los Angeles	22.0	47.9	21.6	51.1
New York	12.3	53.8	12.2	54.1
Philadelphia	17.8	50.8	12.5	54.5
Phoenix	15.6	52.3	14.2	55.3
St. Louis	19.0	52.8	22.0	47.2
San Antonio	8.6	51.5	8.4	53.5
San Diego	14.2	50.9	13.6	53.9
San Francisco	10.0	53.9	8.9	56.1

Source: U.S. Department of Labor, Bureau of Labor Statistics, *Geographic Profile of Employment and Unemployment, 1988* (Washington, D.C.: Government Printing Office, 1989), table 27.

Despite their social isolation, inner-city neighborhoods continue to survive and, in some cases, prosper. This prosperity and growth, however, has occurred through "informal" or extralegal means. Informal economic activity, for the purposes of this discussion, consists of the transactions and exchanges that take place outside of the legal system or legal institutions. An unregistered small tool shop operating out of someone's basement, for example, would be considered on informal business. Someone who is paid in cash to provide a service, such as electrical work or plumbing, where the transaction is not recorded for tax or legal purposes, would also be considered informal activity. Some forms of economic activity, such as drug trafficking, are defined as informal since the transaction is illegal. In some cases, the growth of informal activity, has been dramatic. The remainder of this chapter concentrates on the import-ance of informal economic activity in sustaining these neighborhoods.

Estimates of the size of the informal economy in the United States vary significantly, from only 3 percent of Gross National Product (GNP) to almost 30 percent.[36] For example, in 1987, the U.S. Department of Commerce estimated GNP at $4.5 trillion. Three percent of GNP would translate into an underground economy of around $130 billion. On the other extreme, an underground economy valued at 30 percent of GNP would generate an income of $1.3 trillion. A consensus seems to have emerged in the somewhat sparse literature on the underground economy that of a range around 10 percent of GNP is a reasonable estimate.[37] In other words, many experts suggest that the underground economy in the United States generated almost $450 billion in 1987. Moreover, many observers estimate that informal economic activity is increasing, partic-ularly in the industrialized countries of North America and Western Europe.[38]

Estimates of the underground economy vary significantly, largely because it has eluded precise definition.[39] Scholars focusing on the industrialized countries have tended to define underground employment and firms with respect to their legality. Most analysts, for example, have been more concerned about the effects of informal economic activity on tax revenues rather than its implications for inner-city economic devel-opment.[40] Thus, James Smith includes only those activities that are inherently legal in his estimates of the informal economy in his survey of underground economic activity.[41]

One of the most important trends found in the growing literature on informal economic activity is the correlation between informality and economic growth. In fact, scholars attempting to assess the cyclical variations in underground economic activity have discovered that infor-mality becomes more common in periods of low economic growth, strongly indicating that informality is tied to economic cycles.[42]

Most workers (employers) prefer work in the formal sector since their labor (contracts) is (are) protected and enforced by the formal legal system. The informal sector operates outside the legal economy, thus increasing the vulnerability of workers to unscrupulous employers or employers to a breach of contract. During times of recession or depression, workers may have little choice but to look for work in the informal sector. Similarly, businesses may find the informal sector the only alternative to closing their doors if informality allows them to reduce costs and remain competitive. In American cities, recent demographic and economic trends have pushed work and other economic activity in central cities outside normal formal or legal channels.

In New York, for example, the high cost of production and increasing tax burdens encouraged firms to either move to the suburbs or go underground during the 1980s.[43] Informality can be characterized by the degree people work in unregistered businesses or perform unregistered work, and the amount of unregistered economic activity detectable in the New York City economy is extensive and growing. In the apparel and garment industry, for example, the number of illegal "sweatshops" increased dramatically from only 200 in the early 1970s to over 3,000 by 1981.[44] Operating outside formal work rules and the legal system, sweatshops employed 50,000 workers and an estimated 10,000 additional workers through homework.

Informal activity is not isolated to garment and apparel workers in New York. Rather, the same study found the similar trends in other sectors of the local economy, such as electronics and furniture. An estimated 90 percent of all interior work and renovation by small construction companies in Manhatten was performed without permits.[45] In addition, the study found that many informal manufacturing firms represent a growth sector in New York. Thus, despite the out-migration of formal manufacturing firms, informal manufacturing facilities "represent one of the few sources of manufacturing jobs in the city, frequently demanding specialized skills."[46] Ironically, attempts to crack down on unregistered manufacturing firms may result in a more pervasive erosion of the city's manufacturing base.

Similar informal activity was found in the immigrant neighborhoods of Miami. In a detailed case study, Alex Stepick found two distinct informal sectors, one linked to the broader economy and the other operating in isolation.[47] Cuban immigration established links to the broader economy that facilitated the economic rise of Miami's middle-class Cuban community. The more recent arrival of Haitian refugees in the early 1980s, on the other hand, stimulated the creation of a largely segregated, isolated informal sector concentrated in a neighborhood referred to as "Little Haiti." As in New York, the largest concentration of informal work was found in the garment industry, construction, and restaurants.

The Haitian informal economy, in contrast to the Cuban informal sector, which works hand in hand with the broader economy, has constructed a "separate ethnic economy . . . distinct from the larger one and is fueled primarily by immigrant survival strategies."[48] Haitian immigrants have experienced severe isolation and discrimination from both the larger white society and the Cuban community. Thus, they have come to depend on themselves for economic progress rather than the more hostile, larger Miami economy. Almost one-third of the workers in Little Haiti are estimated to work in informal enterprises, although, for most, informal work serves as a supplement to wage labor rather than a replacement.

These examples provide illustrations of the methods used by communities to cope with economic and social decline. Much of the discussion on urban decline focuses on trends in numbers and what can be correlated with perceived patterns in aggregates. Little attention is paid to the coping strategies of residents in these depressed areas. The rise of the informal economy is, in essence, a reflection of the ways individuals cope with declining economic opportunities. Thus, as observers of Third World informal economies have emphasized, informality is reflective of shifts in attitudes, cultures, and values and often grounded in the way people interact with each other and the legal system.

Clearly, as the preceding discussion of urban decline has emphasized, residents of inner-city neighborhoods are experiencing declining economic opportunities. In many cases, the neighborhoods most dramatically affected are minority neighborhoods and urban blue-collar communities.[49] Faced with the out-migration of manufacturing jobs and other low-skilled employment, inner-city residents must cope with their new environments. In many cases, as the examples of New York and Miami illustrate, the coping strategies revolve around the creation of informal work and economic activity. In essence, workers and firms go underground and operate outside the legal system.

One of the clearest indicators of the informal activity may be labor force participation rates. Unlike unemployment rates, which measure the number of people who are unemployed but looking for work, labor force participation rates measure the degree to which members of a population or subgroup participate in the legal work force. In conventional analysis, the portion of the labor force not employed or looking for work is considered "discouraged." The increasing recognition of the informal sector in many areas of the country and in central cities, however, suggests that these people are more likely participating in informal work. Hence, the labor force participation rate reflects participation in the official or legal employment market. The employment in the two sectors (formal and informal) should be inversely related.[50]

Yet, to understand the implications of informality on labor force participation rates, knowledge of the impact of the transformation of urban systems in recent years is essential. The transition of cities from manufacturing bases to human-centered, knowledge-intensive economies has created a dual labor market where opportunities for low-skilled, low-educated populations are severely constrained. Since migration to the suburbs has been limited for minority and low-income populations, these neighborhoods represent ideal locations for informal activities. Columbia University's Saskia Sassen-Koob, an observer of New York's informal economy, noted that immigrant communities represent "collections of spatially concentrated resources that facilitate informal production or distribution of certain activities."[51]

Similarly, minority communities, particularly those dominated by young African-American youth, represent a rich source of human capital for informal industries.

Indeed, participation in the formal labor market has declined precipitously over the past two and one half decades (table 1.5). Minority teenage labor force participation rates have declined from over 70 percent in 1960 for eighteen and nineteen year olds to 55 percent in 1984, almost a 28 percent decline. Declines were also evident among young adults, as labor force participation rates declined 17 percent for twenty to twenty-four year olds and 9 percent for twenty-five to thirty-four year olds.

Most African-Americans end up in the official labor force by the time they reach their late twenties. This implies that at some point, they secure full-time work in the formal labor market. Yet, clearly for some, entry into the formal labor market is delayed substantially.

White labor force participation rates, on the other hand, have remained much more stable. In fact, participation rates for teenage whites increased over time, falling only after 1981 as the economy entered into a severe recession. The steep decline in labor force participation rates for minority sixteen and seventeen year olds in the late 1970s and early 1980s may also reflect steep unemployment rates that often doubled the rate for white teenagers.If the prospects for work look bleak, young workers are less likely to continue looking for work in the formal sector. Moreover, they remain even more susceptible to opportunities in the informal sector.

The full implications of the relationship between informal economic activity and labor market decisions of inner-city residents are reserved for chapters 4 and 5, but the link to the drug economy should be clear. Illicit drug trafficking now accounts for well over $100 billion by standard estimates, or over 40 percent of the income derived from underground economic activity.

TABLE 1.5
Civilian Labor Force Participation Rates
by Race and Age, 1960 to 1984

Race/Age	1960	1965	1969	1973	1977	1981	1984
Blacks & Others							
16-17 years old	45.6	39.3	37.7	33.6	31.0	30.0	27.0
18-19	71.2	66.7	63.2	61.3	57.5	54.1	55.4
20-24	90.4	89.8	84.4	81.4	77.7	76.6	77.2
25-34	96.2	95.7	94.4	91.4	90.4	88.3	88.2
Whites							
16-17 years old	46.0	44.6	48.8	52.7	53.8	51.5	47.0
18-19	69.0	65.8	66.3	72.3	74.9	73.5	70.8
20-24	87.8	85.3	82.6	85.8	86.8	87.0	86.5
25-34	97.7	97.4	97.0	96.2	96.0	95.8	95.4

Source: U.S. Department of Labor, *Employment and Training Report of the President* (Washington, D.C.: Government Printing Office, 1982; Ibid., *Employment & Earnings* 32 (January 1985). Reported in William J. Wilson, *The Truly Disadvantaged* (Chicago: University of Chicago Press, 1987), 42, table 2.7.

Data collected by the Federal Bureau of Investigation (FBI) clearly illustrates the dominance of cities in the drug economy. In 1988, offenses related to drug violations were 449.9 per 100,000 population for the nation as a whole.[52] For cities, however, offenses related to drug violations increased to 530.5 per 100,000. Cities with populations over 250,000 experienced a drug violation offense rate of 944.4 per 100,000. Suburban areas, in contrast, reported an overall drug violation rate of only 305 offenses per 100,000 population.

An indication of the extent of drug trafficking activity in cities is the arrest rates for drug sale or possession. In 1987, the National Institute of Justice established the Drug Use Forecasting program to help track the illicit drug trade in the United States. Twenty-two cities participate in the program by providing information on arrest rates and drug use by arrestees. Although very limited in scope, this data can provide information about the relative importance of drug trafficking in U.S. cities. Unfortunately, drug charges at the time of arrest are reported under an all-inclusive category "drug sale/possession," significantly reducing the usefulness of the information for tracking drug trafficking per se. Nevertheless, often arrests for possession are also linked to drug trafficking. In addition, the data are not adjusted for differing levels of enforcement. Some cities, for instance, may place more emphasis on drug enforcement than others.

As a general indicator, the data show that cities that have experienced relative economic declines in their central portions have high arrest rates for drug trafficking and possession (table 1.6). San Diego appears to be a significant exception, although its proximity to the Mexican border (a source for most imported marijuana) and its function as a port make the city a natural distribution center for illicit drugs. Detroit and Chicago, on the other hand, experienced substantial declines in their inner city even though their metropolitan areas prospered. San Antonio has the median arrest rate among this sample.

Cities arresting larger proportions of people for drug sales and possession were more likely to experience negative growth or slower growth than cities arresting smaller proportions of people for the same crime. Moreover, in each case, the central city grew at a slower pace than the metropolitan area. Even though the central city may have been growing, it was not able to grow as quickly as adjacent suburban areas. Thus, the relative position of the central city within the metropolitan area declined even further.

Interestingly, the major drug trafficking cities reported lower proportions of their total arrests devoted to drug trafficking than several other cities that experienced more severe central city declines. This may suggest that drug trafficking may be a smaller problem in these cities than news reports suggest, although the overall volume of drug trafficking may be significantly higher than in other, interior cities.

TABLE 1.6
Percentage of Arrests for Drug Charges

City	Arrested drug sale/ possession	Population Growth 1980 to 1986 City	Metropolitan
Major Drug Trafficking Cities			
Miami *	24	7.8	10.1
Los Angeles *	22	9.8	13.7
New York	18	2.7	2.4
Other Cities			
San Diego *	24%	15.9%	18.2%
Detroit	32	- 9.7	-3.2
Chicago	27	0.0	2.3
Houston*	26	8.4	17.2
Cleveland *	22	- 6.6	- 2.4
San Antonio	19	16.3	19.1
Philadelphia *	17	- 2.7	2.7
St. Louis	13	- 6.0	2.6
Phoenix	9	13.1	25.9
Dallas	3	11.1	24.7
Indianapolis	2	2.7	3.9

Source: Arrest data from National Institute of Justice. *1988 Drug Use Forecasting Annual Report* (Washington, D.C.: U.S. Department of Justice, Office of Justice Programs, March 1990), 24; growth rates calculated from population data from the U.S. Bureau of the Census.

* Represented largest percentage of arrests among violent, property, and nonproperty crime.

The data suggest that a link may exist between drug trafficking and economic development. The inability of central cities to adapt readily to the challenges of metropolitan economic development have created the supply-side conditions necessary to support the drug trade. Combined with the continued demand for illicit drugs, some inner-city neighborhoods are now fueled principally by the drug economy. This has dramatic implications for economic development in central cities and public policy on local, state, and federal levels. The remainder of this book will focus on developing this thesis in more detail.

An Economic Development Perspective

The analysis presented in this chapter has startling implications for public policy. The rise of the drug economy in inner cities and its attendant social costs are not solely a function of a nation's wild "addiction" to illegal drugs, or to prohibition. Rather, the drug economy is also a function of economic development in central cities.

The function of the central city has shifted dramatically over the past several decades from a center for economic growth to a centralized coordinating role for advanced services. Services now dominate the employment and industry mix of most central city cores. The drug trade is a service and distribution industry: very little production of most illicit drugs occurs within the United States. In cocaine trafficking, for example, virtually all of the growing and processing occurs in Latin America (often Bolivia and Colombia). Similarly, most of the opium growing and processing occurs in source countries in Southeast Asia. American central cities serve as the distribution hub for the multi-billion dollar drug trafficking industry in the United States.

More important, perhaps, is the growing importance of the drug economy in "capitalizing" the poorest sections of the inner-city economy. Higher-skilled manufacturing jobs paying well in previous decades are now located in suburban and exurban ring cities rather than in the central city. The jobs left in central cities are increasingly characterized as high-wage, high-skilled professional jobs and low-wage, unskilled minimum-wage jobs with few opportunities for immediate advancement. The drug economy offers an income-generating alternative for many of these underskilled inner-city residents, particularly young men.

Unfortunately, as chapter 5 details, the jobs that dominate the drug trade are contributing to the erosion of the life chances of their employees. The very jobs that seem attractive to a young man in his late teens or early twenties do not prepare him for the job he eventually takes for the rest of his life in the legal employment sector.

The government's current policy of complete drug prohibition must bear most of the responsibility for the erosion of the life chances of these inner-city laborers. Skyrocketing drug prices and the allure of drug industry employment result directly from a public policy of prohibition with respect to recreational drug use.

Yet, even if the illicit drug industry were eliminated tomorrow through comprehensive legalization, the problems of the inner city would persist. Central cities are inhospitable places for businesses in today's competitive environment. Public policy, then, must also concentrate on promoting economic and community development in inner cities. Yet, as chapter 3 will demonstrate, governments have produced significant obstacles to meaningful development here as well. The "War on Drugs" has allowed most analysts to ignore the consequences of public policy on urban economic development despite the fact that drug trafficking and economic development are interwoven.

The Plan of the Book

The remainder of this book develops these themes in more detail. The next two chapters develop the context for analyzing economic development in urban environments through a discussion of institutions and their role in allowing individuals to pursue diverse goals. The legal institutions and the values they promulgate are important for understanding the "constitutional" foundation of urban economic growth. More specifically, institutional restraints on government and guarantees of fundamental civil liberties provide the necessary conditions for successful entrepreneurship and economic development. The mechanics of this framework will be illustrated through an analysis of the economic environment in contemporary American cities, drawing inferences to the conditions that permit underground economies to flourish and grow. By implication, an analysis of the black market in illegal drugs becomes an exercise in constitutional economics and development theory.

Chapter 2 examines the relationship between institutions and economic growth. Institutions that protect the freedom to create and innovate also promote and sustain growth. This chapter provides a historical background important for understanding how public policy has altered incentives to innovate and subdue diversity in contemporary cities.

Chapter 3 extends the general discussion of institutions and growth to current trends in urban policy. The institutions that promote entrepreneurship and development are being weakened by the expansion of local government and the systematic attenuation of private property rights. This chapter discusses the role of rules and institutions in defining the "rules of the game" for exchange and transactions. These trends parallel changes in the respect for property rights in the urban drug economy. In essence, the rules constraining individual behavior are weakening in both the formal economy and the drug economy.

Chapter 4 provides an extensive discussion of the demand side of the drug economy. A brief history of drug use is included as well as an analysis of recent trends in drug use, addiction, and narcotics control. The persistence of illegal drug use is placed in context of other drugs widely used (and abused) in the United States. This chapter explores the relationship between drug use, drug abuse, and the ability of public policy to significantly affect consumption behavior.

The supply-side aspects of the drug economy are discussed in detail in chapters 5 and 6. Chapter 5 concentrates on the labor market for young drug traffickers in urban areas. The evidence suggests that drug trafficking reflects an economic decision by most of the participants, lending support to the general observation that the drug economy must be viewed in the context of urban economic development.

Chapter 6 focuses on the market structure of the drug trafficking industry. The effects of the recent War on Drugs is explored within the context of the responses and adaptation of trafficking organizations and individuals. This chapter, then, focuses more on how the employers of young traffickers described in chapter 5 operate and the likely effects of public policy.

Chapter 6 also discusses in-depth the role of public policy in determining the structure of the drug industry. In contrast to some observers of government policy and the drug economy, this approach emphasizes the role government plays in setting up the rules of the game for industry participants. Many of the most negative elements of the current drug economy are a direct consequence of the policies implemented to enforce drug prohibition. The rise of gangs and violent Colombian cartels is a direct outgrowth of an aggressive government strategy targeted at mid-level and high-level traffickers. This chapter will set the stage for a detailed discussion of the consequences of legalization as a policy option for limiting the social costs of illegal drug use.

Chapter 7 evaluates attempts to enforce drug prohibition laws. Trends in drug enforcement are tracked through arrest data on national and city levels. Levels of drug smuggling are discussed, as well as changes in smuggling strategies. This chapter also further accentuates the unique role cities play in the illicit drug industry. The chapter concludes with an assessment of the effects of the supply-side strategy pursued by law enforcement agencies on the national and local levels.

Chapter 8 assesses the arguments in favor of comprehensive decriminalization as a first step toward developing a more realistic and effective drug control strategy. The arguments favoring and opposing decriminalization are outlined and discussed. The chapter speculates on the potential consequences of adopting comprehensive decriminalization as a cornerstone of a national drug control policy.

Chapter 9 summarizes the main themes of the book with a special emphasis on economic development in inner cities. Insights into how urban markets work are fused with an analysis of the drug economy as it has prospered in inner cities. The conclusion attempts to integrate the themes of each of the earlier chapters as part of an overall framework for analyzing the drug economy, public policy, and the potential consequences for economic development.

Notes

1. Quoted in Todd S. Purdum, "Perpetual Crime Wave: 4 Childrens' Killings May Be Coincidental, But Crime is Up and Officials are Groping," *New York Times*, 1 August 1990, sec. B, p. 12.
2. Ibid.
3. "D.C. Mayor Gets 6 Month Prison Term," *Dayton Daily News*, 27 October 1990, sec. A, p. 8.
4. Mizzell Stewart III, "Candidate Hunts for Pot of Gold: Kentuckian Wants Marijuana Legalized," *Dayton Daily News*, 29 October 1990, sec. A, p. 4.
5. Timothy J. Flanagan and Kathleen Maguire, eds., *Sourcebook of Criminal Justice Statistics 1989* (Washington, D.C.: U. S. Department of Justice, Government Printing Office, 1990), 126, table 2.1.
6. Ibid; 127, table 2.2.
7. Ibid; p. 130, table 2.4.
8. David F. Musto, *The American Disease: Origins of Narcotic Control*, exp. ed. (New York: Oxford University Press, 1987).

9. Using data from the mid-1980s, a common estimate of the size of the illegal drug economy fluctuated around $80 billion. New data from drug seizures and the dismantling of large drug marketing organizations suggest that previous estimates of the drug economy significantly underestimated its actual size. Most observers now concede that the drug economy exceeds $100 billion. See James Ostrowski, "Thinking About Drug Legalization," *Policy Analysis No. 121* (Washington, D.C.: Cato Institute, May 1989).

10. Steven Wisotsky, *Beyond the Drug War: Overcoming a Policy Failure* (New York: Prometheus Books, 1990).

11. See "Marijuana in America: NORML's 1986 Domestic Marijuana Crop Report," *Common Sense for America* 2, no. 1 (Spring 1987): 11-12, 23, 26-34.

12. See "Nation's Richest Harvest: $41 Billion Just for Pot," *Omaha (NE) World-Herald*, 14 September 1989, p. 39.

13. U.S. Department of Justice, *Drug Trafficking: A Report to the President* (Washington, D.C.: Office of the Attorney General, August 1989), 3.

14. An extensive discussion of the trafficking organizations of major drug organizations is contained in U.S. Department of Justice, *Drug Trafficking*.

15. See the discussion in Dennis R. Judd, *The Politics of American Cities: Private Power and Public Policy*, 3d ed. (Glenview, Il: Scott, Foresman, 1988), 179-92.

16. Kenneth Jackson, *Crabgrass Frontier: The Suburbanization of the United States* (New York: Oxford University Press, 1985), 203-6.

17. Kenneth A. Small, "Transportation and Urban Change," in *The New Urban Reality*, ed. Paul E. Peterson (Washington, D.C.: Brookings Institution, 1985), 197-223.

18. Virginia D. McConnel, "Automobile Use and Locational Interdependence," *Journal of Regional Science* 26, no. 3 (1986): 475-98.

19. William Fulton, "Office in the Dell," *Planning* 52, no. 2 (July 1986): 13-17.

20. Ruth Eckdish Knack, "The Once and Future Suburb," *Planning* 54, no. 2 (February 1988): 6-12.

21. John Blair and Robert Premus, "Industrial Location: A Review", *Economic Development Quarterly* 1, no. 1 (February): 1-28.

22. Ann Markusen, Peter Hall and Amy Glasmeier, *Hi Tech, America: The What, How, When, and Why of the Sunrise Industries* (Boston: Allen & Unwin, 1986), 25.

23. David Birch, *Job Creation in America* (New York: Free Press, 1987).

24. Katherine Bradbury, Anthony Downs, and Kenneth Small, *Urban Decline and the Future of American Cities* (Washington, D.C.: Brookings Institution, 1982). Peter F. Drucker, however, argues that non-high-tech firms still provide the largest proportion of manufacturing jobs. See Peter F. Drucker, *Innovation and Entrepreneurship: Practice and Principles* (New York: Harper & Row, 1985), 7-11.

25. James Fallows, "America's Changing Economic Landscape," *Atlantic Monthly*, March 1985, 47-68.

26. The results were reported in *The New England Economic Review* (July-August 1984): pp. 39-55. See the discussion in Anthony Downs, "The Future of Industrial Cities" in *The New Urban Reality*, ed. Paul E. Peterson (Washington, D.C.: Brookings Institution, 1985), 281-83.

27. These trends are well documented in the literature. See, for example, Richard B. McKenzie, *The American Job Machine* (New York: Universe Books, 1988); Thierry Noyelle and T.M. Stanbach, *The Economic Transformation of American Cities* (Totowa, N.J.: Rowman & Allenheld, 1985); Timothy K. Kinsella, "Traditional Manufacturing in Transition to Human-Centered Cities," *Journal of Urban History* 12, no. 2 (1986): 31-53; Peter Hall, "The Anatomy of Job Creation: Nations Regions and Cities in the 1960s and 1970s," *Regional Studies* 21, no. 2 (1987): 95-106; Barry Bluestone and Bennett Harrison, *The Great American Job Machine: The Proliferation of Low Wage Employment in the U.S. Economy* (Washington, D.C.: Joint Economic Committee, U.S. Congress, 1986).

28. John D. Kasarda, "Urban Change and Minority Opportunities," in Peterson, *New Urban Reality*, 45-46. See also Bradbury, Downs, and Small, *Urban Decline*.

29. George E. Peterson, "Urban Policy and the Cyclical Behavior of Cities," in *Reagan and the Cities*, ed. George E. Peterson and Carol Lewis (Washington, D.C.: Urban Institute Press, 1986), 23, table 7.

30. David L. Birch, *Job Creation in Cities* (Cambridge, Mass: M.I.T. Program on Neighborhood and Regional Change, 1980), p. 19. The author notes that the exception to this general pattern appears to be the central business district in prospering areas.

31. Ibid., 19-22. For extension of the argument that declining regions tend to be more dependent on small business job creation, see also Catherine Armington and Marjorie Odle, "Small Businesses—How Many Jobs?" *Brookings Review* (Winter 1982): 17-24.

32. Birch, *Job Creation in Cities*, 25.

33. Kasarda, "Urban Change," 34-35.

34. The underclass has received substantial attention in the recent literature on poverty. The most comprehensive analysis of the underclass can be found in William J. Wilson, *The Truly Disadvantaged: The Inner City, the Underclass, and Public Policy* (Chicago: University of Chicago Press, 1987). Recent work has attempted to more systematically define the underclass and measure its growth. See Erol Ricketts and Ronald Mincy, "Growth of the Underclass: 1970-1980," *Changing Domestic Priorities Discussion Paper* (Washington, D.C.: Urban Institute, 1988).

35. See the discussion in Wilson, *Truly Disadvantaged*. Whether or not minority communities are actually "isolated" from mainstream employment opportunities will be discussed more thoroughly in chapter 4.

36. A review of recent estimates of the size of the informal economy can be found in Barry Molefsky, "America's Underground Economy," in *The Underground Economy in the United States and Abroad*, ed. Vito Tanzi (Lexington, Mass.: Lexington Books/D.C. Heath, 1982), 47-67; James D. Smith, "Measuring the Informal Economy," *Annals of the American Academy of Political and Social Science* 493 (September 1987): 83-99; Anne D. Witte, "The Underground Economy in the United States and Western Europe," in *Examination of Basic Weaknesses of Income As the Major Federal Tax Base*, ed. Richard W. Lindholm (New York: Praeger Press, 1986), 204-29; Alfred L. Malabre, Jr, "Underground Economy Grows and Grows," *Wall Street Journal* 20 October 1980, p. 1.

37. See the discussion in Molefsky, "America's Underground Economy," 48-57.

38. Manuel Castells and Alejandro Portes, "World Underneath: The Origins, Dynamics, and Effects of the Informal Economy," in *The Informal Economy: Studies in Advanced and Less Developed Countries*, ed. Alejandro Portes, Manuel Castells and Lauren A. Benton (Baltimore, Md.: Johns Hopkins University Press, 1989), 11-37; Louis A. Ferman, Stuart Henry, and Michele Hoyman, "Issues and Prospects for the Study of Informal Economies: Concepts, Research Strategies, and Policy," *Annals of the American Academy of Political and Social Science* 494 (September 1989): 154-72; Raffaele De Grazia, "Clandestine Employment: A Problem of Our Times," in Tanzi, *The Underground Economy* 29-43; and Witte, "The Underground Economy in the United States."

39. Informality has received the most attention in the academic literature on economic development in the Third World. For a useful review, see Lisa Peattie, "An Idea in Good Currency and How It Grew: The Informal Sector," in *World Development* 15, no. 7 (1989): 851-60.

40. Excellent examples of this approach can be found in Tanzi, *The Underground Economy* and Lindholm, *Examination of Basic Weaknesses*.

41. See Smith, "Measuring the Informal Economy," 83-99.

42. See M. Patricia Fernandez-Kelly and Anna M. Garcia, "Informalization at the Core: Hispanic Women, Homework, and the Advanced Capitalist State," in Portes, Castells and Benton, *The Informal Economy*, 247-64 and Juan Carlos Fortuna and Suzana Prates, "Informal Sector versus Informalized Labor Relations in Uruguay," in Portes, Castells and Benton, *The Informal Economy*, 78-94.

43. Saskia Sassen-Koob, "New York City's Informal Economy," in Portes, Castells and Benton, *The Informal Economy*, 60-77.

44. Based on estimates from the International Ladies Garment Workers Union reported in Sassen-Koob, "New York City's Informal Economy," 66.

45. Ibid., 65.

46. Ibid., 75.

47. Alex Stepick, "Miami's Two Informal Sectors," in Portes, Castells and Benton, *The Informal Economy*, 111-31.

48. Ibid., 121.

49. For extensive discussion of minority community isolation and declining employment prospects, see Kasarda, "Urban Change," 33-67; Jonathan S. Leonard, "The Interaction of Residential Segregation and Employment Discrimination," *Journal of Urban Economics* 21 (1987): 323-46; and William J. Wilson, *The Declining Significance of Race* 2d ed. (Chicago: University of Chicago Press, 1982).

50. This relationship may not be a one-to-one correlation. Informal work in Miami is used to supplement legitimate employment. Similarly, as chapter five details, work in the drug economy is often used to supplement income from the legitimate sector as well

51. Sassen-Koob, "New York City's Informal Economy," 71.

52. Flanagan and Maguire, *Sourcebook* 419, table 4.2.

2

Law, Order, and Economic Development in the Modern City

Economic growth has been the source of debate and discussion since at least 1776, when moral philosopher Adam Smith wrote his classic treatise on economics, *The Wealth of Nations*. Smith, of course, was concerned with the wealth of nations rather than of cities. Nevertheless, his work laid the foundation for contemporary economic analysis of development and what constitutes growth.

Smith, writing in the early stages of the industrial revolution, marveled at the productive capacity of the factory and the ability of people to market products despite the complexity of the production process. The "invisible hand" became Smith's metaphor for economic markets that directed the productive capacities of people toward the common good through the pursuit of self-interest. A market, as this chapter will discuss, is an important economic institution that is essential for promoting growth and development.

Smith's invisible hand was an important abstraction that has since become an indispensable tool of economic analysis. Indeed, modern economies are judged according to how well the invisible hand—or the institution of the market—works (or is allowed to work). Most important, markets do not work in isolation. Rather, social and political institutions are essential to ensure that competitive market economies can function.

The decline of many large cities in the United States suggests that the institutions currently in place may not be capable of sustaining vibrant, entrepreneurial market economies. Entrepreneurship requires a tolerance for diversity and experimentation. Consumer preferences change quickly and buyer decisions incorporate knowledge that is explicitly unknowable to producers and suppliers in the market. The entrepreneur attempts to discover these preferences through the price system embodied in economic markets. To the extent that cities encourage this entrepreneurial behavior, they will prosper. To the extent that cities discourage this behavior, they will fail.

The relationship between institutions, entrepreneurship, and urban development will be discussed in two parts. Humans are fundamentally social beings and rarely exist in isolation. Individual behavior is defined by rules that set out the bounds of socially acceptable behavior. These rules are a common ground on which others can be judged. They become the political, social, and economic institutions which define communities, nations, and cultures.

A market is a social institution since it facilitates exchange and trade between people. Markets are responsible for coordinating economic resources in most of the developed and developing industrial world. Yet, Smith's invisible hand works because laws, customs, and traditions allow it to function. Public policy plays an exceptional role in laying the formal ground rules for market activity. The last sections of this chapter will concentrate more specifically on this relationship.

Economic markets as social institutions have been relevant in human history only for a limited period, beginning with the Enlightenment in the seventeenth and eighteenth centuries. Previously, the institutions conducive to the kind of economic activity observed by Smith did not exist or, at the very least, functioned haphazardly and inefficiently.

The great economic leap forward resulting from the industrial revolution contrasts starkly with the depressed inner cities of the late twentieth century. As the first chapter detailed, the problems of urban development have become more pressing in recent years as central cities have stagnated and, in most cases, declined. Millions of urban residents have plunged into poverty as central cities struggle to rebuild their economic bases. Meanwhile, underground economies have emerged as important sources of income for the poor and unemployed. Depressed inner-city economies, restrictive public policies, and sustained domestic demand for illicit substances have all contributed to the emergence of a vast underground drug economy.

As central cities have failed to prosper, their institutions have failed to provide the environment necessary to stimulate economic growth and development in the legitimate economy. Understanding the full implications of an urban economy dominated by drug trafficking requires an understanding of the institutions that provide the foundation for that economic activity. The institutional foundations of the drug economy differ markedly from those necessary for fostering economic development in the legitimate economy.

The irony of this analysis lies in the observation that the growth of the drug economy (or any underground economy) is integrally tied to the legitimate economy. Drug trafficking, in particular, is the product of events and processes occurring in the legitimate sector. Thus, understanding events in the legitimate economy are also essential to comprehend the role and function of the drug economy in American cities.

Institutions also imply a broadly defined body of ethics. The analysis presented in the next several sections argues that the institutions that form the basis for America's market economy—the protection of private property, civil liberties, and tolerance of diversity—are essential elements of any productive economy. The drug economy, on the other hand, is characterized by institutions that are fundamentally destructive to economic and social progress despite apparent short-run gains. Nevertheless, the values and characteristics of the drug economy mirror recent shifts in public policy in the legal economy.

A complex array of institutions continually interact to promote certain forms of behavior and discourage others. The final outcome depends on the way rewards and benefits are structured by the institutions defining appropriate and successful behavior. For example, if the institutional system rewards innovation and creativity, the economy will be characterized by invention and technological progress. On the other hand, if the social system rewards loyalty and subservience, at the expense of individual creativity, the economy will be stagnant and lethargic.

Institutions, Law, and Order

Institutions are the established customs, laws, and traditions that provide the underpinnings of any society.[1] The particular arrangement of institutions in the social, political, and economic spheres of interpersonal contact define the the general "ground rules" for individual behavior. This institutional "framework" is thus comprised of several, less comprehensive institutions that span less inclusive social groups such as the family, the business, government, or friendship. Institutions, then, provide "services" to human action by providing a common framework within which individuals can interact and accomplish more than they could separately.[2]

Institutions pervade all forms of community and human action. Individuals take cues concerning appropriate behavior from these traditions and customs that form the core of their culture. The Judeo-Christian ethic, for example, provides the moral foundation for most Western cultures. Systems of rules and customs such as the Ten Commandments define right and wrong and "socially acceptable" behavior.

The market is a social institution that coordinates resource allocation, production, and consumption decisions. Economic activity is the result of people making choices about what and how to produce. The market provides an institutional framework for using resources based on consumer preferences registered by the price system. "Correct" behavior is rewarded by profits and "incorrect" behavior is punished by losses.

Similarly, political institutions, such as representative democracy, define the appropriate role and function of political behavior in different societies. By making politicians accountable to their constituencies, democracy minimizes the risk of dictatorship. As long as the political culture tolerates dissent and political opposition, the system will check the arbitrary power of elected politicians.

Rules provide an essential function for decentralized human societies. Each person has a perspective on the way the world works based on past experiences. Yet, people cannot read each other's minds to ensure that action is well coordinated. Rules provide a means for reducing uncertainty in human behavior.[3] Although we cannot know someone else's intentions telepathically, we can make a reasonable guess if the person follow's certain behavioral rules with which we are familiar. Thus, these rules lift the individual to the social realm of human interaction.

Institutions in the moral, social, political, and economic realm interact over time, evolving with constituent attitudes and needs. Understanding how these institutions evolve is essential for understanding the nature of urban economic development as well.

Large cities, for example, can also be considered institutions. Their high densities, fragmented populations, and extreme diversity provide the general framework necessary to stimulate creative and innovative individual behavior. The rules that define city life—tolerance of diversity and fragmentation—are substantially different from those defining rural life, which depends more on a homogeneity and consensus.[4]

Jane Jacobs pioneered the idea that cities were important for their ability to harbor and encourage export- induced economic growth.[5] The inherent diversity of a city's population and work force provides an opportunity for discovering new markets as well as developing new ways to accomplish old tasks. Large cities provide an environment that encourages specialization and heightened productivity. Eventually, through progress and innovation, "new work" could be added to "old work," increasing the material well-being of city residents.

Economic progress occurs because cities are "messy" and "impractical" social institutions according to Jacobs.[6] The large, vigorous cities do not enforce social and economic conformity. To the extent that the city's social and economic systems do reflect narrowly defined goals and characteristics, they are imposed through processes external to urban life per se. The ability to experiment with different processes, to succeed or fail, combine to make city economies vibrant.

Institutions are beyond the control or influence of any particular individual at any specific time. Nevertheless, institutions change. What is perceived as appropriate today may have been inappropriate at an earlier time. Large cities, for example, were often run as political machines by influential politicians. Municipal jobs were often patronage positions used to payoff political loyalists. City politics is now more inclusive and open. In many states, patronage is illegal and city political machines are rare.[7] In most major cities, political success depends on broad public support and less on who you know.

Institutional change is not deterministic, capable of being arranged by an omniscient, benevolent dictator (or planner). Rather, institutions evolve. Each new rule, custom, or tradition embodies the history of past human behavior circumscribed by rules and customs of an earlier period. Current tradition, then, embodies information that has survived through centuries of human activity.

The growth of cities in contemporary metropolitan areas embodies many of these institutional changes. Communities outside of large cities began as primarily agricultural villages. As city residents moved out to more rural environments, spurred by easy access to the city through the interstate highway system and cheap credit, the demographic composition of these towns evolved into suburban, residential towns. These towns began to take on citylike characteristics as their populations increased. Small shops appeared, serving suburban families rather than farmers. Professional services such as commercial banks, lawyers, doctors, insurance salesmen, and so on emerged as a budding commercial sector adapted to the changing needs of the village's residents. Eventually, a small manufacturing plant may locate in the hinterland of the town, which has now incorporated as a city, and ancillary services may locate nearby to serve the factory.

At each stage of the city's development, new rules emerge that govern behavior of individual residents. For example, restrictions on land use appear more frequently to protect the value of suburban home owners. The farmer, sitting on 200 or more acres of farmland, now must have new buildings approved by the local planning commission or zoning board. Similarly, educational standards in the public school may change as the local school system attempts to steer larger proportions of its graduates to colleges and universities. Even the ways people relate to each other will alter everyday life in the town. Residents will be less likely to recognize one another as, with urban growth, life becomes more impersonal and complex.

Several decades of development will transform the small farming village into a bustling small city. At any particular point in this development, no one may be able to point to a particular individual or event that stimulated the growth. In retrospect, community historians may be able to isolate events and individuals who contributed to the growth, such as the first farmer to sell his land to the housing developer, or the first "pro-growth" mayor. Rarely can a city's growth be attributed to one event or one person. The changes are incremental and marginal.

Institutions implicitly reflect past patterns of social behavior as well as expectations about future behavior. Those institutions that are able to sustain progress and human betterment tend to prosper, while those that do not tend to stagnate. This process of institutional self-selection can take centuries.

Feudal society, for instance, gave way to capitalism after several centuries of social turmoil, war, and political change. Capitalism promised a better life for the masses as factory workers developed production techniques that lowered costs to the point where significant consumer markets could be tapped. Human history is replete with examples of civilizations dying out and rejuvenating as tradition and customs adapted to the changing attitudes of people.

Sometimes, the process of institutional change appears to backpeddle. The decline of the Roman Empire, for example, signaled a degeneration of European civilization into a less sophisticated society based on feudal principles. Western civilizations emerged as powerful world powers only after the philosophical and political resurgence of the Enlightenment during the seventeenth and eighteenth centuries. The industrial revolution further solidified the institutional framework of Western civilizations by entrenching concepts of private property and democratic government. Whether these precepts survive over the long run, of course, remains an open question.

The moral, social, political, and economic institutions that dominate a social system also establish the incentive structure for individual behavior. For example, the protection of private property and the right to the proceeds of personal labor in market societies provide rewards to individuals for innovation and initiative through wealth accumulation. A society whose economic institutions focus on equalizing the distribution of wealth will be less likely to reward individual achievement through the natural play of economic activity. Thus, a complex array of institutions provides the "constitution" for individual participation in society, forming the basis of social behavior.

These institutions may differ depending on the type of market or the particular circumstances of the transaction. Generally, economic transactions in the legal economy are protected by social, political, and legal institutions. If someone goes into a small boutique to purchase a pair of pants or a shirt, the legal system will protect the rights of both the purchaser and the seller of the item. A court system provides a third-party forum in which "injuries" to person or property can be adjudicated without resorting to "shotgun justice."

Underground economies, on the other hand, are often driven by a completely different set of institutions. Without a court system to resolve conflicts peacefully, justice is often determined by the parties directly involved. In many cases, the most forceful of the parties involved in the dispute dominates the outcome. Justice, in these cases, is determined by the size of the gun.

A street-level drug dealer, for example, faces tremendous risks to person and property (as chapters 6 and 7 will discuss). If a dealer's inventory (cache of drugs) is stolen by another dealer or robber, his only recourse is often to recapture the stolen drugs or follow through on a threat to the thief's life. Moreover, while in the legitimate economy creativity and innovation may be rewarded, secrecy and loyalty often dominate successful underground organizations at the expense of economic progress. Thus, cartels are much more interested in loyalty to the organization than product development or marketing.

Knowledge, Uncertainty, and Rules

The importance of institutions such as economic markets for facilitating human interaction follows directly from what is now known as the "knowledge problem."[8] People live in an uncertain world, with limited access to information about the people and events around them. Most of our information is gained directly through experience. This knowledge, combined with what we learn from others, allows us to form judgments about behavior and to form expectations about the future. The particular way we integrate these bits of information is unique to each individual. We can only infer from what we observe about how others are interpreting the same events.

Adam Smith, for example, used the example of a pin factory to illustrate the complexity of the knowledge problem in economic life. Hundreds of people are involved in the production of pins, from the mining of the ores that are refined into needles, to factory workers who produce the pins, to the retailers who make the pins available to consumers.

No one individual has the knowledge necessary to understand or comprehend the entire production process. The retailer does not have the knowledge necessary to mine the ore, nor does the miner understand the finer points of pin marketing. Yet, through successive stages of production, the product is eventually supplied on the market for purchase by consumers.

The activities of consumers and producers at each stage are mediated by market prices, which provide signals concerning the cost of producing pins compared to other products (e.g., a shirt). The market for pins remains an intangible for most people except for the final product.

Pin production occurs only as a result of supportive institutional structures that permit consumers and producers the freedom to allocate scarce resources to fit each others needs. "Almost all of us serve people whom we do not know," observes F.A. Hayek, a leading economist and political theorist,

> and even of whose existence we are ignorant; and we in turn constantly live in the services of other people of whom we know nothing. All this is possible because we stand in a great framework of institutions and traditions - economic, legal, and moral - into which we fit ourselves by obeying certain rules of conduct that we never made, and which we have never understood in the sense in which we understand how the things that we manufacture function.[9]

The miner of the ore for pin production would not mine if he did not expect the manufacturer to pay for the ore. Similarly, the manufacturer would not produce pins if he did not expect the retailer to pay him for the pins he sells on the market. The entire system is dependent on people at every stage of production trusting others to follow through on contractual obligations.

Honoring voluntary agreements sets the entire system in motion. A simple rule such as "honor all contracts entered into voluntarily" permits trust to evolve among merchants without detailed knowledge of the personality or background of the other.

Clearly, rules such as these become very important in forming expectations about the future behavior of others. If people can count on others following certain rules, human action becomes more predictable and expectations become more consistent with reality. For example, drivers on major surface streets in a city expect other cars entering from side streets to yield to them. If, however, the driver could not reasonably expect other cars to observe this traffic rule, the trip would become significantly longer and more difficult since the driver would be forced to drive under the suspicion that any car could pull out in front of him.

The behavioral rule that "cars on side streets yield to cars on major surface streets" becomes an economizing rule allowing for smoothly flowing traffic. The driver on the major thoroughfare does not need to know who the driver of the car on the side street is. Widespread adherence to the traffic rule alleviates the need for a detailed knowledge of the personalities involved in the situation.

Similarly, many drug dealers work only with well- established clients in order to avoid detection by law enforcement authorities. As chapter 6 will explain in more detail, the drug distribution system on the retail level is highly decentralized and very risky. Adopting a rule that permits drug transactions to occur only among known buyers substantially reduces the risk to the dealer and the organization. Thus, those dealers who remain in business for a long period of time often service long-time repeat customers.

This approach to knowledge and human behavior contradicts popular interpretations that presume complete knowledge and a full understanding of the consequences of personal decisions. In reality, detailed information about a particular situation, event, or person is unobtainable. Rules, then, become essential in the routine aspects of human behavior.

Efficient resource coordination is the hallmark of successful market systems. Yet, economic systems are built on the rules, traditions, and other social institutions that evolve out of human behavior designed to cope with routine problems. Thus, social institutions in the form of rules that guide behavior reflect the experience of previous generations, experience that is, in turn, transferred through tradition and custom to more recent generations.

Many societies have social mores that forbid the consumption of certain foods. Often, these customs are based on actual experience with certain foods. In some cultures, wine replaced water as the primary drinking beverage to avoid health problems associated with contaminated wells. The custom that embraces wine drinking may in fact represent an attempt to avoid illness. Or, in areas where water is in short supply, wine could have served as a convenient substitute. In this case, the custom of wine drinking served as a means of conserving water. In the present day, individuals may be unaware of the origins of this tradition. Yet, these customs often reflect practical solutions to social problems from earlier times.

Similarly, rules are used in the underground drug trade. In his detailed study of a teenage Dominican cocaine ring in New York City, sociologist Terry Williams describes how street-level suppliers regulate the amount of cocaine allocated to street-dealers.[10] "Overindulging" in cocaine cuts into the profits of the trade. When a supplier sees one of his dealers indulging in cocaine, he "corrects" the situation by reducing the amount of cocaine supplied to maintain the profitability of the operation. Since dealers have an "aversion to buying cocaine," the reduced supply of cocaine reduces the amount of "partying" by skimming inventories.

Other, more traditional rules, follow conventional good business practices. When cocaine and crack surged in popularity in the early

1980s, street-level dealers began diluting the purity of the cocaine they sold on the retail level. While dealers were able to reap short-term profits from this practice, their longer-term success was less clear. Consumers became more sophisticated and quickly diverted their business to dealers selling cocaine with higher purity levels. "By the end of the summer of 1984," observed Williams, "only the most naive buyer would tolerate cocaine with any adulterant."[11] Selling a quality product promotes a steady and profitable business.

Rule-following behavior thus represents a form of social learning that evolves from the experiences, successes, and failures of previous generations. Ultimately, a system of rules develops that evolves into a set of institutions called "culture." States Hayek, "The process of selection that shaped customs and morality could take account of more factual circumstances than individuals could perceive, and in consequence tradition is in some respects superior to, or 'wiser' than, human reason."[12]

Hayek has called the social institution of "the market" an "extended order"[13] because of its ability to facilitate and encourage human cooperation beyond what could be accomplished by each person individually.

One of the most striking examples of how extended orders embody experience from previous generations may be the evolution of language.[14] Children learn languages by adopting rules of grammar. Rules concerning word usage, sentence construction, conjugation, etc., all become part of the child's method of interpreting events around him. Each one of these rules embodies knowledge accumulated through centuries of evolution in language building. Language, in a very real and important sense, is a product of human action but not human design. English, for example, would lose its meaning if people did not communicate with it. At the same time, no one individual planned the development of English as a language, nor did a single individual or group consciously choose English as their language.

Thus, language develops as a process. Rules change as uses change. For example, words evolve as their meanings change or become fully integrated into social communication. The word *businessman* may have started as two words, business and man. In the beginning, *business* was used as an adjective to describe an occupational characteristic of a man. Then, as the two words were used jointly, the word may have evolved to *business-man*, finally becoming one word *businessman* after a long process of social integration. In addition, the meaning of the word may have changed. In early times, the term may have described men only. In current times, the term is used more generically to mean anyone involved in a commercial enterprise. The evolution of the word, then, is a process of socialization and adaptation.

Similarly, although on an infinitely more complex and grander scale, "civilization is not only a product of evolution, it is a process; by establishing a framework of general rules and individual freedom it allows itself to continue to evolve."[15] Thus, culture is not permanent or unchanging as many social scientists tend to view it.[16] Cultures are continually evolving to reflect a myriad of adjustments needed for sustained social progress. Changes in culture, however, reflect changes in society's institutions.

These institutions do not change autonomously, without cause. Rather, institutional change is itself the result of human behavior, if not human design.

Institutions and Entrepreneurship

The possibility that institutions change over time and that these changes are reflected in alterations in custom, tradition, and the broader culture suggests that something serves as a catalyst for change.

The "ground rules" for behavior are determined by customs, traditions, and rules, but individuals push the bounds of these institutions and alter them incrementally. "Institutional analysis," notes economic historian Douglass C. North, "is at base the study not simply of the rules of the game but of the individual responses to such rules."[17] Individual behavior in the context of these rules becomes important to fully understand the importance of rules in structuring human behavior. While individuals influence the direction in which rules change, the existing rules of the game determine the pace and the pattern of change.

Within societies that encourage initiative and creativity, the catalyst for change often takes the form of entrepreneurship. The entrepreneur is the person looking for new opportunities.[18] In market economies, entrepreneurs are usually identified as small businessmen. The entrepreneur starts out with an idea and tries to parlay it into a successful business enterprise. Those that reach the peak of this process are hailed as examples of success and persistence (e.g., "the Horatio Algers of the world").

Entrepreneurial behavior is found in the underground economy as well. A Haitian carpenter may begin a small construction company to remodel or renovate apartments or homes in low-income immigrant communities. The carpenter may see a demand for his skills and background and provide his services at reasonable prices in the community. Tailors, plumbers, electricians, and accountants may provide similar services that cater to the particular tastes and cultural traditions of homogeneous populations.

In the drug trade, new methods may be invented to increase profits and facilitate distribution on the retail level. Reducing the purity of cocaine is one example already mentioned. Another "innovation" was the "crack house." Terry Williams observed that

> between 1984 and 1988, cocaine distribution increasingly came to resemble a fast food chain. Cocaine and crack houses proliferated, offering low prices, fast service, and good quality. Most houses operate more than one office in a single building, which allows for high-volume purchasing by buyers who need not be referred by other buyers.[19]

Indeed, crack itself is a technical innovation induced by a desire to develop a more powerful, cheap form of cocaine more easily accessible to low-income communities in inner cities.[20] Obviously, profits in the drug trade are important inducements to technical innovation.

If, on the other hand, someone is merely substituting one job for another, his behavior is not necessarily entrepreneurial. Entrepreneurs are motivated by a search for new opportunities. The distinction is important since the entrepreneurs who are "alert" to new opportunities push the boundaries and limits set by social institutions.[21] In this context, institutions change through entrepreneurial behavior that tests the limits imposed by established customs and traditions. When Ford developed the Mustang in the early 1960s, the automobile company was testing existing conceptions of what consumers wanted in a car. By stretching the bounds of convention, Ford was able to successfully develop a new product and develop a previously untapped consumer market. In contrast, income substituters work within the bounds of existing rules.[22]

Entrepreneurs use the market and its profit opportunities as a vehicle for producing new products. As David Birch has noted with respect to small businesses, entrepreneurs are builders and "are driven by a desire to create an innovative force in the corporate world."[23] For them, the market serves as a convenient institution, driven by a company balance sheet that encourages "discovery." The market encourages success by imposing one rule on its participants: they must make money. Profits are the standard of success and failure in all economic markets whether they are aboveground or underground.

Entrepreneurs determine which areas of the market may yield the highest profits by observing consumer demand through movements in prices.[24] Prices serve as signals to the entrepreneur concerning consumer preferences that are unknowable directly to the entrepreneur. The demand for a product is discovered through the quantities people are willing to buy at certain prices. Individually, these preferences are too fragmented for the entrepreneur to interpret individually. The price system, however, allows the entrepreneur to ascertain patterns in consumer preference that give her information about the potential market for her product.

For example, higher prices for cocaine in the late 1970s and 1980s provided signals to suppliers to shift their efforts to cocaine importation. Marijuana, an extremely bulky product, became a higher-risk import. As drug enforcement efforts increased interdiction along the borders and made foreign based supplies more unstable, more and more marijuana was grown domestically. Cocaine, on the other hand, is easier to conceal, has higher profit margins, and is an expanding market.

In some cases, preferences may be well-defined. In others, preferences have yet to be discovered. The market system, by rewarding successful economic decision making through the profit and loss system, allows entrepreneurs to take risks based on their expectations of consumer behavior. In the words of the nineteenth-century economist J. B. Say, "The entrepreneur shifts economic resources out of an area of lower and into an area of higher productivity and greater yield."[25]

Knowledge, as the previous section emphasized is highly decentralized. Institutional arrangements, such as economic markets operating through freely flowing price systems, allow individuals to collect this information simply by following their tendencies to buy products that are offered on the market. Trends in consumer behavior often provide the basis for forming expectations about future behavior that provides incentives to invest in new products. Thus, the rewards to an entrepreneur that manifest themselves most often in higher incomes also represent an ability to interpret price signals as indicators of consumer preferences.

Institutions and Economic Growth

Yet, as the recent experiences of the planned economies in Eastern Europe attest, entrepreneurship is not present in every economy despite relatively close cultural links. Nathan Rosenberg and L.E. Birdzell, Jr., for example, note that Imperial China did not experience dramatic economic growth compared to Western European countries despite a more highly developed culture and social structure during the period preceding the Protestant Reformation of the fourteenth and fifteenth centuries in Europe.[26] Chinese culture, they observe, was dominated by a hierarchical social structure that centralized economic, political, and social activity. China's advanced technological state produced an entrenched elite that discouraged innovation and change. In contrast, the European countries, particularly the English and Dutch, were breaking away from traditional, hierarchical feudal structures. Competition among nation-states and the rise of a wealthy merchant class contributed to the breakdown of centralized social structures that inhibit entrepreneurial activity.[27]

Clearly, the institutional structures that define the costs and rewards of economic activity have a role in sustaining economic growth. A centralized political structure like the system dominated by feudal societies and the Catholic church during the Middle Ages in Europe tends to stifle innovation and growth. Decentralized political systems like the breakdown of feudal hierarchies during and after the Protestant Reformation tend to encourage entrepreneurship and technological innovation. As Rosenberg and Birdzell note in their survey of the causes of economic growth in the industrialized world, "In the West, the individual centers of competing political power had a great deal to gain from introducing technological changes that promised commercial or industrial advantage and, hence, greater government revenues, and much to lose from allowing others to introduce them first."[28] The institutions in the Western world that tended to encourage the growth of a merchant class, or entrepreneurial class, included the decline of the arbitrary confiscation of personal wealth, the growth of business enterprises as separate entities from the individual managers and owners, stable financing and insurance networks to cover the risks of business, and a moral climate that encouraged individual hard work and honesty in contractual obligations. These social and cultural changes manifested themselves in a set of modern-day institutions such as double-entry bookkeeping, insurance companies, banks and other lending institutions, taxation (rather than arbitrary confiscation), and autonomous national governments constituted to protect private property. In essence, the development (or evolution) of these institutions made it safe for entrepreneurs to invest in industry and commerce without the fear of forfeiting their profits to their ruler.

Property Rights and Economic Growth

The acceptance of the Magna Carta in 1215 was a watershed in the development of complex industrial economies. The charter represented an agreement between the king of England and his subjects guaranteeing the right to own property without fear of arbitrary expropriation by their rulers. While the document was established during the feudal era, the Magna Carta recognized individual property rights for the first time in modern history. As long as individuals had the right to own property and benefit from its productive use, legal trade could occur. Governments were forced to turn to the more stable and predictable revenue-raising tactic of taxation. Out of this early acknowledgement of property rights, a system of common law emerged, supporting individualism over the collective will of governments or feudal lords. The protection of property rights, and the ability to transfer property rights through contract, allowed for the voluntary and peaceful transfer of wealth among individuals as gifts or loans. [29]

The development of personal property rights, or "several property," is the source of social growth and development. As long as property was held by one person as a collective good, the information embedded in the price system could not be unleashed in a decentralized market economy. Only by allowing the creativity of individual minds to work toward a common goal —the satisfaction of consumer wants—could rapid economic growth be sustained and raise the bulk of Western civilization from poverty. As F.A. Hayek notes, "the prior development of several property is indispensable for the development of trading, and thereby for the formation of larger coherent and cooperating structures, and for the appearance of those signals we call prices."[30] As long as people were afraid their property could be confiscated at any moment (e.g., to finance a war with a rival lord), economic activity would be stunted and forced underground.[31]

Through the emergence of common law, legal systems introduced enough stability and predictability to support substantial investments in long-term projects such as factories and complex distribution networks. The long-term investment necessary to promote industrial expansion was very risky as long as local rulers were arbitrarily confiscating private property. Thus, the evolution of laws anchored in abstract principles, such as the right to own property, made industrial economies possible. As Douglass North observes, "Modern economic growth results from the development of institutions that permit an economy to realize the gains from specialization and division of labor associated with the sophisticated technology that has developed in the Western World in the last several centuries."[32]

Ethics, Civil Liberties, and Public Policy

A close connection exists between private property, individual liberty, and economic growth. Civil liberties are grounded in the respect for self-expression. The right to own and use private property is the tangible manifestation of the inalienable right to self-ownership that underlies the constitutional restraints on government power in the United States. Protecting private property is essential for protecting and maintaining civil liberties. Without the freedom to use private resources to innovate and create, individual expression would be impossible.

Liberty is inseparable from the concept of several property. The material aspects of personal life are expressions of the individual and must be acknowledged as such under law. The protection of civil liberties, then, becomes a tangible restraint on coercion by protecting private property.

Thus, abstract rules that protect private property and preclude arbitrary coercion by third parties are necessary to protect liberty and individual freedom:

> Freedom requires that the individual be allowed to pursue his own ends: one who is free is in peacetime no longer bound by the common concrete ends of his community. Such freedom of individual decision is made possible by delimiting distinct individual rights (the rights of property, for example) and designating domains within which each can dispose over means known to him for his own ends. That is, a recognizable free sphere is determined for each person.[33]

The development of abstract rules constraining government power and protecting private property form the foundations of economic development. Historically, the protection of profits derived from the productive use of personal resources provided incentives for individuals to innovate and take risks with the reasonable expectation of some future return for their efforts. Previously untapped knowledge, much of it known only to the individual, could now be harnessed to increase the productive capacity of society more generally.

Abstract rules oriented toward protecting the property of its citizens, rather than enforcing the arbitrary wishes of a ruler, necessitated the emergence of modern constitutional democracies. Within a constitutional democracy, government power is derived from the governed and tangibly constrained by the protection of personal property and freedom. Modern representative democracies, then, are founded on the principles of the "protective state."[34]

The protective state, in the words of political economist Richard E Wagner, "maintains a framework of security and order within which liberty can reign."[35] The government enforces rather than enacts laws, reflecting its subordinate position to its citizens. Rights are not designated or granted by government. Instead, the rights of the people are prior to the very formation of government. While this concept of government appears to be on the wane,[36] it still forms the cornerstone of American constitutional law.

More important, the concept driving the protective state is essential for understanding the context for the development of economic markets in modern industrial societies. This, in turn, has wide-ranging implications for analyzing the changing institutional structure of the inner city and the full significance of the drug economy in many of these neighborhoods.

The "rules" or laws that restrict individual behavior within society— or, the legal institutions—are the products of change and evolution. At any given moment, the institutional structure reflects contemporary social attitudes toward individual behavior. At another time, these institutions reflect further developments in attitudes, sometimes contradicting earlier attitudes and sometimes supporting them. To a large extent, then, the state of civilization (reflected in its legal system) will determine "the scope and the possibilities of human ends and values."[37]

American political institutions supported racial segregation through the middle of the twentieth century. With the Supreme Court officially barring segregation in *Brown vs. Board of Education*, the legal system slowly began to dismantle the vestiges of legally institutionalized racism. While other forms of racism exist in the form of social attitudes and mores, the legal system has been purged of legally sanctioned racist policies.

This change of heart did not occur at once. Rather, these political changes occurred over a prolonged period. Continual pressure from organizations such as the NAACP slowly nibbled away at the system until it eventually cracked. The political gains of the civil rights movement, however, could never have occurred without changing racial attitudes among the dominant white political elite through the 1940s, 1950s, and 1960s.

Personal property rights, or the Lockian idea of self-ownership, did not appear all at once. Rather, they were part of an evolution of ideas and institutional change. These processes are reflective of broad-based social movements beyond the control of any individual mind.

> That rules become increasingly better adjusted to generate order happened not because men better understood their function, but because those groups prospered who happened to change them in a way that rendered them increasingly adaptive. This evolution was not linear, but resulted from continued trial and error, constant "experimentation" in arenas wherein different order contended.[38]

Thus, adaptation is essential to the survival of rules over time. Tradition and custom, then, lie between instinct and reason, representing an evolutionary process of learned behavior modification and adaptation. For customs to survive, they must provide some benefit to the group that adopts them, "thereby enabling them to expand more rapidly than others and ultimately to supersede . . . those not possessing similar customs."[39]

The dismantling of an officially segregationist political system also allowed African-Americans to develop their productive capacities without the arbitrary obstacles imposed on them through the coercive power of the state. The social benefits of a more tolerant social system are reflected in rising incomes and productivity in segments of the minority population.[40]

The role of public policy and government is to support and encourage behavior conforming to established rules and customs. Policymakers achieve this by defining who has access to the institutions that facilitate market transactions, enforcing voluntary agreements and contracts, resolving conflicts through peaceful (civil) procedures, defining criminal behavior, and defining the relationship between legal and extralegal behavior.

In recent years, public policy has become an unwitting accomplice in promoting underground economies and, more directly, the drug trade. As the next chapter will elaborate in more detail, public policy has altered the institutional environment of the inner city in two fundamental ways. On the one hand, urban policy has systematically undermined the institutions necessary to promote economic development by severely attenuating property rights. On the other hand, drug policy has provided the institutional environment necessary to harbor and promote a lucrative drug trade.

As a result, economic development in some of America's largest low-income inner-cities is an outgrowth of the development of the drug trade. In the long run, however, the institutions capable of sustaining significant economic development do not exist in the drug economy. The widespread abridgement of civil liberties and private property rights seriously circumscribes its potential to promote meaningful economic development. Economic development is predicated on peace, tolerance, and trust in the most prosperous market societies and the drug trade is fundamentally violent, dictatorial, and repressive. Unfortunately, urban policy in recent years has reinforced these characteristics of the drug trade rather than suppressed them.

Notes

1. The classic statement of this view of rules can be found in T. W. Schultz, "Institutions and the Rising Economic Value of Man," *American Journal of Agricultural Economics* 50 (December 1968): 1113-22.
2. See Schultz, "Institutions," 1116.
3. See Ron Heiner, "The Origins of Predictable Behavior," *American Economic Review* 73 (September, 1983): 560-95.
4. For the distinction between city and small towns, see Claude S. Fischer, *The Urban Experience*, 2d ed. (New York: Harcourt Brace Jovanovich, 1984), 116-17.
5. See Jane Jacobs, *The Economy of Cities* (New York: Random House/Vintage Books, 1961).
6. These ideas are developed further in Sam Staley, "Disequilibrium and Time in the Urban Economy: Reassessing the Contributions of Jane Jacobs to Development Theory," *Market Process* 7, no. 1 (Spring 1989): 16-21.
7. Some cities, however, are still run as machines. Powerful mayors can still create machinelike political operations that override professional managerial decisions. For an example, see the case of William Donald Schaefer as the mayor of Baltimore in Paul E. Peterson, Barry G. Rabe, and Kenneth K. Wong, *When Federalism Works* (Washington, D.C.: Brookings Institution, 1986), 75-76, 208-13. Other contemporary mayors running political machines were Richard Daley in Chicago and Marion Barry in Washington, D.C.

8. The knowledge problem was first introduced by economist F.A. Hayek in the early 1940s. Since then, a number of economists and social theorists have developed these ideas further. See F.A. Hayek, "The Use of Knowledge in Society," *American Economic Review* (September 1945); reprinted in F.A. Hayek, *Individualism and Economic Order* (Chicago: University of Chicago Press, 1948), 77-91, and "The Pretence of Knowledge," in *New Studies in Philosophy, Politics, Economics, and the History of Ideas* (Chicago, University of Chicago Press, 1978), 23-34. For a review of the literature and application to current policy problems, one of the best works available is Don Lavoie, *National Economic Planning: What is Left?* (Cambridge, Mass.: Ballinger, 1985).

9. F.A. Hayek, *The Fatal Conceit: The Errors of Socialism* (Chicago: University of Chicago Press, 1988), 14.

10. Terry Williams, *The Cocaine Kids: The Inside Story of a Teenage Drug Ring* (New York: Addison-Wesley, 1989), 58- 59.

11. Ibid., 43.

12. Hayek, *The Fatal Conceit*, 75.

13. The full meaning of an "extended order" goes beyond the purposes of this book. For those interested in pursuing this issue in more depth, see F.A. Hayek, *Law Legislation and Liberty*, vol. 1, *Rules and Order* (Chicago: University of Chicago Press, 1973), 35-54; *Studies in Politics, Philosophy, and Economics* (Chicago: University of Chicago Press, 1967), 22-41.

14. F.A. Hayek, "Rules, Perception and Intelligibility," in *Studies in Politics, Philosophy, and Economics*, 43-65.

15. Hayek, *The Fatal Conceit*, 74.

16. The contemporary view of culture common in much social science literature is to view it as a constant. Individual behavior is defined by the culture in which it occurs. As the following sections will outline, this view is challenged by the Hayekian notion that culture, tradition, and values are part of a broader, evolutionary spontaneous order. While a particular event within a specified time period may experience constraint based on cultural factors, a longer-run view would incorporate some notion of cultural or institutional change.

17. Douglass C. North, "Institutions, Transactions Costs, and Economic Growth," *Economic Inquiry* 25, no. 3 (July 1987), 419-28.

18. This interpretation of entrepreneurship is consistent with the concept developed by Israel Kirzner, *Competition and Entrepreneurship* (Chicago: University of Chicago Press, 1973). For how this distinction can be used in a more practical context, see the discussion of differences between income-substituting behavior and entrepreneurial behavior in job creation in David Birch, *Job Creation in America* (New York: Free Press, 1987), 29-36.

19. Williams, *The Cocaine Kids*, p. 52.

20. Richard C. Cowan, "How the Narcs Created Crack," *National Review* 38, no. 23 (December 1986): 26-34.

21. By some estimates this type of entrepreneur accounts for the bulk of job creation in the United States. See Birch, *Job Creation*, 36.

22. Thus, not all drug dealers are entrepreneurs. Many are simply income substituters attracted by the promise of higher incomes. Although this phenomenon is described more thoroughly in chapter 5, Williams observes that the leader of the teenage cocaine ring in New York draws "from a sizeable labor pool of teenagers who have dropped out of high school and are unemployed. Like workers in the above-ground economy, the kids have a chance to be promoted and make more money..." p. 45.

23. Birch, *Job Creation*, 31.
24. F.A. Hayek, "The Market As a Discovery Procedure" in *New Studies*, 179-90.
25. Quoted in Peter F. Drucker, *Innovation and Entrepreneurship: Practice and Principles* (New York: Harper & Row, 1985), 21.
26. Nathan Rosenberg and L.E. Birdzell, Jr. *How the West Grew Rich: The Economic Transformation of the Industrial World* (New York: Basic Books, 1986), 86-88.
27. Ibid., 137-38.
28. Ibid., 137.
29. Hayek, *The Fatal Conceit*, 30-31.
30. Ibid., 31.
31. In fact, this was common in a number of commercial activities until institutions could be developed sufficiently that businessmen would trust their governments. Significant investment in industry, for example, did not begin until the late seventeenth century (the beginning of the industrial revolution in England). In banking, the centralized authority of the Catholic church forced lending activities underground through the prohibition of usury. Not until after the rise of the merchant class and competition from Protestant religions did the Catholic church begin to allow interest payments on loans.
32. North, "Institutions," 422.
33. Hayek, *The Fatal Conceit*, 63, emphasis in the original.
34. For a discussion of various roles and responsibilities of government, see James M. Buchanan, *The Limits of Liberty* (Chicago: University of Chicago Press, 1975), 68-70.
35. Richard E. Wagner, *To Promote the General Welfare: Market Process Vs. Political Transfers* (San Francisco, Calif.: Pacific Research Institute for Public Policy, 1988), 3.
36. See Wagner, *To Promote the General Welfare*; Terry L. Anderson and Peter J. Hill, *The Birth of a Transfer Society* (Stanford, Calif.: Hoover Institution Press, 1980); Richard Epstein, *Takings: Private Property and the Power of Eminent Domain* (Cambridge, Mass.: Harvard University Press, 1985).
37. F.A. Hayek, *The Constitution of Liberty* (Chicago: University of Chicago Press, 1960), p. 24.
38. Hayek, *The Fatal Conceit*, 20.
39. Ibid., 43.
40. As the first chapter noted, however, economic progress has been unequal. See the discussions in Ronald B. Mincy, *Paradoxes in Black Economic Progress: Incomes, Families, and the Underclass*, Changing Domestic Priorities Discussion Paper (Washington, D.C.: The Urban Institute, 1989), and William J. Wilson, *The Declining Significance of Race*, 2d ed. (Chicago: University of Chicago Press, 1982).

3

The Changing Values
of the Central City

The institutional environment of the city has changed dramatically since the beginning of the twentieth century. These changes have fundamentally altered the way urban systems work and contributed to the rise of the underground economy. Generally speaking, the institutions that cultivate social development—the respect for property, contract, and tolerance of diversity—have eroded since the 1920s. The transition of rural towns into sprawling suburban communities has hastened this institutional change by validating trends in public policy that continually subvert the spontaneous adjustment processes of metropolitan economies.

A complete survey of the issues, problems and effects of these changes is beyond the scope of this book, although the following analysis relates directly to the concerns underlying the growth of the drug economy. Thus, changing values and attitudes that manifest themselves in the legitimate economy are also implicit in the illegitimate economy.

The Rule of Law

The overarching change evident in every area of urban political economy has been the trend toward rule by men rather than rule by law (fig. 3.1). Under the rule of law, human action is bounded by larger social institutions such as custom, tradition, the legal system or broader values of their society (e.g., "respect your elders"). These boundaries of individual conduct can be formalized through statutory law, or they may exist through less formal channels (e.g., "prevailing" standards or beliefs), or well-established social rules. The rule of law subsumes the individual to the will of the larger community. A strict religious order that holds each individual strictly accountable to a higher order is an example of an extreme form of the rule of law.

FIGURE 3.1
The Rule of Law versus the Rule of Men

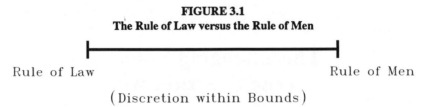

Rule of Law   Rule of Men

(Discretion within Bounds)

The rule of man, in contrast, is characterized by the arbitrary will of men acting irrespective of the bounds of important social, political, and economic institutions. This activity consists of any action directed primarily by the will and interests of individuals or well-organized interest groups. A dictatorship where one man serves as the supreme ruler serves as an example of an extreme form of the rule by man.

The American legal system is a peculiar blend of both the rule of law and rule of men. The rule of law manifests itself in the Constitution, which restrains the powers of government by requiring the State to protect the rights, liberties, and privileges of citizens and local governments. Political behavior is constrained by abstract principles such as the inalienable right to own and use property, the right to free speech, or the right to face accusers in a jury trial.

The rule of man manifests itself in the democratic features of the system. Personal rights are determined by the legal system and can be abridged by those controlling the government. In democracies, citizens are permitted substantial control over the functions and activities of the federal government. In a pure democracy, citizen rights and responsibilities are not determined by abstract rules. Instead, they are determined by the majority vote.

The rule of law breaks down when events and behavior are judged by the arbitrary will of men. For example, a criminal suspect is presumed innocent until proven guilty by the judicial system. The standard places limitations on the power of the State or other third parties to deprive the suspect of basic liberties until she can be formally convicted or acquitted. As long as this standard is upheld as law, the suspect is protected by the law and allowed to use the privileges of citizenship (e.g., to be represented by a lawyer, face her accusers, receive trial by jury, etc.).

If the suspect were no longer protected by the law, she would be subjected to the unrestrained and arbitrary will of other people. The police could deprive her of basic freedoms depending on the subjective judgement of individual police officials. Victims could exact retribution from the suspect before she was proven guilty. Justice retreats into a state of formal lawlessness where rules are determined case by case and standards set by the arbitrary whim of powerful individual interests.

Many consider the breakdown of "law and order" unique to the drug economy, symbolically illustrated by random, "drive-by" shootings. Yet, this behavior reflects a more general and subtle breakdown of law and order within the broader, formal urban system. The violence and apparent lawlessness of the drug economy is an extreme extension of a deeper abrogation of the social values necessary to sustain economic growth and community development. The drug economy should thus be interpreted as near the endpoint of rule by men, where law is determined individually and through force rather than through the social evolution of complex orders.

Private Property and the "Police" Powers of the City

One of the most blatant examples of how the institutional environment of the city has changed in the post-World War II era concerns the expansion of government power through the use of eminent domain. Legally, the power of local governments to appropriate private property for public purposes is permitted through the fifth amendment of the Constitution, as long as "adequate" compensation is provided to the original owner based on "fair market value."

Thus, while the power of the State to seize private property is permitted in principle, it is constrained by the general rule of just compensation. The intent of the Constitution lies in its belief that certain actions by government are necessary to promote the general welfare.

The powers of local governments to expropriate property for government purposes have expanded significantly in recent years. "Public purpose" is defined increasingly broadly to include virtually any local government action justified on the grounds of "promoting the general welfare." Moreover, federal courts have consistently upheld the right of local governments to use eminent domain and zoning powers as long as some ostensibly public purpose is identified in the action.[1]

Restraints on the police powers of local governments have weakened, allowing the expansion of the government's ability to transfer benefits from one interest group to another. As a result, the rights to property and the benefits from the productive use of that property are subject to the whims of government officials and politicians.

Eminent domain was often used to help provide public goods that were difficult if not impossible to provide without the assistance of government. In the early nineteenth century, for example, the government's power of eminent domain enabled it to build roads, canals, and railroads. The ability of individual transportation companies to purchase a comprehensive agreement with enough landowners to permit the construction of a coherent and efficient transportation network was considered virtually impossible without government intervention. Yet, rarely did the powers of government move beyond simple public goods problems, often deferring to the rights of individual property owners.

More recently, governments have expanded their use of eminent domain to include most projects designed to promote general goals and objectives. In 1981, the city of Detroit seized the homes of over one thousand families to make way for a new factory.[2] Governments have also used the takings clause of the U.S. Constitution to redistribute land because ownership was concentrated among a few landowners, creating, in the words of the court, "oligopolistic" tendencies in local housing markets. In 1984, the U.S. Supreme Court upheld the Hawaii Housing Authority's right to require landlords to sell their land to tenants based on issues of "affordable housing."[3]

Restrictions on the governments power to seize private property for "public use" have also eroded significantly in recent years. Public use has been interpreted by U.S. courts very broadly to include virtually "any end otherwise within the authority of Congress."[4] The federal courts have routinely upheld the power of a local government to use the takings clause of the U.S. constitution to appropriate property for broadly determined public interests.

Moreover, the power of eminent domain has also moved far beyond the power of Congress and is increasingly used by local governments to further local political and business interests. Some of the most celebrated cases of local governments' using eminent domain to further local political interest in recent years centered on professional sports teams. For example, the Colts football team moved from Baltimore to Indianapolis overnight, infuriating local football fans and politicians. The city attempted to obtain eminent domain powers to keep the team in Baltimore, arguing that the city had a compelling interest in the sports team to maintain the general welfare. Similarly, the states of New York and California sought the same powers based on a compelling public interest to force teams to remain in their local area.

Increasingly private organizations are using the government's powers of eminent domain to further their own interests. In Dayton, Ohio, the University of Dayton, a private Catholic University, received approval to use eminent domain to acquire 114 properties near its campus.[5] Ohio law permits private colleges and universities to appropriate lands through eminent domain if the land is used for educational purposes.

The university claimed that its acquisition of the land would help the school maintain minimum physical standards for student housing and "there is increasing awareness at the university that behavioral standards can be better maintained with respect to students living in university-owned facilities than in privately owned housing."[6] While other public universities had used the law to acquire property, the University of Dayton was the first private school to use the law's privileges in Ohio.

The law stipulates that the university must make a "reasonable" attempt to negotiate a price for the property. Yet, the university offered to buy the property for $5 million while a group of private investors offered the landlord $6.25 million. The university's refusal to match the private investor's commitment resulted in a breakdown in negotiations. Presumably the university's offer represented a reasonable attempt to acquire the property, justifying its request for eminent domain powers to seize the property. In other words, since the university did not want to match the offer of private investors, it would force the landowner to take their offer through the police powers of the state.

More significantly, objections to the "taking" centered on the separation of Church and State rather than on the ability of local governments to transfer eminent domain powers to private parties.

The University of Dayton case is a blatant example of how private interests have edged their way into using local governments to force contracts unsustainable through voluntary bargaining. More often, the exercise of private power is more subtle. Downtown redevelopment projects routinely use eminent domain powers to seize entire blocks of commercial property for private developers through the appearance of public-private joint development projects. The case of seizing homes to make way for a factory serves as a way a city government justifies the expropriation of private property for a public purpose, but the beneficiaries are private developers and business interests.

Contemporary public-private joint ventures blur the distinction between government power and private gain. Downtown redevelopment programs often use eminent domain to seize businesses for new office towers and high rises. In one downtown project, over forty businesses were displaced to make way for a twenty-storey office tower financed by a group of local banks, private developers, and the city. In one instance, a property owner was offered only $67,000 for his business. When the building's owner took the city to court, he was awarded $235,000.[7]

The expanding use of eminent domain is only one case in which the rule of law is breakingdown under the aegis of personal interests. While private parties may have legal title to their land, their control over their property is continually challenged by the expanding power of the local state. As a result private property owners must continually be wary of attempts by others to seize their property. The local state has emerged as a threat to the underlying institutions of the liberal society rather than its protector. This trend promises to continue as local governments become increasingly involved in local development efforts. Already, almost three quarters of all location decisions by manufacturing firms involve some form of government assistance.[8]

Urban Governance and Attenuated Property Rights

In many circles, the subversion of private interests to the authority of an aggressive local government is welcomed. Some urban scholars have recently suggested that cities develop and exploit "public property rights" to ensure private interests work toward goals of social justice. The primary function of cities, they contend, is to protect the disenfranchised and promote an equal distribution of economic and political power.

In a highly acclaimed article on property rights and urban political economy, Judith A. Garber recently wrote:

> In the end, we must understand that cities cannot achieve justice without property rights that are significantly more far reaching than what they have now. Because the present status of the city within American democracy is bound so tightly to a celebration of private property, new forms of land policies will contribute to a revised conception of the city.... If local officials are willing to tap the vein of regulatory innovation and extract what is useful from an evolving judicial doctrine, perhaps they can work around a recalcitrant legal status to achieve more just policy outcomes.[9]

To promote "just policy outcomes," cities will need to expand the concept of property rights to include the "collective rights" of city residents exercised through municipal public policy. The use of city funds to finance downtown development projects is an obvious example of local governments exploiting collective interests. The use of local government financing for projects provides prima facie justification for imposing social obligations on those using the funds. "The notion that municipal rights might actually exist in somebody's private property," notes Garber, "has been offered as a justification for local governments to claim part ownership in plants and sports franchises that have benefitted from public spending."[10] Ultimately, municipal rights supercede private property rights to achieve just outcomes.

What Garber and others have missed, however, is the importance of restricting arbitrary encroachments of government on private property. As Richard Epstein notes, "it is the ability to act at will and without need for justification within some domain which is the essence of freedom, be it of speech or of property."[11] The institutions that contributed the most to the development of modern industrial civilization are those that are being subverted by the aggressive local state.

The public interest view of public policy contends that if only democratic government were unleashed from the chains of constitutional restrictions and guarantees of private property, a just social system could be achieved. This view is increasingly at odds with evidence on the way local governments actually work.

Local governments do not operate on the basis of rational decision models taught in organizational behavior classes. Local decision makers work within a political environment that sharply circumscribes their behavior.[12] Understanding the political and economic environment in which a public official operates provides a better understanding of how policy is developed and implemented. This research suggests that local governments may be incapable of developing rational public policies that have the precise political outcomes (e.g., equal justice) that their proponents contend. A more likely consequence is the emergence of political coalitions that develop and implement policy regardless of the impact on noncoalition members.

Instilling social obligations through the political process undermines the very institutions that facilitate social progress. Eminent domain is one example of how the right to own and use property, even when that use does not harm others, is jeopardized by local government action. Eminent domain controls private use by transferring ownership rights from one party to another. As the previous examples illustrate, these transfers can be from a private party to a public party (e.g., individual to government), or from a private party to another private party.

Planning and Land-Use Regulation

A far more serious threat to the institutional environment of urban areas lies in the expanding responsibilities of planners and regulation. As local governments become more aggressive in their attempts to control private property rights, ownership and use are becoming dichotomized. While individuals may own their property, their uses are typically highly circumscribed by local public policy.

The existing system of land-use regulation is extremely decentralized in the United States. This has caused many people, particularly planners, endless amounts of frustration. Planners are expected to "rationalize" the chaotic development that occurs through economic growth. The "messes" that Jane Jacobs extolled as part of the virtues of urban innovation and experimentation are seen as examples of how uncoordinated and unplanned land uses reduce social welfare by allowing inappropriate and harmful applications. Social harms and inappropriate uses are, of course, determined by the values and visions of the planner. Planners are charged with ensuring that land is put to its highest valued use according to the standards of contemporary planning practice (not necessarily the preferences of the community).

The American system of land use reflects the domination of local government in determining zoning policy. As such, the American system is highly fragmented and decentralized, which works against attempts by planners to unify the complex development process under one coherent plan. The internationally known planning specialist Peter Hall, for example, laments,

Far too much funding has been spread indiscriminately across the country, both among areas in great need and areas in less need. This is because a philosophy of economic development, based on careful analysis of goals and objectives, has not been clearly worked out at the centre.[13]

More comprehensive national and regional planning, Hall contends, would have created a far more even and just distribution of benefits from development and economic progress. For the planner, land use should be coordinated through a vast network of standards that avoid "errors" such as mixed uses.

Yet, the critics of economic development in the United States fail to realize that if a system of comprehensive planning were put in place, the pace and pattern of economic growth would have been substantially different. Economic development must be seen from the perspective of how public policy determines how the costs and benefits of economic activity are calculated.

This approach is known as a "constitutional perspective" and developed from public choice theories of politics. "Central to the constitutional perspective," writes Richard Wagner, an economist and editor of *Constitutional Political Economy*, "is the presumption that political outcomes are largely governed by constitutional rules, so 'better' outcomes result more from developing alternative constitutional rules than from given alternative information and advice to politicians and other public officials."[14] Thus, the problem with policy, on the local level as well as the federal level, is systemic rather than situational.

The very existence of government in the American system rests on the consent of the governed. Personal freedoms and individual rights constrain the powers of government and public policy. This notion of government evolving out of the Enlightenment thinking of the sixteenth and seventeenth century permitted the industrial revolution to unfold in the eighteenth and nineteenth centuries.

Attempts by some scholars and urbanists to expand the scope of government power by attenuating private property rights (particularly the right to own *and* use property) is to overthrow the essence of democratic government and the precepts underlying the economic transformation of the modern industrial world. Although observers of legal trends such as Garber may welcome the expanding powers of local government as a tool for social justice, these trends also undermine the very notions of freedom and liberty that permit social progress to occur. Those advocating restrictions on private property rights and the expansion of government rights over private action ignore the long-term effects of these actions on the social and economic development of a community. Urban development is a dynamic process, continually changing as the needs and desires of residents and citizens change. Advocates of more restrictions on the use of private property implicitly employ a static, short-term perspective concerning the nature of urban development and policy.

Zoning and land-use regulations provide a telling example of how important these influences can be in stifling economic development, particularly in urban areas.

Land-use controls evolved out of concerns over nuisances or externalities.[15] Zoning as a tool for land-use control emerged during the early part of the twentieth century as the federal judicial system validated local government attempts to restrict land uses. During the 1920s, the U.S. Supreme Court officially sanctioned zoning policies that invoked the "police" powers of local governments to protect and promote the general welfare of the community.

With the expansion of local government's capacity to coordinate uses, zoning has emerged as the most important tool in the planner's toolbox. More important, zoning has become the primary method for segregating land uses according to "appropriate" applications. In other words, zoning is the primary means by which planners ensure that everything goes in its proper place.

Some degree of planning always takes place whether in private or public spheres. Firms form plans based on expectations of future demand and prices. Planning, as Peter Hall has noted, "is the making of an orderly sequence of action that will lead to the achievement of a stated goal or goals."[16] Plans are essential in order for people to perform any action as long as human action is defined as purposeful behavior.[17]

Contemporary planning, as it is practiced in cities, regions, and nations, is rooted in geography and viewed within a spatial context. The most important concepts driving planning models, then, focus on how land uses are allocated among divergent functions. Elaborate master plans are devised in which highly specialized land uses are allocated to specific areas of a municipality to control the growth of the community. By arranging land uses appropriately, planners can define the optimal growth path for the community.

The influence of planners has grown steadily with the rise of suburban communities during the post-World War II development era. In some cases, the planner has become the supreme arbiter over land-use development. In Hawaii, for example, the state supreme court upheld the right of county councils to maintain exclusive control over land use over the wishes of voters in a referendum. "Zoning by [voter] initiative," the court claimed, "is inconsistent with the goal of long-range comprehensive planning."[18]

While Hawaii represents an extreme case,[19] the trend is relevant and important for this discussion of public policy and urban economic growth. Gradually, control of land use and development has been abdicated to a set of professional planners. While individuals retain ownership of their property privately, public officials exert control over their use. Without control over the use of private property, the social institutions of private property breakdown.

If someone owned a parcel of land in a city, she could not build anything there without the approval of her local government through the planning department or zoning commission. She would have to check with the local planning commission to determine whether the property was zoned for that use. If the property is not zoned for that specific use, the developer will need to obtain a "variance," permission to use land for a nondesignated use.[20] In other words, the builder could not initiate development without the explicit approval of a professional planner or elected planning commission.

If, for example, the builder wanted to construct a commercial building that would house a few small neighborhood businesses, but the land was zoned for multifamily housing, the landowners would have to petition the local commission for a zoning variance. Only after a hearing was held on the prospective change and, usually, the staff planner evaluated the request, would the variance be approved or rejected.[21] If the request were to be rejected, there would be little the landowner could do.

If the request was approved, the developer could move onto the next stage. Most often, the builder must submit a plan to the city planning department. The planning department will either approve the business plan or return it for modifications. This process will often take several months and lengthy negotiations between the building and the planning department. After the plan is approved, the developer can secure the appropriate building permits and begin construction. An occupancy permit that allows tenants to use the building will not be issued until the city's building inspectors clear the structure through all the city's codes.

The process is not neutral in its affects on development.[22] Unfortunately, it serves more to inhibit development than promote it.

The emergence of the underground economy discussed in chapter 1 illustrates the potential impact of regulation on economic growth. Scholars found that underground economies flourished during periods of recession in the local formal economy. For example, instead of leaving the city center entirely, many manufacturing firms moved into the underground economy.

More important, these firms went underground in order to survive. The transactions costs (e.g., permits, license fees, inspections, etc.) faced by these informal firms are so high that they could not exist profitably in the formal sector. The requirements necessary to maintain a legal profit-making enterprise may entail large diversions of entrepreneurial labor by the small business owner, constraining his ability to adequately supervise production and produce efficiently. Similarly, formal manufacturing facilities may be required to pay higher wages through union contracts. These labor costs could eat into potential profits, providing more incentives for the firm to move underground.

Public policy determines which costs will be part of the formal business sector and which will not. If regulators moved to bring the underground manufacturing facilities into the formal sector, these firms would likely die and further reduce manufacturing employment opportunities in poor minority neighborhoods.

Planners, unfortunately, have ignored the human element in their models. Unlike laws of physics, human growth patterns are unpredictable. Without the appropriate forecasts, many of the benefits of planning and zoning cannot be realized. These effects can be quite significant if the barriers to new development become so important that development ceases.

The implications for economic growth are significant and dramatic. Development, particularly in vigorous and bustling cities, does not progress in an orderly manner. Cities are laboratories for experimentation and diversity. In fact, the entrepreneur's ability to experiment and fail may be as important to the process of economic growth as success.

Planning in contemporary cities, on the other hand, does not allow for failure. The purpose behind master plans and, more recently, comprehensive plans, is to avoid failure by forcing new development to go through a rigorous evaluation procedure. The result is stifled economic growth and deflation of expected profits from successful ventures.

The planning process can work only if land uses are controlled by a centralized body of professionals who pass judgement on the merits of each proposed project. Simply by requiring entrepreneurs to have their plans approved, planners presume that existing allocation of land uses are optimal and that any proposed change must be justified.

Yet, the very nature of entrepreneurship defies prediction, as the previous chapter emphasized. Entrepreneurs base their business plans and judgments on explicit information, which could be transmitted to third parties (such as planners), and tacit knowledge, which is untransferable. While the entrepreneur may be able to transfer the explicit parts of his knowledge through reports, graphs, tables, impact analyses, etc., the tacit element is forever excluded from formal discussion. "Hunches" are rarely considered as part of the objective criteria for approving projects. Planners and public officials can never tap into the tacit elements of human knowledge. Moreover, by restricting the use of tacit knowledge, a tremendous amount of waste is encouraged through the inability of entrepreneurs to change land uses according to the changing preferences of consumers and community.

The responsibilities of ownership have been abdicated to the government or planning body in matters of land use and economic development. This has dire consequences for the future of urban economic growth in inner-city areas. In the modern economy, based on high technology and an educated work force, economies have to adapt quickly and efficiently.

The institutional changes that have occurred within the central city can be summarized through three broad observations about public policy and property rights. First, private property is no longer respected. Control over land uses resides completely within the municipal government. Moreover, cities use their control frequently to abrogate private property rights and force contracts by exercising their police powers for public programs. For most municipal projects, economic exchange by contract has been replaced by coerced exchange, with local governments playing the role as enforcer.

Second, control over development is highly centralized and power is concentrated at the top. New development must be approved by planning or zoning commissions, or city departments responsible for permits and licenses. Spontaneity is virtually outlawed since any use of land that contradicts the master plan is, by definition, a nonconformity and treated as an exception. This places the burden on the developer to "prove" that the prospective use is appropriate or justified. Thus, institutional change is discouraged since entrepreneurial opportunities are truncated by the bureaucratic policy-making process.

Third, the values that are promulgated in urban economies promote conformity rather than risk taking. Public policy governing land use and economic development dampens entrepreneurial tendencies by attempting to weed out failures and guarantee successes. Development in urban economies is characterized by organizational accountability rather than market accountability. Whether a project is approved or not depends on how well the developer can fight through the local bureaucracy to secure the appropriate variances, permits, and licenses to operate. Market accountability, on the other hand, requires only that the entrepreneur produces a product that will satisfy untapped demand.

Ultimately, the underlying institutional framework of many cities is regressive since it strengthens the arbitrary whims of special interest politics over the more abstract concerns of the rule of law. Spontaneous development is viewed with hostility and creativity with suspicion. To the extent entrepreneurship occurs at all, it is in spite of these obstacles rather than because of them. The rules and customs have changed dramatically from the days when the main concern of the building and inspections department was safety. Now, the emphasis is on political conformity in most cities.

The change evident in these trends in public policy is related to the breakdown of institutions discussed in chapter 2. Economic growth is fostered by institutions that respect creativity and individuality. Tangibly, this respect manifests itself in the respect for private property and self-expression. The broadening of the police powers of government, combined with fewer restrictions on the use of these powers, has contributed to an erosion of these traditions, customs, and rules that form the institutional context for economic development. This transition in urban policy has validated rule by men through the political process over the rule of law.

The Drug Economy and Economic Growth

The institutional foundations of the drug economy appear, at first, substantially different from those of the legitimate economy. Ironically, they are similar in very important respects. In both spheres of social interaction, the rule of law has diminished as an important constraint on the coercive behavior of others. Increasingly, the rules of the game in the inner city encourage the acceptance of institutions that support the arbitrary rule of men over abstract principles. In the informal economy, these trends are most evident in the drug economy and general changes within the criminal justice system.

The Institutional Foundations of the Drug Trade

The most obvious difference between market activity in the formal sector and market activity in the informal sector is its legal status. Informal transactions, by definition, take place outside the formal legal system. By implication, informal transactions are not supported by the legal system. The drug economy's illegality may, in fact, be the primary source of the social costs of the drug use and abuse in the United States.[23]

The lack of a formal legal system does not mean that there is a complete absence of order. Markets are institutions that organize human activity to facilitate exchange even though markets do not exist via statutory law. Markets exist as means for allocating scarce resources among competing uses within a society. Market prices act as signals to entrepreneurs who direct their activities to satisfy consumer desires. Thus, through the price mechanism, markets are "ordered" and have rules governing market-based activity (e.g., profits and losses). The absence of a legal system codified by statute simply suggests that other, less formal institutional factors are at work.

In constitutional systems, explicit constraints are placed on govern-mental power to protect specific rights deemed inalienable prior to the creation of the government. The role of the judiciary is to interpret the meaning of statutory law with respect to the intent of the constitution and the more abstract principles of the right to life, liberty, property, and happiness. No individual or branch of government is empowered with the right to supersede the constitution. Moreover, to further constrain the power of government over the rights of the citizens, strict rules exist for amending the constitution.[24]

Similarly, order exists in illegal drug markets as market participants conform to certain rules and customs. Drug dealers, for example, tend to limit their transactions to relatively small, confined markets where buyers can be monitored and tracked. Any buyer is a potential police informant or undercover officer. Small-scale, face-to-face transactions reduce the dealer's probability of arrest by allowing more intimacy between buyer and seller. A dealer may more easily detect an undercover police officer in a face-to-face meeting than in a more distant mail order transaction where addresses and accounts can be traced. Similarly, virtually all drug deals use cash transactions to avoid detection by drug enforcement authorities.

These may seem like obvious rules to follow for illegal businesses, but they form the basis for an extended order in the underground economy. A set of rules for behavior emerges that allows these agents to interact in meaningful economic exchange. When these rules are violated, the underground enterprises must also find ways of punishing offenders. The rules of punishment eventually become accepted as a part of the general context in which business is transacted.

Exchange could not take place without some element of consistency in routine business practices. For example, when a drug user purchases drugs from a dealer, he does not expect the dealer to kill him. Similarly, the drug dealer does not expect the buyer to kill him once his cache of drugs has been sold. Some element of trust exists between the buyers and sellers of the product. This element of trust forms the basis for all economic transactions in the drug economy.

In fact, millions of peaceful transactions take place every day in some of the most violent sections of American cities. These transactions are punctuated by intermittent violence as dealers and buyers attempt to enforce contracts. The violence, however, is not arbitrary and is often provoked by someone's failure (or suspected failure) to follow through on a previously negotiated transaction.

Nevertheless, the illicit nature of the drug trade also implies that market participants are willing to take more risks. The personalities of the participants themselves will have an impact on the dynamics of the drug trade. Generally, those entering into the drug trade tend to be poor minority men with little hope of obtaining well-paying jobs in a high-tech, high-touch information economy. As chapter 5 details, these individuals expect little (and receive little) from the legitimate economy. The underground drug economy at least *promises* short-term income gains.

These gains can be rather substantial. In a recent analysis of the Washington, D.C. drug trade published by the RAND Corporation, the expected benefits and costs of drug trafficking were calculated.[25] On average, regular drug dealers were reporting incomes of $24,000 per year (tax free). Almost two-thirds of these dealers also held jobs in the formal sector, although their average pay was $7.00 per hour (about $14,000 per year or about $11,000 after taxes).

These earnings have induced larger numbers of young people into the potentially lucrative drug trade. From 1981 to 1986, juvenile arrests for drug trafficking in Washington, D. C. increased from 58 to 1,550.[26] The proportion of juveniles arrested for distribution increased from 17 percent to 82 percent in the same period (fig. 3.2). In contrast, the number of arrests for possession increased at a substantially lower rate from 285 in 1981 to only 344 in 1986. While the larger number of juvenile arrests may be a result of the increased crackdown on drug trafficking in the late 1980s, juvenile distribution arrests grew faster than adult distribution arrests.[27]

FIGURE 3.2
Juvenile Arrests for Drug Offenses
in Washington, D.C.: 1981 and 1987

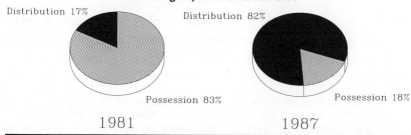

Distribution 17%   Distribution 82%

Possession 83%   Possession 18%

1981   1987

Source: Peter Reuter, Robert MacCoun, and Patrick Murphy, *Money From Crime: A Study of the Economics of Drug Dealing in Washington, D.C.* (Santa Monica, Calif.: The Rand Corporation, 1990). 29

Moreover, these trends paralleled trends on the national level among adult convictions. The number of people convicted for distribution in federal courts almost doubled, from 5,429 in 1982 to 10,564 in 1986.[28] Convictions for possession, on the other hand, decreased from 1,353 in 1982 to 1,225 in 1986. Of the 380,160 inmates in local jails in 1989, 12 percent were in jail for drug trafficking alone - the largest single group of offenders.[29] Moreover, incarcerations for trafficking offenses increased much faster than for possession offenses: while the proportion of offenders in local jails for drug possession doubled from 1983 to 1989, the proportion incarcerated for trafficking tripled.

These trends are at least partly explainable by the potential income opportunities from drug dealing. Taking into account the probabilities for death, physical injury, and incarceration in Washington, D.C. for drug dealing, a regular, full-time risk-neutral drug dealer would need to earn at least $20,000 per year to compensate him for the risks associated with the profession.[30] In terms of pure monetary returns, the risks associated with drug dealing seem to be more than adequately compensated by the market. Thus, the authors of the study on the Washington drug trade found that almost 25 percent of Washington's young, African-American male population was involved to some extent in the drug trade.[31]

A common criticism of drug prohibition is that by making drug purchases illegal, the system forces normally law-abiding consumers to interact with criminals.[32] By making drugs illegal, the general public works routinely with people who survive by violating normal rules of conduct (embodied in statutory law). In addition, by criminalizing drug use, otherwise law-abiding citizens automatically become criminals. The drug user is not considered substantially different from the mugger or the burglar.

Similarly, an unintended consequence of drug prohibition is to bring normally law-abiding young people into a violent and corrupt business enterprise. The primary motivation of younger drug dealers is money. As Peter Reuter, Robert MacCoun, and Patrick Murphy observe,

> Drug dealing now offers poorly educated young males potential earnings that appear far higher than any other activity—at least in the short-run. A tax-free $40,000 per year is much more than such persons might reasonably expect to earn from working hard at unskilled or semiskilled jobs. For some, drug dealing may also be associated with the prospect of making higher incomes if they move up in the drug trade (an unlikely outcome for most persons in conventional employment).[33]

Most inner-city teenagers are faced with high unemployment, or employment in low-paying jobs with few prospects for advancement. The perceived possibility of making a thousand dollars a week selling drugs part-time more than compensates many young men for abrogating any moral inhibitions against selling drugs. To the extent involvement in the drug trade increases the frequency of drug use and experimentation with other drugs, a lucrative drug market could even further corrupt dealers.

Unfortunately, the rules that young traffickers learn work against the rules necessary to sustain economic growth and development in the formal economy. Drug dealers are consistently circumventing the law. They attempt to abridge existing rules or values in their attempts to stay out of jail and supply their product. In many cases, drug dealers may be forced to extreme lengths (e.g., murder) to protect their market or prevent "hostile takeovers" from other dealers. While this behavior fosters a form of self-reliance, the context of the drug economy (e.g., its legal status) prevents the emergence of more stable rules that could more fully develop the skills and abilities of the young dealers. The short-term profits gained from the drug trade reinforces attitudes that ignore socially accepted rules and norms codified into law.

The most extreme example of how these factors work against sustained social development concerns the respect for human life. As discussed in chapter 2, development emerged out of institutions that preserved and protected human life through the institution of private property. By restraining a ruler's ability to arbitrarily confiscate property, these institutions permitted individuals to invest resources in longer-term, more productive endeavors such as factories. The institutions respected liberty and the freedom of individuals to use their privately owned resources to whatever end they felt proper. The core of the slowly evolving system of rules and customs respected the individual's life as preeminent.

The drug economy is notorious for its use of violence to enforce discipline in its enterprises and enforce contracts. The Colombian cartels, in particular, are well-known for using kidnapping and murder to enforce loyalty within their organizations. They have also been willing to move beyond the confines of their businesses to attack politicians, judges, police, and other potential opponents to their trade and methods. As Steven Wisotsky noted recently, Colombians are even willing to kill groups of people who are associated with their targets.[34]

Drug-related killings currently makeup substantial proportions of all homicides in major American cities. In Washington, D.C., an estimated

60 percent of all homicides were considered drug related.[35] In Dade County, Florida, officials estimate that over one-third of the homicides were connected in some way to the drug trade, while one-fourth of homicides in New York City were classified as drug-related.[36]

Indeed, most law enforcement officials blame the recent rise in urban violence on the drug trade.[37] "In much the same way that the traditional Mafia uses professional contract killers to settle its disputes," notes Wisotsky, "cocaine traffickers also require private methods of security, discipline, and punishment."[38]

American drug laws send mixed and confusing signals to unemployed, undereducated inner-city teenagers. On one level, the legal system is set up to protect the right of citizens to do what they want as long as they do not harm others in the process. The legal system supposedly protects the right of people to engage in voluntary exchanges as long as the transactions respect their respective individual rights (as stipulated in the Constitution and the legal code).

On the other hand, the most visible part of the criminal justice system is geared toward an activity that, in addition to being one of the few lucrative employment activities, does not directly harm others. Drug sales are completely voluntary. No one can be forced to buy drugs. In addition, street-level sales rarely involve violence. In fact, if a dealer developed a reputation for violence among his normal customers, he would likely be out of business quickly as his customers found more passive suppliers. Yet, the legal system does not protect those contracts. Contract enforcement is left to the specific needs and individual judgement of the dealer.

In the absence of the peaceful dispute resolution available through the legal system, contract enforcement inevitably becomes violent. Violence is also becoming an accepted part of drug dealer behavior because the trade is inherently constrained by uncertainty, deception, and theft. A dealer often does not know if his customer is a undercover policeman, a rival drug dealer moving in on his territory, or a normal customer. In order to protect his market and reduce the likelihood of being arrested, the drug dealer is forced to consider anyone a potential enemy and demonstrate a willingness to take whatever means necessary to protect his business. If large segments of a neighborhood accept violence and distrust as a normal element of life, the institutions necessary to promote economic progress and community development breakdown.

The breakdown of the values, customs, and traditions necessary to sustain development has already begun. *Chicago Tribune* columnist Clarence Page has written that "frontier justice" has returned to New York City as citizens take "the law" into their own hands. Bernard Goetz's case was only the beginning, as larger numbers of people take measures to protect themselves. Cases of "jiffy justice in the Big Apple have become so common that they seldom make national news anymore," says Page, "unless . . . the victims and their assailants cross racial lines, as they did in Goetz's case."[39]

The willingness to use violence to settle disputes reaches deep into the social fabric of inner-city neighborhoods. Even minor disputes can become legitimate reasons for murder. Numerous instances of teenagers attacking and killing each other over tennis shoes and jogging clothes have emerged in cities as disparate as Detroit, Atlanta, and Hapeville, Georgia. During the early 1980s, profits from drug dealing have fueled a multi-billion-dollar market for athletic shoes and sportswear in many large central cities.[40] One sportswear shop in Connecticut was earning an estimated $2,000 per week from drug dealers. Drug dealers in cities are setting more than fashion trends in sportswear. They are also teaching survival values to those who engage in the trade.[41]

Ironically, these changes are encouraged by current trends in public policy. The importance of abstract principle or law has diminished significantly. Already, restraints on municipal power over private property have bowed to interest group pressure. Similarly, the legal system is bending to popular will in the drug war at the expense of principled justice.

Constitutional protections against unreasonable search and seizure have practically collapsed in recent years in order to support the government's War on Drugs. A review of over two hundred federal appeals court rulings during 1989 found that "judges are routinely upholding the legality of searches involving citizens who fit no profile at all - people who are stopped simply at random in bus, train or airplane terminals."[42] Appeals courts are defining search and seizure in increasingly narrow ways. For instance, police officers on an Amtrack train blocked an exit from a cabin to question a passenger. The court ruled that the search was legal since the passenger was "free to leave" and not technically "seized." Craig Bradley, a law professor at the University of Indiana has observed a national trend toward expanding the powers of police to search citizens without cause. Courts, he continued, "are influenced by the drug scare in much the same way courts were influenced by the Red Scare."[43]

Politicians have weakened constitutional protections against the arbitrary use of force by altering the standards of proof necessary to confiscate private property for legal purposes. Many local police forces are allowed to use the assets confiscated in drug-related arrests to fund their drug enforcement efforts. This clearly provides an incentive for police departments to emphasize drug-related operations over others such as non-drug-related murder, burglary, theft, arson, etc.

More important, police can routinely seize assets even if the suspect is not convicted of the crime. Houses, cars, and land are constantly seized by police through civil court proceedings with lower standards of proof than in criminal courts. Civil law requires that the police's behavior is justified by "probable cause," not guilt beyond reasonable doubt. Indeed, more lenient standards in civil courts may well reflect the current emphasis by drug enforcement authorities on civil law. While all states and the District of Columbia have laws allowing for the forfeiture of assets in civil courts, only nine—or 17 percent—have provisions for asset forfeiture through criminal proceedings.[44] Thus, even if the police cannot prove that someone was trafficking drugs, they can seize his property as long as there was evidence suggesting the suspect could traffic the drugs.

In one case in Ohio, the home and property of a family of four was seized after police found twenty-five marijuana plants on the property.[45] The suspect claimed the plants were grown for personal consumption and were not intended for sale. An agent from the Federal Bureau of Investigation in Cincinnati noted that the law does not require that the home owner be convicted or that the amount of marijuana found be significant. In principle, a home could be seized if police found a few marijuana seeds somewhere on the property.

Drug dealers have also been singled out for special prosecution and punishment by the legal system. The Bush Administration's former "Drug Czar," William Bennet, has advocated the death penalty for "drug kingpins."[46] In Los Angeles, a twenty-two-year-old man received a life sentence for possessing five and one-half ounces of cocaine.[47] This is the same sentence that could be given to cocaine drug cartel leaders like Carlos Lehder and Juan Matta Ballesteros. The administration has also enlisted the use of the military to assist in drug enforcement efforts.[48] The

Customs Service has asked for authorization to shoot down planes suspected of carrying drugs. The recent drug trial of Washington, D.C. mayor Marion Barry provides one of the most visible cases of the extent to which corruption has permeated local governments. The jury convicted Barry on only one count of cocaine possession despite testimony suggesting hundreds of cases where the mayor used drugs during the 1980s.[49]

As the War on Drugs escalates, the powers of government are becoming increasingly broad and arbitrary. The rule of law is eroding. Legal rules are no longer applied equally within a commonly accepted set of standards of fairness or justice. Lawmakers and law enforcement officials have slowly carved special niches within the criminal justice system for drug dealers. The end result is to promote values that place personal values (e.g., do all that is necessary to put drug dealers out of business) over commonly accepted customs and norms.

Institutional Consequences of the Drug Economy

The rise of the drug economy is seriously undermining the institutional foundations of limited government and individual liberty. As chapter 2 detailed, these values formed the cornerstone of the economic development experienced during the eighteenth and nineteenth centuries. The drug economy undermines these principals in three general ways

First, the drug economy is driven by short-term profits. For many young men in American inner cities, employment prospects are dim. The drug economy promises short-term income gains at the price of forsaking the legal system and socially accepted behavior, such as finding employment in the legitimate sector. In contrast, sustained economic development is driven by long-term objectives. Typically, factories are built to last decades and, sometimes, generations. As the next chapter details, most drug dealers have left their profession on a full-time basis by the time they reach their mid to late twenties.

Second, the drug economy is driven by violence. This violence works against the conditions necessary for sustained economic development. The economic advances of the eighteenth and nineteenth centuries built on the evolution of peaceful institutions embracing respect for negotiated contract, nonviolent dispute resolution and trust. The drug economy, in contrast, is driven by suspicion and distrust. Law is determined by the individual as judge, jury, and enforcer, and enforcement is arbitrary.

Third, the drug economy limits personal development. The drug economy is hierarchical and intolerant.

Sustained economic development is driven by creativity and innovation, which enhances individual productivity. Individual initiative in the drug economy is encouraged only if it is geared toward satisfying superiors or the collective consciousness/identity of the family or gang. Sustained economic development can only be achieved through an institutional environment facilitating contract, agreement, and productive investment. Public policy in American cities, the criminal justice system, and the drug economy currently discourage this behavior by making contracts unpredictable and subjecting agreements to the arbitrary machinations of individual actors or special interests.

Notes

1. For a review of the relationship between federal courts and local government powers, see William A. Fischel, *The Economics of Zoning Laws: A Property Rights Approach to American Land Use Controls* (Baltimore: Johns Hopkins University Press, 1985), 39-58.
2. Reported in the syndicated column by Frank Wilner, "Power of Eminent Domain Being Stretched Beyond 'Public Use,'" *Hampton (VA) Daily Press*, 18 September 1984.
3. Richard A. Epstein, *Takings: Private Property and the Power of Eminent Domain* (Cambridge, Mass.: Harvard University Press, 1985), 180-81.
4. Epstein, *Takings*, 161.
5. Sandy Theis, "Regents Back UD Plan to Use Eminent Domain to Get Property," *Dayton Daily News*, 15 July 1989, sec. A, pp. 1, 5.
6. Ibid., p. 5. The university is a Catholic school and some observers have expressed doubt that the eminent domain privileges would be upheld in court based on the separation of Church and State.
7. "Building Gone: Battle Goes On: Ownership Says City Took Structure Illegally for Arcade Centre," *Dayton Daily News*, 26 January 1988, p. 5.
8. John P. Blair, *Urban and Regional Economics* (Homewood, Il: Richard D. Irwin, 1991), 39.
9. Judith A. Garber, "Law and the Possibilities for a Just Urban Political Economy," *Journal of Urban Affairs* 12, no. 2: 12.
10. Garber, "Law and the Possibilities," 11.
11. Epstein, *Takings*, 66.
12. For an excellent review of the literature and an original contribution to the literature on city management, see William A. Pammer, *Managing Fiscal Strain in Major American Cities* (New York: Greenwood Press, 1990).
13. Peter Hall, *Urban and Regional Planning* (Boston: George Allen & Unwin, 1982), 271.

14. Richard E. Wagner, *To Promote the General Welfare: Market Processes vs. Political Transfers* (San Francisco: Pacific Research Institute for Public Policy, 1989), 17.
15. An excellent review of the literature and development of zoning law can be found in Fischel, *The Economics of Zoning Laws*; Richard F. Babcock, "Zoning," in *The Practice of Local Government Planning*, ed. Frank S. So, Israel Stollman, Frank Beal, and David S. Arnold (Washington, D.C.: International City Management Association, 1979), 416-43.
16. Hall, *Urban and Regional Planning*, 6.
17. Human action as purposeful behavior has been the subject of numerous discussions in economics. See Ludwig Von Mises, *Human Action: A Treatise on Economics*, 3d ed. (Chicago: Henry Regnery Gateway Company, 1966).
18. Quoted from "Hawaii Court Says No to Ballot Box Zoning," *Planning* 55, no. 8 (August 1989): 31.
19. The influence of planners, registered by the number of existing planning positions, varies considerably across the United States. For a discussion of recent trends and their implications, see Frank J. Popper, "Understanding American Land Use Regulation Since 1970: A Revisionist Interpretation," *Journal of the American Planning Association* 54, no. 3 (Summer 1988): 291-301.
20. In reality, a variance is an admission that planners forecast land use incorrectly. Many planners are highly critical of variances, particularly when used frequently, because it allows land uses to deviate from the plan. See the discussion in Arthur B. Gallion and Simon Eisner, *The Urban Pattern: City Planning and Design*, 5th ed. (New York: Van Nostrand Reinhold, 1986), 230-31.
21. Planners have a substantial influence over the zoning process. Although zoning and zoning variances are usually considered highly contentious and politicized, a recent case study of the Atlanta metropolitan area revealed the professional planners and administrators have a substantial influence on the final outcome of requests. In fact, only a small minority of requests that are rejected by planners are overridden by the planning board. See Arnold Fleishmann, "Politics, Administration, and Local Land-Use Regulation: Analyzing Zoning as a Policy Process," *Public Administration Review* 49, no. 4 (July/August 1989): 337-44.
22. In fact, this problem is recognized within the literature and has resulted in several recent attempts to modify planning practices. See the discussions in Ruth Eckdish Knack, "Repent Ye Sinners, Repent," *Planning* 55, no. 8 (August 1989), pp. 4-13; "Rules Made to Be Broken," *Planning* 54, no. 11 (November 1988): 16-21; "The Once and Future Suburb," *Planning* 52, no. 2 (February 1986): 24-27; John King, "Protecting Industry from Yuppies and Other Invaders," *Planning* 54, no. 6 (June 1988): 4-8; Charles A. Setchell and Dan Marks, "4 Rms Hwy Vu," *Planning* 50, no. 9 (September 1984): 21-24.
23. See chapters 7 and 8 for a more thorough discussion of these issues. For a general introduction to this approach to the drug problem, see David Boaz, ed., *The Crisis in Drug Prohibition* (Washington, D.C.: Cato Institute), 1990.
24. This does not imply that governments do not abridge civil liberties or that economic agents do not attempt to abrogate contracts in formal economic markets. On the contrary, these infractions occur all the time. The formal sector, however, has allowed the development of peaceful institutions for resolving conflicts to the satisfaction of most members of the community. Even though private individuals or governments attempt to abridge civil liberties, they do not have the *right* or statutory authority to arbitrarily abridge freedom.

25. Peter Reuter, Robert MacCoun, and Patrick Murphy, *Money From Crime: A Study of the Economics of Drug Dealing in Washington, D.C.* (Santa Monica, Calif.: The Rand Corporation, 1990).
26. Ibid., 29.
27. Ibid.
28. U.S. Department of Justice, "Drug Law Violators, 1980-86," *Bureau of Justice Statistics Special Report* (Washington, D.C.: Bureau of Justice Statistics, 1988), 3, table 3.
29. Allen J. Beck, "Profile of Jail Inmates, 1989," *Bureau of Justice Statistics Special Report* (Washington, D.C.: U.S. Department of Justice, Bureau of Justice Statistics, April 1991), 4.
30. Reuter, MacCoun, & Murphy, *Money from Crime*, 104-5.
31. Ibid., 46.
32. See the discussions in David Boaz, "The Consequences of Prohibition," Boaz, *Crisis in Drug Prohibition*, 2; Randy Barnett, "Curing the Drug-Law Addiction," in *Dealing With Drugs: Consequences of Government Control*, ed. Ronald Hamowy. (Lexington, Mass.: Lexington Books/D.C. Heath & Company, 1987), 83-86.
33. Reuter, MacCoun & Murphy, *Money from Crime*, 102.
34. Steven Wisotsky, *Beyond the War on Drugs: Overcoming a Failed Public Policy* (Buffalo, N.Y.: Prometheus Books, 1990), 150-52.
35. "Drugs Blamed for Bloody Year," (AP) *Dayton Daily News* 28 December, 1989, sec. A, p. 4.
36. Wisotsky, *Beyond the War on Drugs*, 151.
37. Note this comment from a recent news report: "This was the bloodiest year on record in at least a half-dozen of America's big cities, and law enforcement officials are viturally unanimous in blaming drug wars for the violence. . . . One expert suggested that violence has ebbed in some cities because drug dealers have already killed their rivals and divided their turf." See also note 36.
38. Wisotsky, *Beyond the War on Drugs*, p. 152.
39. Clarence Page, "Frontier Justice Invades Big Apple," *Dayton Daily News* 21 June 1990, sec. A, p. 11.
40. For a journalistic review of how violence has become a part of this business, see Rick Telander, "Senseless," *Sports Illustrated* 14 May 1990, pp. 36-49.
41. It is important to note that trends in violence are not specific to any one ethnic group. A recent study found that demographic variables such as sex, age, and urban versus nonurban residence were better predictors of attitudes toward violence than ethnic background. The authors conclude that "the data suggest that blacks and American Indians have had more violence experiences than the general population. Blacks and Hispanics were less tolerant of violence than the general population, although the fuller contexts of these experiences were not available from the surveys being analyzed." See Donald J. Shoemaker and J. Sherwood Williams, "The Subculture of Violence and Ethnicity," *Journal of Criminal Justice* 15, no. 7 (1987): 461-472.
42. Tracy Thompson, "4th Amendment is Trampled in Drug Offensive, Critics Say: More Courts Upholding Random Searches," *Washington Post* 7 May 1990, sec. A, p. 1.
43. Ibid.
44. Timothy J. Flanagan and Kathleen Maguire, eds., *Sourcebook of Criminal Justice Statistics 1989.* (Washington, D.C.: U.S. Department of Justice, Bureau of Justice Statistics, Government Printing Office, 1990), 118, table 1.101.

45. Wes Hills, "Pot Growers Might Lose Their Homes," *Dayton Daily News* 11 March 1990, sec. B, p. 1.
46. See the review of the drug war strategy in Jack Kelley, "President Wants Broader Use of Death Penalty in Drug War," *USA Today* 12 January 1990, sec. A, p. 2.
47. "Man Gets Life for 5 1/2 Ounces of Cocaine," *Dayton Daily News* 11 September 1990, sec. A, p. 11.
48. For a discussion of the issues surrounding the military waging the drug war, see Ted Galen Carpenter and R. Channing Rouse, "Perilous Panacea: The Military in the Drug War," *Cato Institute Policy Analysis no. 128* (Washington, D.C.: Cato Institute, 1990).
49. See B. Drumman Ayres, Jr. "Final Arguments Begin in Barry Trial," *New York Times* 2 August 2 1990, sec. A, p. 8, and "D.C. Mayor Gets 6-Month Prison Term," *Dayton Daily News*, 27 October 1990, sec. A, pp. 1, 8.

PART II

FOUNDATIONS
OF THE DRUG ECONOMY

4

Drug Use and Abuse in America

The underground economy operates like all market economies. Prices mediate between consumers who want the product on the market and suppliers who ensure that consumers get what they want. Variations in price send signals to consumers and producers about the relative costs of maintaining the market for illicit drugs. Higher prices tell consumers that the relative costs of supplying illegal drugs in the black market will be high, while lower prices suggest that the costs will be low. The way the two sides of the economic equation work is essential for evaluating the prospective role of public policy.

All markets are ultimately driven by consumer behavior. While some suppliers may be able to influence the price of their product, they cannot force people to consume it. Thus, as economists frequently observe, demand curves slope downward: at higher prices consumers demand less of a product and at lower prices they demand more.

Although a consumer base is necessary for a market in illegal drugs, the supply side operates through a separate set of incentives and goals from the demand side. More specifically, the supply side is profit-driven while the demand side is utility-driven. Producers attempt to find the most efficient methods of supplying a product to the market. Consumers, on the other hand, are simply attempting to satisfy their preferences for illicit drugs.

The drug economy is often presented as fundamentally different from traditional markets because of the addictive properties of illegal drugs such as heroin, cocaine, and, more recently, crack. The physically and psychologically addictive qualities of heroin and cocaine are widely cited in the contemporary "war" on drugs. The increased use of "crack," or rock cocaine, has accompanied fears that new, synthetic versions of cocaine may be "instantly" addictive. Thus, public service antidrug announcements carry the slogan, "don't even try it once."

Indeed, clinical evidence suggests that many harder drugs are very addictive. At the same time, as more work appears on the addictive qualities of these drugs, researchers are finding that drug use, even among addicts, is controllable. Even the classic heroin addict, who refuses to quit his habit for fear of withdrawal, will alter his behavior to accommodate the accessibility of the drug. As the following sections will show, the ability of the drug user to control drug use is essential for understanding the dynamics of the illegal drug industry and the role of public policy. The ability of users to control their drug intake makes consumers responsive to price changes.

Nevertheless, addiction certainly has an important impact on the structure of demand for illicit drugs in the United States. Yet addicts do not necessarily dominate drug use in the United States. In fact, the largest and most profitable sector of the drug economy is the market for cocaine, which is considered less addictive than heroin. The second largest sector is the market for marijuana, which is considered one of the least addictive psychoactive substances (even when compared to alcohol and tobacco). Early estimates suggest that more than half of heroin trafficking exists to support an addict population. As evidence mounts that substantial numbers of users are not addicts, however, even the demand for heroin can be seen as responsive to price fluctuations.

Drug Use and Availability

Drug use in the United States is extensive, although trends since 1975 suggest a slight decline. Lloyd D. Johnston, Patrick M. O'Malley, and Jerald G. Bachman, of the University of Michigan's Institute for Social Research, have published the most widely recognized analysis of trends in drug use.[1] Their analysis of survey data from 1975 to 1986 reveal that older age groups have higher levels of "lifetime" experience. In other words, older people experiment with more types of drugs. The authors, however, did not find a corresponding increase in the daily or monthly use of drugs in this age group. Thus, despite the fact that young adults continue to experiment with drugs, few become heavy users.

Cocaine use appears as a unique exception. They observe,

> *Cocaine* presents a somewhat unique case in that lifetime, annual, and current use *all* rise substantially with age, at least through age 24....In 1986, lifetime prevalence by age 27-28 was roughly 40%, vs. 17% among today's high school seniors (and 10% among the 27-28 year-old cohorts when they were seniors in the mid 1970's). Annual prevalence for 27-28 year-olds today is about 20% and 30-day prevalence around 8%—again, appreciably higher than for 1986 seniors. Clearly this is a drug which is used much more frequently among people in their twenties than among those in their late teens; and at the present time this fact distinguishes it from all of the other illicit drugs. (Emphasis in original.)[2]

In contrast, experience with marijuana rises from under 50 percent to 76 percent by the time students are nine to ten years out of high school. Yet, daily use remained the same. In contrast, daily alcohol consumption increased with age (at least through age 28).

These data are confirmed by earlier studies tracking the age of first use among drug users (fig. 4.1). A study of over 27,000 participants in federally supported drug- treatment programs between 1973 and 1975 found that most were exposed to heroin and cocaine at later ages than marijuana (table 4.1). While over half of the participants had used marijuana before they were fifteen, only 14 percent had used heroin. Exposure to cocaine, however, tended to spread out more evenly, with peak exposure occurring between sixteen and twenty years old.

In fact, the percentage of high school seniors ever having used marijuana, cocaine, or heroin has declined (table 4.2). The most popular drugs are the ones most entrenched in American social custom: alcohol and cigarettes. The prevalence of alcohol among seniors increased from 90.4 percent in 1975 to 93.2 percent in 1980, although alcohol use seems to have declined somewhat during the 1980s. While tobacco is the second most used drug, its use has declined significantly since 1975.

These data should be qualified, since a general trend exists toward lower-tar cigarettes and less-potent alcoholic beverages such as beer. Even though alcohol and tobacco remain the most used drugs, their use has been accompanied by reduced health risks. Nevertheless, in absolute terms, smoking has declined among high school seniors from 73.6 percent in 1975 to 67.6 percent in 1988.

In contrast, the proportion of high school students reporting use of either marijuana, cocaine, or heroin is substantially lower. Nevertheless, marijuana remains the most popular of the three drugs (fig. 4.2). It is important to note that the proportion of high school seniors indicating that they had used marijuana at least once declined from 60.3 percent in 1980 to 47.2 percent in 1988. Perhaps more important, cocaine experienced an increase in popularity in the 1980s but has declined substantially toward the end of the decade.

FIGURE 4.1
Age of First Use for Cocaine, Heroin, and Marijuana

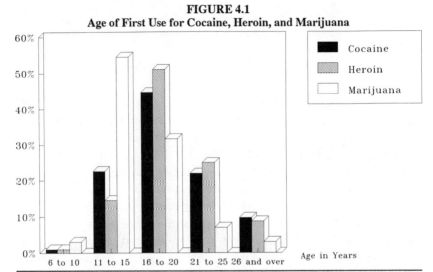

Source: Leon Gibson Hunt, *Assessment of Local Drug Abuse* (Lexington, Mass.: Lexington Books, 1977), 59, table 7.1

These trends persist when frequency is considered (table 4.3). In 1986, over half of the high school seniors surveyed indicated they had used marijuana. Only 23 percent, however, indicated they had used marijuana within the last thirty days. Only 6 percent of high school students indicated they had used cocaine in the last thirty days. Although cocaine use increased significantly since the mid-1970s, cocaine users remain a small minority of the drug-user population. The heroin user formed a negligible part of the general drug-user population and has not increased significantly in recent years. On the other hand, almost two-thirds of the students polled said they had used alcohol.

When seniors were asked about their daily consumption of these drugs, very few students indicated they used them on a daily basis (table 4.4). Based on data for the years through 1986, the most frequently abused illicit drug appears to be tobacco: almost one-fifth of high school seniors said they smoked on a daily basis. Daily cocaine use and heroin use constituted less than 1 percent of the drug use among American high school seniors. Even the popular drugs alcohol and marijuana were used daily by only 4 percent.

TABLE 4.1
Age of First Use of Selected Drugs

Age	Cocaine (in %)	Heroin (in %)	Marijuana (in %)
6 to 10 years old	1.0%	1.0%	3%
11 to 15	22.6	14.5	54.5
16 to 20	44.6	51.0	31.7
21 to 25	22.0	25.0	7.0
26 to 30	6.9	7.7	3.0
Over 30	2.8	1.0	-

Source: Leon Gibson Hunt, *Assessment of Local Drug Abuse* (Lexington, Mass.: Lexington Books, 1977), 59, table 7-1.

Note: Data for heroin and marijuana users are from 1973. Data for cocaine users are from 1975.

TABLE 4.2
Prevalence of Selected Drugs among High School Seniors, 1975-1988

Drug	1975	1980	1985	1986	1988
Percent ever having used:					
Marijuana	48.3%	60.3%	54.2%	50.9%	48.2%
Cocaine	9.0	15.7	17.3	16.9	12.1
Heroin	2.2	1.1	1.2	1.1	1.1
Alcohol	90.4	93.2	92.2	91.3	92.0
Cigarettes	73.6	71.0	68.8	67.6	N/AV

Source: Lloyd D. Johnston, Patrick M. O'Malley, and Jerald G. Bachman, *National Trends in Drug Use and Related Factors Among American High School Students and Youth Adults, 1975-1986* (Washington, D.C.: U.S. Department of Health and Human Services, 1987), Table 7; Timothy J. Flanagan and Kathleen Maguire, eds., *Sourcebook of Criminal Justice Statistics* (Washington, D.C.: U.S. Department of Justice, Bureau of Justice Statistics, Government Printing Office, 1990), pp. 308-9, tables 3.89-3.90.

Thus, while almost 17 percent of the high school seniors surveyed in 1986 said they had tried cocaine, less than 1 percent used cocaine at least once every day. While over half of the students polled said they had tried marijuana, only 4 percent indicated they used marijuana daily. Given that the indicators of use have steadily declined during the late 1980s, daily prevalence has probably also continued to decline.

FIGURE 4.2
Percent of High School Seniors Ever Using Selected Drugs

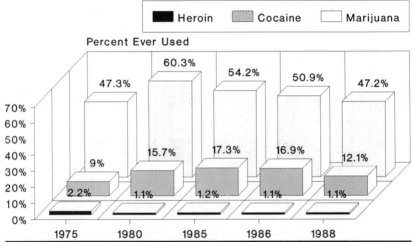

Source: Johnston, O'Malley, and Bachman. *National Trends in Drug Use*, table 7; Flanagan and Maguire, *Sourcebook*, 308-9, tables 3.89-3.90.

TABLE 4.3
Thirty-Day Prevalence of Selected Drugs among High School Seniors, 1975-1989

Drug	1975	1980	1985	1986	1989
Percent having used within last 30 days:					
Marijuana	27.1%	33.7%	25.7%	23.4%	16.7%
Cocaine	1.9	5.2	6.7	6.2	2.8
Heroin	0.4	0.2	0.3	0.2	0.3
Alcohol	68.2	72.0	65.9	65.3	60.0
Cigarettes	36.7	30.5	30.1	29.6	28.6

Source: Johnston, O'Malley, and Bachman, *National Trends in Drug Use*, table 9; Flanagan and Maguire, *Sourcebook*, 311, table 3.92.

To the extent that these data reflect actual trends in drug use, the drug-abuse story appears extremely complex. Whether illicit drugs are a "social problem" depends at least in part on where you start. Clearly, currently illicit drugs are less prevalent than the more socially acceptable substances such as alcohol and tobacco.

TABLE 4.4

Daily Prevalence of Selected Drugs among High School Seniors, 1975-1986

Drug	1975	1980	1985	1986
Percent ever having used:				
Marijuana	6.0%	9.1%	4.9%	4.0%
Cocaine	0.1	0.2	0.4	0.4
Heroin	0.1	0.0	0.0	0.0
Alcohol	5.7	6.0	5.0	4.8
Cigarettes	26.9	21.3	19.5	18.7

Source: Johnston, O'Malley, and Bachman, *National Trends in Drug Use*, table 5.

If the yardstick used to gauge the extent of the "drug problem" is the proportion of children ever having used a psychoactive drug, then the numbers reported by Johnston, O'Malley, and Bachman are serious. If, on the other hand, the standard is daily prevalence, then the problem does not appear nearly as severe as newspaper headlines and TV "sound bites" suggest. Without a doubt, addiction will adversely affect the lives and families of the students and their friends. Yet, heavy regular drug use does not appear to be the norm among high school students.

Indeed, the "drug problem" is normally defined as the rate of addiction to any psychoactive substance. Illicit drugs are considered dangerous because of their addictive qualities and the inability of users to control their personal behavior when on these drugs. The data suggest that substantial control is exerted by drug users, even teenagers. Only a small minority—with the notable exception of users of tobacco—use psychoactive drugs on a daily basis.

Moreover, these controls are substantial given the availability of these drugs (table 4.5). Although data were not reported for alcohol and tobacco, their extremely high use rates reported by seniors suggest that supplies are plentiful. Of more interest for this discussion, however, is the prevalence of the more traditional illicit drugs, marijuana, cocaine, and heroin.

Eight out of every ten high school seniors surveyed in 1989 claimed that marijuana is either "fairly easy" or "very easy" to get. Over half the seniors (58.7 percent) felt that cocaine would be easy to obtain as well. Even heroin was obtainable, if they wanted it, by almost one-third of the seniors polled. Moreover, the availability of these drugs increased throughout the 1980s. Given the availability of these drugs and the experimental nature of younger people, the proportions of students ever using these drugs may be considered remarkably low. Other factors are clearly important in decisions by young people to experiment and use illicit drugs.

TABLE 4.5
Trends in Availability of Selected Drugs among High School Seniors, 1975-1989

| Drug | Percent Saying Drug Would be "Fairly Easy" or "Very Easy" for Them to Get | | | | |
	1975	1980	1985	1986	1989
Marijuana	87.3%	89.0%	85.5%	85.2%	84.3%
Cocaine	37.0	47.9	48.9	51.5	58.7
Heroin	24.2	21.2	21.0	22.0	31.4

Source: Johnston, O'Malley, and Bachman, National Trends in Drug Use, table 22; Flanagan and Maguire, Sourcebook, 193, table 2.72.

Accessibility has two principal components: availability and affordability. The first relates to whether or not the drug is available to the potential drug user. The data from table 4.5 strongly suggest that availability is not a serious problem for most high school students who would want to use them. Their geographic location may also have important implications for accessibility in many cases. For example, 50 percent of the seniors in the Northeast have used drugs illicitly while only 37 percent of the seniors in the South reported the same behavior.[3]

Cocaine use showed the largest regional differences in preferences observed by Johnston, O'Malley, and Bachman, and was most prevalent on the Northeastern and Western seaboards. Annual prevalence of cocaine use was 20 percent in the West and 28 percent in the Northeast. In contrast, only 10 percent of the seniors in the North Central United States and 7 percent of the seniors in the South reported annual cocaine use.

Geography also plays a role when the statistics are broken down by population density (table 4.6). Nonmetropolitan areas, which are predominantly rural, experience the least amount of illicit drug use. Some of these differences are small. For example, 92 percent of the seniors in large metropolitan areas have used alcohol. Seniors in nonmetropolitan areas report a slightly lower proportion. Cocaine experience, on the other hand, seems to vary more significantly. The proportion of students using cocaine at some point in their lifetime in large metropolitan areas is double the rate in rural areas. The prevalence of cocaine use in smaller metropolitan areas is also substantially less than in the larger, more dense metropolitan areas.

TABLE 4.6

Prevalence of Selected Drugs among High School Seniors by Urban Area, 1986

Drug	Population Density		
	Large SMSA	Other SMSA	Non-SMSA
Percent ever having used:			
Marijuana	55.8	51.5	45.9
Cocaine	23.5	16.4	12.2
Heroin	1.2	1.2	0.8
Alcohol	92.8	91.0	90.6
Cigarettes	67.7	66.1	69.6

Source: Johnston, O'Malley, and Bachman, *National Trends in Drugs Use*, table 7.

Note: Large SMSAs consist of the twelve most populous metropolitan areas defined by the 1980 census.

Significant differences exist among cities as well. The National Institute of Justice sponsors the Drug Use Forecasting Network, which attempts to track drug use in major cities. The cities that participate in the program perform drug tests on people arrested, reporting the data to the Institute. The percentage of arrestees testing positive for any drug in 1988 varies widely among the cities, from a high of 83 percent for New York to a low of 54 percent in Indianapolis (table 4.7).

Moreover, tests for specific drugs vary significantly. In New York, 74 percent of the arrestees tested positive for cocaine while 30 percent tested positive for marijuana. In San Antonio, 44 percent tested positive for marijuana while only 27 percent tested positive for cocaine. In Indianapolis, 42 percent tested positive for marijuana, 15 percent tested positive for cocaine, and only 4 percent tested positive for heroin. In New York, the proportion of arrestees testing positive for heroin reached 24 percent.

TABLE 4.7
Drug Use by Male Arrestees in Selected Cities, 1988[1]

City	Percent Testing Positive			
	Any Drug	Marijuana	Cocaine[2]	Opiates
New York	83	30	74	24
San Diego	82	49	43	21
Philadelphia	81	32	72	11
Chicago	80	50	58	18
Los Angeles	75	32	60	13
Miami	75	32	64	1
Cleveland	68	26	52	4
Detroit	68	33	51	12
Dallas	66	36	49	6
Houston	65	43	49	4
Phoenix	63	44	30	7
San Antonio	63	44	27	18
St. Louis	56	17	38	6
Indianapolis	54	42	15	4

Source: National Institute of Justice, 1988 Drug Use Forecasting Annual Report (Washington, D.C.: U.S. Department of Justice, Office of Justice Programs, March 1990), 4-8.
[1]Results were obtained through urinalysis, January through December, 1988.
[2]Data for cocaine includes crack use.

These differences are partially related to the distribution network of particular drugs. New York serves as a primary importing and distribution center for cocaine and heroin. By some accounts, New York State is home to over half of the national heroin addict population.[4] Similarly, cities in the interior and in the South (except for Miami) may be heavily influenced by trade in marijuana. Many Midwestern states are also major growers of domestic marijuana. Higher proportions of cocaine use would be expected in cities that serve as major drug distribution centers (New York, Miami, and Los Angeles).

In fact, drug use may vary within cities depending on the specific characteristics of the drug-using population. For example, New York City heroin users apparently start earlier than users in the nation as a whole. Among users entering a New York City methadone maintenance treatment program in 1973-74, the age of first use among addicts was 18.2 years while the national average was 19.3.[5] Heroin use spreads through small groups of friends rather than through shifts in mass behavior. "Most commonly," notes John Kaplan, "heroin use spreads within a peer group in areas where use is already endemic. Typically, these are the cores of our large cities where . . . there are always more heroin users and sellers than police can apprehend or the courts process."[6] Similarly, the use of "crack" cocaine varies significantly by city.

Thus drug use in the United States is highly varied, among regions, cities, and people. For the most part, addictive behavior is not as automatic nor as prevalent as the press or many politicians claim.[7] This, of course, does not imply that drug use is benign or should be encouraged. Rather, this evidence merely suggests that popular notions of drug abuse may be misplaced. The real costs of drug use manifest themselves in lower productivity on the job, socially harmful behavior while using the drug, and harms associated with acquiring the drugs themselves.

Drug Abuse and Addiction

Anyone who looks deeply into the literature on drug abuse quickly discovers that controversy abounds over the term and meaning of addiction. In fact, even the term drug abuse is vague and difficult to identify. The hope that neat, consensual definitions may emerge out of scientific research is quickly dashed as the reader discovers that published studies often contradict one another.

Some physiological characteristics of certain drugs are easy to discern. Other psychological properties, such as most forms of addiction, are often difficult to assess. Often, when a researcher asserts that a drug is "highly addictive," the statement implies a comparison with other drugs. For example, alcohol is considered less addictive than cocaine, which is considered more addictive than marijuana.

These distinctions may seem obvious (and they are well acknowledged in the literature on drug use and abuse), but public discussion and debate often presumes drugs can be rated on some abstract absolute scale of addictiveness. For instance, public discussion often assumes that some drugs, such as heroin, can be rated on a scientifically determined scale that is universally applicable to everyone.

The reality is much different. For most drugs, researchers are unable to determine the extent that drugs are addictive among individuals. Apart from individual physiology (human beings are chemically different), a host of other factors influence the likelihood of addiction. A more fruitful approach to understanding drug addiction and its consequences may be to focus on who becomes an addict rather than what drugs are addicting.

This does not imply that drug use is not associated with changes in behavior or the emergence of mental disorders. In fact, the abuse of any drug can result in behavior changes. The ingestion of alcohol, for example, can result in more aggressive behavior, impaired judgment or "impaired social or occupational functioning." According to the *Diagnostic and Statistical Manual of Mental Disorders* published by the American Pyschiatric Association (APA), there are seven mental disorders attributed to the the direct effect of alcohol on the nervous system. These are effects attributed directly to the drug, irrespective of how it is used.

The APA distinguishes between the direct effects of drugs and the effects resulting from the use of the drugs.[8] The effects of drug use are often considered socially undesirable. For example, cocaine abuse would be signified by disturbances such as fights, loss of friends, job impairment, and other behavioral changes that may create confrontation and conflict. Often, the direct effects of drugs and the effects of drug use are experienced together (although not always).

Physical and Psychological Dependency

Physically, of the three major drugs forming the core of the illicit drug traffic, heroin is the only one capable of inducing a strong physical dependence. Research on heroin addicts dating back to the nineteenth century determined that heroin withdrawal could be extremely painful and the addict would experience extreme discomfort. Yet, even with heroin, physical withdrawal can be completed within six and ten days.[9]

For heroin addicts, the most difficult part of withdrawal is often overcoming the psychological dependency. Moreover,

> there is little evidence that addiction to heroin . . . actually results in organic damage to the human body. We know that heroin typically has to be injected three to five times daily, and that immediately after a fix addicts may nod off and thus be recognizable, but afterward they can act as normal as anyone. They can hold a job, perform manipulative tasks, and . . . even perform surgery. As long as addicts obtain their drug and do not overdose, they can function normally in society.[10]

In fact, alcohol and cigarette smoking inflict much more damage on the human body than heroin.

Deaths associated with heroin overdoses are misleading as well. The amount of heroin required to become toxic is substantially greater than what is found in a typical dose available on the street.[11] In many cases, the addict suffers from acute reactions to impurities in the quality of the heroin. To the extent that quality control is restricted in the black market, the public health risk of heroin use is increased.

Thus, the belief that heroin addicts are a necessary drag on society is inconsistent with the experience of heroin addiction. While a subset of the heroin population may be involved in criminal activities, crime is not a necessary result of the pharmacological properties of the drug.

In fact, the crime associated with heroin addiction is largely induced by factors that limit the supply of heroin to the addict. Addicts will, for example, often steal in order to raise money to support their habits. Yet this behavior is not induced by the drug itself. On the contrary, the criminal behavior is a direct result of constraints placed on the addict in acquiring more of the drug.

Continuing research on heroin addicts is discovering that the addict population is extremely diverse. Current estimates indicate that 500,000 people use heroin, and perhaps half of the addict population is concentrated in New York City.[12] While the typical image of the street addict may be of someone who is "dirty, sickly, infected, and living in squalor," the reality can be very different.[13] In fact, many professionals, particularly doctors with access to the drug, are heroin users (if not addicts).

Moreover, the addictive qualities of heroin have become suspect in recent years. Discussions surrounding heroin addiction often presume that once someone starts using the drug, he or she becomes physically and emotionally dependent on it. Most addicts become addicted within one or two years of heroin use and two-thirds of all heroin addicts are between fifteen and twenty-five years old.[14] This implies that most people end their addiction as they become older.

Indeed, in a survey of over one hundred heroin addicts in London, England, psychiatrist Rolf Wille found that the mean length of opiate use was 6.3 years.[15] Most had started using opiates at nineteen years old (consistent with the findings of Hunt) and stopped at twenty-five years old. Moreover, of the heroin addicts that stopped during the time of the survey, 30 percent of the sample, only one relapsed into opiate use.

Many addicts also end their addiction without treatment or help from another source.[16] As Kaplan has noted, "a number of investigators have concluded that the number of controlled heroin users probably matches, and may even exceed, the number of addicts at any one time."[17] In other words, a significant population of heroin users may exist who do not habitually or compulsively consume the drug.

The experiences of returning Vietnam veterans may provide the most important insights into heroin addiction and the future of addicts. Heroin addiction among Vietnam servicemen became widespread as a direct result of the Army's antimarijuana campaign. By severely restricting the supply of marijuana, the campaign inadvertently led servicemen to substitute heroin.[18]

The result was a significant heroin addiction problem. Studies indicate that over one-third of the enlisted men in Vietnam tried heroin and 54 percent of those who tried it became addicted. After returning home, about 10 percent relapsed into addiction. More important, "although 95 percent of heroin-addicted Vietnam returnees did not become addicted in the United States, 88 percent did take heroin occasionally, indicating that they had developed some capacity to use the drug in a controlled way."[19]

This ability to control heroin use has also been noted among certain social circles in major cities. In these groups, heroin is injected only in the presence of a small, well-knit social circle. This environment allows the group to use heroin within the safety of the group and minimize the risks of an adverse reaction. In addition, heroin addicts commonly go through stages of voluntary withdrawal and abstinence.[20]

These examples strongly suggest that heroin use may not be as addictive as previously thought.[21] The addage "once an addict, always an addict" is breaking down under closer scrutiny of the actual behavior of drug users. As many researchers have already pointed out, most empirical work until recently has attempted to assess the effects of drugs by looking at the drug-abusing population. The most readily available subjects for studies were those in addiction treatment programs. This group almost always represents the worst cases. Current studies now estimate that only 10 to 20 percent of the drug-using population becomes addicted, even to heroin.[22]

This evidence suggests that important social institutions are working to control the use of drugs. Norman Zinberg, a psychiatrist who has studied drug problems extensively, argues that the key to understanding drug use and abuse is to look at the values, social mores, sanctions, rituals, and other rules that control social behavior. The interaction of the pharmacological properties of the drug being used with the attitude and personality of the user and the environment in which the drug is consumed is far more important.

All drug users, Zinberg observes, exert some form of control over their behavior. Alcoholics, for example, do not drink continually. The discussion should center on how the three variables—drug, personality, and setting—combine to create rituals or controls over drug use. Through a process of social learning, most drug users establish limits on their consumption to avoid abusing their drug. "Know your limit," "never drink alone," or "never smoke marijuana until after the children are asleep," are all rules that have been internalized through social rituals.

The probability of addiction is determined by how these factors interact in different social settings.

> The issue, therefore, is not one of obtaining gratification from substance abuse, for most users do. The issue is the degree to which an individual can balance and hence control those wishes for substance gratification with other factors, such as moral revulsion, the desire to enhance gratification in the long run, automatic acceptance of peer group standards, or unconscious utilization of available social sanctions and rituals.[23]

Steven Wisotsky has noted recently that "people have natural defenses to drug abuse."[24] Among these are the natural tendencies for people to get bored with a particular experience.[25] In the jargon of economics, the vast majority of drug experimenters have diminishing marginal utility for psychoactive experiences. If addiction were determined purely by the chemical makeup of the drug, large proportions of the drug-using population would be addicted to drugs.

In fact, human tolerance to drug use varies significantly among individuals, depending on the chemical makeup of the drug and the personality of the user.[26] As psychiatrist Robert Byck notes,

> Although "drugs" are commonly assumed to have unitary and specific effects, this is not the reality. Each drug has a spectrum of effects depending on *form, dosage, route* of administration, and *chronicity.* The human variables of personality structure and circumstance of drug administration are equally important in judging the psychopharmacological results of drug taking. (Emphasis in original.)[27]

Laboratory tests can provide indications of the range of effects from various drugs. By using subjects with similar chemical makeups, for example, researchers can vary the form of the drug (e.g., refined cocaine versus chewing on a coca leaf), dosage, route (e.g., smoking or injecting), and chronicity (or frequency). Most of what is known about the effects of these drugs derives from controlled laboratory experiments that carefully monitor how these drugs affect the human body.

Scientists can thus categorize drugs. Heroin is a narcotic, which induces insensibility or stupor. Narcotics are often used medically to reduce pain. Examples of narcotics available over the counter or by prescription include such common drugs as codeine, demerol methadone, or darvon. Thus heroin and other opiates are considered depressants.

Cocaine, in contrast, is an upper and stimulates the central nervous system. Cocaine is classified as a narcotic for political reasons. As Ken Liska observes in a popular textbook on the effects of drugs on the human body,

> There is no way it [cocaine] can properly be grouped with heroin or the opiates for they are CNS [central nervous system] depressants and cocaine is a stimulant. But the description stuck, and courts have held that it is valid to classify cocaine as a narcotic for purposes of punishment.[28]

The effects of cocaine vary significantly from individual to individual and, in the case of crack, are extremely unpredictable. Some people can take cocaine repeatedly with little long-term effect. Others can overdose and die on their first trip.

Marijuana is the most popular illicit drug in America. Almost seventy million people have tried it at some point in their lives. The pharmacology of marijuana is extremely complex, with over one hundred species of the plant. Although the active ingredient is THC, over sixty other chemicals have also been found in marijuana. The effects of short-term marijuana use appear minor, although long-term use may be correlated with several respiratory problems. Marijuana, like cocaine, is not a narcotic but is classified as such by the legal system through the Marijuana Tax Act of 1937.

Claims that particular drugs are "irresistible" should be considered with skepticism. If the effect of cocaine, for example, was so powerful that the typical user would prefer cocaine to food, water, or sex, millions would be dying in the streets either through starvation or overdoses. The reality is more sobering. The National Institute of Drug Abuse's (NIDA) 1988 survey of drug use estimates that 2.9 million Americans used cocaine during the previous month, 8.2 million used cocaine during the previous year, and 21.2 million had used cocaine at least once in their lifetime. In fact, these numbers are probably low. A recent survey of over fourteen hundred adults in the United States commissioned by the Drug Policy Foundation discovered that 11 percent had tried cocaine at some time in their lives.[29] This would translate into over twenty million people who have tried cocaine.

The term *addict* has been used somewhat loosely up to this point. According to a recent survey of ninety-nine experts in twenty-three organizations working in the drug abuse and treatment field, a drug addict is a "person who is physically dependent on one or more psychoactive substances, whose long-term use has produced tolerance, who has lost control over his intake, and would manifest withdrawal phenomena if discontinuance were to occur."[30] *Drug addiction* was defined as a "chronic disorder characterized by the compulsive use of a substance resulting in physical, psychological, or social harm to the user and continued use despite that harm."[31]

These definitions, which were the result of a study designed to develop a consensus among professionals to clarify terms in the substance-abuse profession, are largely inconsistent with the pattern of drug use for the vast majority of illicit drug users in the United States. Most people stop using drugs after a period of steady use or abstain altogether after their first experiments.

This may be most dramatically demonstrated by the poll commissioned by the Drug Policy Foundation in Washington, D.C., and conducted by Targeting Systems, Inc., a northern Virginia polling firm. When each person was asked whether they had ever tried drugs, 35 percent admitted they had tried marijuana and 11 percent admitted they had tried cocaine. The survey thus polled slightly higher proportions of marijuana and cocaine users than the survey performed by NIDA. (Using numbers derived from the NIDA survey, 10 percent of the American public had used cocaine and 25 percent had used marijuana at some point in their lives.)

Yet the Drug Policy Foundation study revealed that 81 percent of those polled would not use marijuana if it were legal. Another 8 percent said they would not be likely to use marijuana if it were legal. Only 10 percent indicated that the legalization of marijuana would make them "somewhat likely" or "very likely" to use the drug. Similarly, 97 percent of those polled said they would not use cocaine if it were legal and another 4 percent indicated they would not be very likely use cocaine if it were legal.

Two observations can be made about the responses to the survey. The lopsided results indicate that those who have experimented with drugs, as well as those who have not, would not use either marijuana or cocaine in the absence of an important legal control over their behavior. Very few people appear to abstain from using the drug for purely legal reasons.

This suggestion is corroborated by recent research on alcohol consumption during the Prohibition Era in the United States. Economists Jeffrey Miron and Jeffrey Zwiebel recently compared alcohol consumption before, during, and after Prohibition to determine the effects of public policy on behavior.[32] During the early years, Prohibition seemed to work: alcohol consumption fell to levels of only 30 percent of the pre-Prohibition levels. After the early years, however, consumption began to increase. Toward the end of prohibition, consumption increased to "60-70 percent of its initial value and did not increase substantially immediately following the repeal of prohibition." Miron and Zwiebel conclude that "legal deterrents had little effect on limiting consumption outside their effect on price. Social pressure and respect for the law did not go far in reducing consumption during prohibition."[33]

Determining who becomes an addict or heavy drug user and who does not has become a source of frustration for many researchers. Increasingly, experts are looking at the interaction of nonchemical explanations for drug use, such as the influence of the family and other informal controls on use.[34] A study of 435 mothers and their offspring revealed that the frequency of marijuana use was heavily influenced by the parent-adolescent relationship.[35] Overall, the study's authors concluded that their empirical results strongly suggest that family factors have a powerful effect on drug use.[36]

Similarly, a study of almost five thousand high school seniors from thirty high schools in six states found that alcohol use, despite legal prohibition, was determined by "self-standards," the student's peer group, and "other students' standards."[37] These results reinforce the points underlined by Zinberg and Wisotsky concerning internal checks and social controls on drug consumption. Few drug users become compulsive consumers.

An example of the public hysteria surrounding drug use is contained in a recently released congressional study of cocaine use and addiction in the United States. Senator Joseph R. Biden, Jr., the chairman of the Senate Judiciary Committee, introduced the report as a call to action to thwart the widespread and tragic cocaine addiction problem in the United States. Cocaine use, he continued, is epidemic and "unless we take decisive action to fight the crisis that hard-core addicts are causing in this country, our streets and schools will never be safe—and a large part of this generation of Americans will be lost."[38] Given the evidence discussed earlier and the estimated number of addicts compared to users, Senator Biden's claims should be suspect from the start. The report claims that over 2.2 million Americans can be classified as "hard-core" addicts.

However, the report does not rely on a medical definition of addiction. Elements of a medical definition would include compulsive consumption that results in physical, psychological, or social harm. Moreover, drug use must continue despite the continued infliction of this harm on the user or those around him.

The Judiciary Committee study defines the hard-core cocaine addict as any person who uses cocaine at least once per week. This definition does not require that the behavior be compulsive or inflict harm. Moreover, the report justifies its classification of hard-core addicts to ensure comparability between its results and results obtained from NIDA's Household Survey on Drug Abuse. "Alternative definitions could be used," the report notes, "for example, defining hard-core addicts by the social consequences of their use; thus, addicts who steal or deal drugs to support their habits are 'hard-core' addicts regardless of the number of times they took drugs."[39] Interestingly, Mark A. R. Kleiman, a widely respected researcher on drug problems and policy, supervised the study by the Senate committee staff although he refers to "heavy users" rather than hard-core drug addicts in the text of the report.[40]

The report has confused drug addiction with drug abuse. Drug *abuse*, based on the survey of professionals, is defined as "any use of drugs that causes physical, psychological, *economic, legal, or social* harm to the individual user or to others affected by the drug user's behavior" (emphasis added.)[41] Drug abuse, then, is differentiated by the focus on widely defined injury

This notion of drug abuse is broadly consistent with the APA's definition of substance abuse.[42] In general, there are three components to their definition. First, there must be a pattern of "pathological use" such as intoxification throughout the day or the inability to stop use. Second, social or occupational functions must be impaired through pathological use. Finally, use must continue for at least one month. In addition, drug use is not related to *recreational or medicinal purposes.*

Someone using cocaine once per week (or two or three times per week) could not be classified as an addict based on frequency alone. In fact, if addiction is defined as compulsive behavior or persistent use despite evidence of harm, someone who restrains their cocaine intake to once a week would probably not be classified medically as an addict. The evidence published by the congressional committee showing that there are only 2.2 million people using cocaine once a week or more—roughly 10 percent of all those who have tried cocaine—suggests that a surprising degree of control exists over cocaine use more generally. The true addict population, from a medical viewpoint, is probably much lower than the popular press and politicians claim.

The Persistence of Drug use in America

Drug use is an indelible part of the American sociological landscape. But, as the previous section indicated, drug use moves far beyond the limits of illicit drugs. Alcohol also alters human behavior and is a psychoactive substance despite its social acceptability. What differentiates alcohol use from other drug use is its legal status. Similarly, cigarettes are highly addictive and arguably alter human behavior. Users build up a tolerance to alcohol and tobacco, as they do to other psychoactive drugs. Tobacco smoking can even develop into a physical dependency. Thus, in evaluating the psychological and physical effects of illicit drugs, comparisons to other socially acceptable drugs provide a useful context.

Historically, archeologists have found evidence of alcohol trafficking in prehistoric shipwrecks.[43] Poppy seeds have been found in Turkey dating back several thousand years. Yet, continued substance abuse was unlikely before 1500 A.D. since mental and physical impairment could easily reduce survival rates in hunter-gatherer societies.

Chronic drug use emerged with the agricultural and industrial revolutions, as wealthy elites could abuse substances without threatening their survival. With the industrial revolution, rising real incomes led to the development of consumer markets. "Spread of the Industrial Revolution in the 1700s and 1800s stimulated cash cropping in psychoactive substances, including organized production of opium, tea, coffee, betel-areca, and grains and grapes for beverage alcohol."[44] Thus, as the threat of starvation subsided and incomes rose, incentives to use drugs increased as part of leisure activity.

Drug use has emerged as an important force in American life in the twentieth century.[45] While use among adults has been endemic in American culture, the spread of drugs to children and adolescents dates only to the mid-twentieth century. The use of drugs by children and their growing spending power has "stimulated the search for cheap, readily available psychoactive substances in the home, school, workplace, grocery store, and hardware shop."[46] Thus, cheaper forms of traditional drugs, such as crack cocaine, have become more commonplace.

The pervasiveness of drug use today is illustrated by a recent study of over twelve thousand participants in the National Longitudinal Survey of Youth. In 1984, an analysis of the survey revealed that 81 percent of the participants (aged nineteen to twenty-seven) had used alcohol in the last thirty days. In the last year, 48 percent had smoked cigarettes, 42 percent had smoked marijuana, and 15 percent had used cocaine (table 4.8).

None of the rates in drug use, however, appear to differ significantly among occupations. The percentage of respondents using alcohol within the last thirty days ranges from a low of 74 percent for farm laborers to 86 percent for managers and sales workers. Cigarette use appears to vary the most, ranging from only 30 percent among professionals to a high of 57 percent among general laborers.

Illicit substance use does not vary greatly either. The least popular drug was cocaine. Only 10 percent of farm laborers reported using cocaine in the last thirty days while only 17 percent of craftsman and service workers indicated use. Marijuana, the most popular of the illegal drugs, ranged from a low of 30 percent for farm laborers to a high of 49 percent for service workers.

These drugs are almost all used in leisure activity. Only 5 percent of the respondents indicated that they were "high on the job" with alcohol. On the other hand, 8 percent of the respondents who had smoked marijuana said they were high on the job. The occupations reporting the largest proportions of workers high on marijuana were craftsmen and operatives (10 percent), and transport operatives and laborers (9 percent). Very few workers (2 percent) using cocaine reported they were high on the job. Thus, despite widespread use of licit and illicit drugs among young workers, this use does not translate into abuse on the job.

In fact, the study discovered that drug users are not concentrated in particular industries or occupations. When drug use was analyzed with respect to the pressures and demands of the work environment, few workplace-oriented variables were statistically significant. Thus, the authors conclude "that the workplace per se appears to contribute little to drug use patterns, and that these patterns are brought in by young workers. Substance use by workers is due not as much to conditions of the workplace as to attributes of the work force."[47]

Moreover, low on-the-job drug abuse rates suggest that lost productivity may be smaller than hypothesized. In fact, a recent three-year study of fifty-five Ohio human resource executives suggested that other problems may be more important to lost productivity than drug use.[48] Over half of the executives (57 percent) reported that marital and other personal problems had the greatest impact on productivity. Only 22 percent indicated that drug abuse problems had the largest impact in the work place. One corporate psychologist noted that only 5 percent of the employees his center counsels report drug problems. "Emotional and marital problems are far more pervasive in the workplace," he continued, "and more treatable."[49]

Nevertheless, the social costs of drug abuse are high. A 1984 study by the Research Triangle Institute in North Carolina estimated that in 1983 alone drug abuse accounted for economic costs of as much as $60 billion. James Ostrowski, using the results of the Research Triangle study, concluded that a more accurate representation of the costs of drug abuse were substantially lower, around $26.4 billion.[50] Ostrowski found that drug treatment accounts for $2 billion, lost employment another $405 million, and welfare $3 million. Interdiction accounted for another $677 million.

TABLE 4.8
Drug Use by Occupation and Industry by Young Men in 1984

Occupation	% Using in Last 30 Days	% Using in Last Year		
	Alcohol	Cigarettes	Marijuana	Cocaine
Professional/Tech.	81	30	34	13
Managers/Admin.	86	47	40	16
Sales workers	86	39	43	14
Clerical workers	82	40	37	14
Craftsmen	82	56	45	17
Operatives	83	52	38	12
Transport	82	51	46	15
Nonfarm laborers	76	57	43	14
Far laborers	74	46	30	10
Service workers	79	52	49	17
Total	81	48	42	15

Source: Adapted from Barbara A. Mensch and Denise B. Kandel, "Do Job Conditions Influence the Use of Drugs?" Journal of Health and Social Behavior 29 (June 1988): 174, Table 1a.

Drugs and Crime

A more tangible problem associated with drug use is the connection between drugs and crime. Crime can be either drug-related or non-drug-related. Drug-related crime refers to offenses committed while the perpetrator is using drugs or criminal acts related to the use, purchase, or sale of drugs. Some crimes committed by drug users many not be directly related to drug-related activities. A drug user, for example, may commit a burglary for reasons completely independent of drug use or drug trafficking. Non-drug-related crime refers to criminal acts that are not attributable to the use of drugs or violations of drug laws.

In a study of heroin trafficking in New York, daily heroin users imposed net costs of $22,844 on victims through non-drug-related crime.[51] Irregular users, in contrast, imposed substantially fewer costs on similar victims ($5,592). On average, non-drug-related crime committed by drug users was $14,000. A more recent study published by the RAND Corporation estimated that total non-drug-related crime in Washington, D.C. amounted to between $150 to $225 million.[52]

A substantial body of research shows that drug users constitute a criminally active subpopulation.[53] National Institute of Justice psychologist Bernard Gropper notes, "Recent studies have shown that heroin-using offenders are just *as likely* as their non-drug-using or non-heroin-using counterparts to commit violent crimes . . . and even *more likely* to commit robbery and weapons offenses" (emphasis in original).[54] In all cases, more frequent drug users are more deeply involved in criminal activity. An increasingly prominent feature of drug-related crime is murder. In many cities, drug-related murders make up as much 50 to 80 percent of all homicides.[55]

Yet, this observation must be tempered by a more thorough examination of the types of crimes committed. For instance, interviews with 2,285 heroin addicts in five cities from 1978 to 1981 revealed that they were criminally active.[56] The average number of offenses over the twelve-month period, however, varied significantly among types of crimes. The average annual number of crimes against persons was 12.8, crimes against property 121.6, public order 67.9, and drug sales 162.2. Thus, even though drug users may be criminally active, they are often not involved heavily in violent crimes.

The expression "drug-related crime" does not necessarily denote crime committed while the abuser was under the influence of the drug. For example, driving under the influence (DUI) is a crime defined by behavior induced by drug use (usually alcohol). In most cases, drug-related crime should not be construed as crime committed while the criminal is under the influence. Even when criminals commit crimes under the influence of drugs, their behavior is not a direct result of the effects of the drugs. Rather, the drugs become a tool for the criminal to induce a more "relaxed" emotional state.

A modern exception appears to be crack, which often produces erratic and sometimes violent behavior. In this respect, the effects of crack on behavior are much more similar to those of alcohol than to those of marijuana, heroin, or cocaine.

In a survey of over 215,000 convicted inmates of local jails in 1989, less than one-third (27 percent) indicated they were under the influence of a drug at the time they committed the offense.[57] Less than 5 percent indicated they were under the influence of cocaine or crack. In contrast, 29.2 percent of convicted inmates indicated they committed the offense under the influence of alcohol. Over half of the convicted inmates, 56.6 percent, said they were under the influence of drugs or alcohol at the time of the offense. Yet, only 15.4 percent indicated they were under the influence of drugs only.

The survey also revealed that, among inmates convicted for violent offenses such as homicide, rape, assault, and robbery, less than 10 percent were under the influence of drugs only at the time of their offense. In contrast, over 30 percent were under the influence of alcohol only while 16 percent were under the influence of both. Among inmates arrested for public-order offenses such as weapons, obstruction of justice, traffic, D.U.I., etc., 54 percent indicated they were under the influence of alcohol only, and less than 7 percent indicated they were under the influence of drugs only (9.6 percent indicated they were under the influence of both).

In a summary of the literature on the connnection between crime and drug use, drug-use researcher Paul J. Goldstein found drug use per se does not induce violent behavior.[58] In particular, early reports that attempted to link violent behavior to the properties of marijuana and opiates "have now been largely discredited."[59] In fact, drug use may cause some to become introspective and reduce violent tendencies.

Goldstein admits that the evidence on the drug use- violence connection is not extensive. Nevertheless, he finds that violence is systemic and associated with "traditionally aggressive patterns of interaction within the system of drug distribution and use."[60] Thus, the violence and criminal activity associated with drug use is an outcome of the life- style of users and traffickers rather than an effect of the drug itself.

Clearly, then, when drawing conclusions about drug use, crime, and violence, researchers and analysts must be careful to distinguish between the statistical correlation between drug use and crime and a pharmacological correlation.

The relationship between crime and drug use is not direct. For example, Gropper observes, "The major impetus for most of [daily heroin users'] criminal behavior is the need to obtain heroin or opiates."[61] This statement is consistent with the high correlation found between frequency of drug use and criminal activity. Yet, criminal activity may be the result of something else.

The regular user engages in criminal activity to get money to sustain his habit. The amount of criminal activity will depend on the cost of the habit. To the extent public policy restricts the supply of heroin, causing prices to rise, the heroin addict will commit more crime. Conversely, if heroin were freely available on demand, the cost of the addicts habit would approach the marginal cost of producing the drug. In this case, the drug user's habit would cost a few dollars per day.

More specifically, if a heroin addict consumed an estimated forty milligrams of heroin per day in 1986, he would have spent fifty to eighty dollars per day.[62] Yet, the cost of supplying heroin legally would run less than twenty- five cents per day.[63] Thus, the price of heroin is inflated by anywhere from 200 to 3,200 percent. In this case, the crime used to generate income for a heroin addict is a manifestation of its legal status rather than of heroin use per se. Thus, if drug users are committing property crimes to support their drug habit, and if accessibility is increased by allowing supply to meet demand, property crime rates should drop dramatically.

Drugs and Public Health

Another cost of drug use is a public health concern. Drug users place themselves at risk more than nondrug users. This, of course, is true for all drug users regardless of whether the drugs are legally tolerated or not. For example, the risks of tobacco place smoking at the top of the list among potential killers. Similarly, the risks to users associated with illicit drugs may also be extremely high. While this argument plays well at first, evidence on deaths per capita by type of drug use reveals that drugs other than cocaine, heroin, and marijuana pose far greater health hazards.

James Ostrowski determined the per capita death rate for six drugs: tobacco, alcohol, heroin, cocaine, and marijuana. In his calculations, Ostrowski attempted to isolate only those deaths that were "intrinsically" connected to the drug being used. In other words, he attempted to determine whether an alcohol death was related to the use of alcohol per se rather than to some other influence. Thus, deaths resulting from diseases directly related to alcohol use are included while others such as DUI traffic deaths are not.

The data show that tobacco remains the number one killer, claiming 650 deaths per 100,000 users (table 4.9). Heroin use results in half the death rate of alcohol per capita. Not one death has been attributable to marijuana use. In fact, based on data concerning the number of repeat users of these drugs, Ostrowski notes that the illicit substances are less likely to lead to repeat use than either alcohol or tobacco.

Tallying the number of people killed through substance abuse is only one method of determining its risk. Another risk is dependence. Substantial numbers of people are psychologically dependent on drugs (although the degree of this dependence is contestable). Nevertheless, for the 10 to 20 percent of each drug user population that is dependent, the effects can be devastating.

TABLE 4.9
Estimated per Capita Death Rates for Selected Drugs

Drug	Users	Deaths Per Year	Deaths/100,000
Tobacco	60 million	390,000	650
Alcohol	100 million	150,000	150
Heroin	500,000	400	80
Cocaine	5 million	200	4

Source: James Ostrowski, "Thinking About Drug Legalization," *Cato Policy Analysis No. 121* (Washington, D.C.: Cato Institute, 1989), 47, table 4.

Note: Deaths attributed to heroin and cocaine were adjusted downward to include only deaths attributed to drug use (e.g., not suicide). The unadjusted figure for heroin is 400 per 100,000 and for cocaine, 20 per 100,000.

Drug dependence, however, is manageable. Heroin addicts can lead productive lives even if they require four or five doses a day. The debilitating effects of heroin are related to the drugs availability and affordability, which in turn are due almost exclusively to its legal status.

Cocaine, in contrast to heroin, is more debilitating and interferes more with work performance.[64] Yet, cocaine's effects typically become negligible within two or three hours. After twenty-four hours, cocaine cannot be chemically traced in human urine (two days with heavy doses). Scientific evidence indicates that regular cocaine use affects the heart and causes cardiac death, heart attack, irregular heartbeat, and damage to the muscle tissue surrounding the heart. Other physical problems associated with chronic cocaine use are deterioration of the liver, high blood pressure, convulsions, respiratory failure, and destruction of the nasal passage.

Nevertheless, as table 4.9 detailed, the risks of cocaine are not as significant as those other drugs that are legally and socially tolerated. The number of chronic or compulsive users is probably very small, despite the results of the study released by the Senate Judiciary Committee. Thus, Steven Wisotsky concludes,

> The data lead to one conclusion: even allowing for legitimate concerns about the health consequences of cocaine and fears about the spread of cocaine dependency, the legal prohibition of cocaine and its severe penalties cannot be justified solely on the grounds of public health. At the very least, the health and death toll of legal drugs—cigarettes and alcohol—runs far higher. . . . But for that 10-20 percent minority, . . . a destructive, accelerating pattern of compulsive use can develop over time. Approximately the same percentage fall "victim" to alcoholism or heroin addiction.[65]

Marijuana poses a far less serious threat from addiction, although the long-term health consequences may be greater than heroin or cocaine. Small doses of marijuana appear to have negligible effects on the human body, although moderate use may produce temporary, short-term memory loss. Marijuana's "most significant adverse acute effects are [increased heart rate], impairment of short-term cognitive functioning, and impairment of motor skills."[66] Research also indicates that long-term respiratory problems (e.g., bronchitis and general irritation) are associated with heavy marijuana use. Researchers speculate that, given higher concentrations of tars in marijuana, long-term use may place the user at higher risk of developing cancer.

The Demand for Illicit Drugs in the United States

In sum, the demand for illicit drugs in the United States will continue despite their legal status. Moreover, the physical and psychological effects of the major illicit drugs—heroin, cocaine, and marijuana—appear much smaller than previously thought. A realistic assessment of the drug problem suggests that dependence on illicit drugs should be treated as a health problem similar to smoking and alcohol use. In fact, at current usage rates, the public health risks associated with illicit drug use are far lower than those for alcohol and smoking.

Moreover, unlike currently illegal drugs, the risks associated with the legal drugs will probably persist through their popularity. As James Ostrowski has noted, "not only are alcohol and tobacco inherently more dangerous than heroin and cocaine, but because they are more popular, their danger is magnified."[67] Despite widespread access, illicit drugs appear far less popular than alcohol or cigarettes. Even those who experiment with these drugs are much less likely to use them again.

The true costs of substance abuse lies in the dependence users develop through prolonged use of the drug. In some cases, such as cigarette and alcohol abuse, the physical effects become life-threatening.

Alcohol and cigarette use, however, appear to be declining over time. The proportion of current smokers in the U.S. population has declined from 42 percent in 1955 to under one-third in the late 1980s. Moreover, recent drinking trends show a general move to beverages with lower alcohol content, such as light beer and wine.

Drug use is part of a far reaching cultural tradition. The most traditional forms of drug use manifest themselves in alcohol and tobacco consumption. These forms have been socially tolerated for centuries and have been an omnipresent fact of American life. Illicit drugs have also been around for centuries, but have received more attention in the late twentieth century.

The reasons for the resurgence of public interest in the most common illicit drugs lie principally in the perceived social devastation that lies in its wake. Indeed, social control over these drugs began in the late nineteenth century as politicians responded to heightening public criticism of cocaine and special interests sought to expand their power. Similarly, the recent trend toward widespread intolerance of psychoactive drugs reflects the rising public outcry against "soaring" addiction rates, the diffusion of drug use into schools, and the violence associated with drug trafficking. Against the backdrop of economic devastation in many American urban areas, drugs became an easy target of public criticism.

Indeed, the recent declaration of "war" against drugs can be viewed as a reaction to the rising social devastation evident in urban areas. As this chapter has detailed, while heroin, cocaine, and marijuana have addictive qualities, none of them approach the levels or use or addiction evident in socially tolerated drugs such as alcohol or tobacco. Indeed, the numbers of chronic users are substantially lower than perceptions gleaned from newspaper headlines and evening news reports. Moreover, the classification of users of illicit drugs as addicts or compulsive users is highly suspect. Many so-called addicts demonstrate substantial control over their drug intake and use.

The issue is not whether people will use drugs, but how much is demanded on the market at a given price. For the vast majority of consumers, drug use is not addictive. "Recreational" drug use, or use of drugs in the same sense that most drinkers use alcohol, is reasonably safe and enjoyable although the potentially negative long-term consequences of drug use may become important. Drug use becomes a problem only when a physical or psychological dependence emerges for the drug or individual behavior becomes individually or socially destructive. Thus, many Americans consume large amounts of psychoactive drugs legally (e.g., alcohol) and illegally (e.g., marijuana). Moreover, drug consumption is sensitive to price changes.

The illicit drug trade is accompanied by substantial social costs that are unrelated to the demand for drugs. Yet, the persistent demand for drugs ensures that producers will enter into the market to supply these drugs. Those who control their drug use so that their behavior does not interfere with their personal and work life pose a minimum threat to their lives and those of others. Rather, the "drug problem" is concerned mainly with the addict population that provides a base level of demand to fuel the drug market. Traffickers will always be able to reap large profits from the drug market as long as an addict population maintains a steady demand for the product. More important, as chapter 6 details, traffickers will benefit from any policy that restricts supplies enough to maintain high prices and high profit margins.

The rules by which suppliers provide these products, however, vary significantly from the rules that exist in the legal market. As the illicit drug trade flourishes, the essential institutions of successful, productive economies founder.

Notes

1. Lloyd D. Johnston, Patrick M. O'Malley, and Jerald G. Bachman, *National Trends in Drug Use and Related Factors Among American High School Students and Young Adults, 1975–1986* (Washington, D.C.: U.S. Department of Health and Human Services, 1987).

2. Ibid., 160.
3. Ibid., 42.
4. See the discussion in Arnold Trebach, *The Great Drug War* (New York: Macmillan, 1987).
5. Leon Gibson Hunt, *Assessment of Local Drug Abuse* (Lexington, Mass.: Lexington Books, 1977), 48-49.
6. John Kaplan, *The Hardest Drug: Heroin and Public Policy* (Chicago: University of Chicago Press, 1983), 27.
7. A growing debate is emerging over the proper use of the term drug abuse. Some scholars question whether the focus on abusing drugs is appropriate. As psychiatrist Thomas Szasz observes, *people* abuse drugs. A debate that centers on the drug as the source of addiction ignores the importance of the individual choosing to consume drugs. For a more in-depth analysis of these relationships, see Thomas Szasz, *Ceremonial Chemistry: The Ritual Persecution of Drugs, Addicts, and Pushers*, rev. ed. (Holmes Beach, Fl: Learning Publications, 1985).
8. These distinctions are explained more thoroughly in the APA's *Diagnostic and Statistical Manual of Mental Disorders*, 3d ed. (Washington, D.C.: American Pyschiatric Association, 1980).
9. Ken Liska, *Drugs and the Human Body: With Implications for Society*, 3rd Ed. (New York: Macmillan, 1990), 154. This discussion, which will draw mainly on references in popular textbooks on drugs, is consistent with the standard literature.
10. Ibid., 154-55.
11. Edward M. Brecher et al., *Licit and Illicit Drugs* (Boston: Little, Brown and Company, 1972), 104-9.
12. See Trebach, *Great Drug War*, 287.
13. Liska, *Drugs and the Human Body*, 153.
14. See the discussion in Kaplan, *The Hardest Drug*, 32-34.
15. Rolf Wille, "Processes of Recovery from Heroin Dependence: Relationship to Treatment, Social Changes and Drug Use," *Journal of Drug Issues* 13, no. 3 (Summer 1983): 339.
16. Kaplan, *The Hardest Drug*, 34.
17. Ibid.
18. Edward M. Brecher et al., *Licit and Illicit Drugs*, 188-89.
19. Norman E. Zinberg, "The Use and Misuse of Intoxicants: Factors in the Development of Controlled Use," in *Dealing With Drugs: Consequences of Government Control*, ed., Ronald Hamowy (Lexington, Mass.: Lexington Books, 1987), 265.
20. Kaplan, *The Hardest Drug*, 36-38.
21. This perspective is highly controversial. See the discussion in Brecher et al., *Licit and Illicit Drugs*, 64-89.
22. Steven Wisotsky, *Beyond the War on Drugs: Overcoming a Failed Public Policy* (Buffalo, N. Y.: Prometheus Books, 1990), 29, 207, n 243.
23. Zinberg, "Use and Misuse of Intoxicants," 252. See also the discussion in Stanton Peele, "Control Yourself," *Reason* 21, no. 9 (February 1990): 23-25.
24. Wisotsky, *Beyond the War on Drugs*, p. 207.
25. Zinberg, "Use and Misuse of Intoxicants," 254; Wisotsky, *Beyond the War on Drugs*, 207.
26. For thorough discussions of the physiological and chemical effects of these drugs in human beings, see Liska, *Drugs and the Human Body*, and Brecher et al., *Licit and Illicit Drugs*.

27. Robert Byck, "Cocaine, Marijuana, and the Meanings of Addiction," in Hamowy, *Dealing with Drugs*, 222.
28. Liska, *Drugs and the Human Body*, 174.
29. The study was performed by Targeting Systems, Inc. in Virginia and conducted from 24 January, 1990 through 4 February, 1990.
30. Robert C. Rinaldi, Emanual M. Steindler, Bonnie B. Wilford, and Desiree Goodwin, "Clarification and Standardization of Substance Abuse Terminology," *Journal of the American Medical Association* 259, no. 4 (January 22/29): 556.
31. Ibid.
32. Jeffrey Miron and Jeffrey Zwiebel, "Alcohol Consumption During Prohibition," *American Economic Review* 81, no. 2 (May 1991): 242-47.
33. Ibid., 246.
34. An excellent review of these issues can be found in Thomas J. Glynn and Marianne Haenlein, "Family Theory and Research on Adolescent Drug Use," in *The Family Context of Adolescent Drug Use*, ed., Robert H. Coombs (New York: Haworth Press, 1988), 39-56.
35. Judith S. Brook, Martin Whiteman, Carolyn Nomura, Ann Scovell Gordon, and Patricia Cohen, "Personality, Family, and Ecological Influences on Adolescent Drug Use: A Developmental Analysis," in Coombs, *The Family Context*, 123-61.
36. These effects were also found in an empirical analysis of 2,926 students in the seventh, nineth, and eleventh grades. See Michael D. Newcomb, Bridget N. Fahy and Rodney Skager, "Correlates of Cocaine Use among Adolescents," *Journal of Drug Issues* 18, no. 3 (1988): 327-56.
37. James F. Rooney, "The Influence of Informal Control Sources Upon Adolescent Alcohol Use and Problems," *American Journal of Drug and Alcohol Abuse* 9, no. 2 (1982-83): 233- 245. This is also true of cigarette smoking, see Charles D. Spielberger, "Psychological Determinants of Smoking Behavior," in *Smoking and Society: Toward a More Balanced Assessment*, ed. Robert D. Tollison (Lexington, Mass.: Lexington Books, 1986), 89-134.
38. U.S. Congress, Senate Judiciary Committee, *Hard-Core Cocaine Addicts: Measuring— and Fighting—the Epidemic* (Washington, D.C.: Government Printing Office, 1990), iii.
39. Ibid., 4.
40. See Kleiman's introduction in U.S. Congress, *Hard-Core Cocaine Addicts*, vii-viii.
41. Rinaldi, Steindler et. al., "Clarification and standardization," 557.
42. APA, *Diagnostic and Statistical Manual*, 163-64.
43. A brief and concise history of psychoactive substance use can be found in Joseph Westermeyer, "The Pursuit of Intoxication: Our 100 Century-Old Romance with Psychoactive Substances," *American Journal of Drug and Alcohol Abuse* 14, no. 2 (1988): 175-187.
44. Westermeyer, "The Pursuit of Intoxication," 180.
45. The classic historical analysis of drug use in the United States is found in David F. Musto, *The American Disease: Origins of Narcotic Control*, exp. ed. (New York: Oxford University Press, 1987).
46. Westermeyer, "The Pursuit of Intoxification," 181.
47. Barbara A. Mensch and Denise B. Kandel, "Do Job Conditions Influence the Use of Drugs?" *Journal of Health and Social Behavior* 29 (June 1988): 182.
48. Carol Kleiman, "Drugs Aren't Everyone's Main On-the-Job Problem," *Dayton, Inc.*, 16 July 1990, p. 3.
49. Quoted in Kleiman, "Drugs," 3.

50. Ostrowski did not include the $33.3 billion loss attributed to marijuana by the original authors. See the discussion in James Ostrowski, "Thinking About Drug Legalization," *Cato Institute Policy Analysis* no. 121 (Washington, D.C.: Cato Institute, 1989), 17-20.

51. Bruce D. Johnson, Paul J. Goldstein, Edward Preble, James Schmeidler, Douglas S. Lipton, Barry Spunt, and Thomas Miller, *Taking Care of Business: The Economics of Crime by Heroin Abusers* (Lexington, Mass.: Lexington Books, 1985), 104-5.

52. Peter Reuter, Robert MacCoun, and Patrick Murphy, *Money From Crime: A Study of the Economics of Drug Dealing in Washington, D.C.* (Santa Monica, Calif.: RAND Corporation, Drug Policy Research Center, 1990), 89.

53. For a review of the literature on the relationship between drugs and crime, see Duane C. McBride and Clyde B. McCoy, "Crime and Drugs: The Issues and Literature," *Journal of Drug Issues* 12, no. 2 (Spring 1982): 137-52.

54. Bernard A. Gropper, *Probing the Links Between Drugs and Crime* (Washington, D.C.: National Institute of Justice, 1985), 2.

55. Former Chicago prosecutor Randy Barnett estimates that half of all the homicides in Chicago were drug-related. See Randy Barnett, "Curing the Drug-Law Addiction," in *Dealing With Drugs: Consequences of Government Control*, ed. Ronald Hamowy (Lexington, Mass.: Lexington Books, 1987), 83- 84.

56. Charles Faupel, "Heroin Use, Crime, and Employment Status," *Journal of Drug Issues* 18, no. 3 (1988): 467-79.

57. Allen J. Beck, "Profile of Jail Inmates, 1989," *Bureau of Justice Statistics Special Report* (Washington, D.C.: U.S. Department of Justic, Bureau of Justice Statistics, April 1991), 8, tables 13, 14.

58. Paul J. Goldstein, "The Drugs/Violence Nexus: A Tripartite Conceptual Framework," *Journal of Drug Issues* 15, no. 4 (Fall 1985): 493-506.

59. Ibid., 495.

60. Ibid., 497.

61. Gropper, "Probing the Links," 5.

62. Amount is average consumption of heroin in the United States, reported in Brecher et al., *Licit and Illicit Drugs*, 92. A more recent estimate by Mark Moore suggests that the average heroin habit may be closer to 50 milligrams per day. See Mark H. Moore, *Buy and Bust* (Lexington, Mass.: Lexington Books, 1977), 84. Income spent is calculated based on the 1986 wholesale price per kilogram which ranged from $120,000 to $200,000 according to data published in the Drug Enforcement Administration, *The Illicit Drug Situation in the United States and Canada, 1984-1986* (Washington, D.C.: U.S. Department of Justice, 1987), 21.

63. In England, heroin can be prescribed for terminally ill patients. Twenty 10 milligram tablets of heroin cost approximately one dollar. See the discussion in Robert J. Michaels, "The Market for Heroin Before and After Legalization," in Hamowy, *Dealing with Drugs*, 303-4.

64. See the discussion in Liska, *Drugs and the Human Body*, 174-79. For a critical review of the scientific evidence concerning the effects of cocaine, see Wisotsky, *Beyond the War on Drugs*, 17-30.

65. Wisotosky, *Beyond the War on Drugs*, 29.

66. Liska, *Drugs and the Human Body*, 274.

67. Ostrowski, "Thinking About Drug Legalization," 48.

5

Drug Trafficking as an Understandable Market Response: Urban Youth and the Drug Economy

As discussed in chapter 1, cities in America experienced dramatic declines in population and economic activity over the past several decades. The decentralization of population and employment since the 1950s has drained many central cities of resources needed for sustained economic growth, finding them with fewer businesses, jobs, and tax revenue and with more unemployed, indigent, and poor.[1] The decline of America's central cities precipitated a dramatic rise in "informal" or "underground" economic activity. A wide range of products and services, from child care to drug trafficking, has become part of the informal sector. While estimates vary, many observers estimate that the extralegal economy generates income well into the hundreds of billions of dollars.

Particularly hard hit in this urban decline have been inner city youth, particularly minority teenagers just entering the employment market.[2] Yet, despite the rise of the underground economy and the simultaneous decline of entry-level jobs in the legal labor market, few observers in the policy arena have linked this extralegal economic activity to degenerating urban labor markets (particularly those for inner-city youth). Typically, the presence of extralegal trade (e.g., drug trafficking) is employed to exemplify urban decay, while the implications remain outside the realm of policy analysis. Even the burgeoning literature on the economics

119

of crime largely ignores the incentives and institutions that contribute to the existence of extralegal economic activity.[3]

A neglected but important cost to the current drug war lies in its effects on our cities' youth and minority communities, particularly since the future of urban America will be determined in large part by its minority population.[4] In essence, the decline of America's central cities and the growth of the drug trade has created a "segmented" labor market for teenagers, one legal and the other extralegal. While employment in the legal job market often prepares youth for the challenges of future employment in the larger economy, the institutions that govern behavior in the underground economy are likely to severely handicap those employed within it. The implications of a growing underground economy, particularly one as violent as the drug trade, could be staggering for cities desperately looking for ways to develop economically.

Urban youth are rational in the sense that they try to maximize the economic and psychic benefits from employment. This observation has significant implications for evaluating public policy and assessing the role for the drug market in this discussion. In fact, a recent study of drug trafficking in Washington, D.C. found that younger traffickers were distinguished from their older counterparts by their instrumental use of drug trafficking as an alternative income source. High profits have lured younger nonusers into drug trafficking for monetary reasons.

Contrary to common perception, most drug abusers are white teenagers. Moreover, higher proportions of young whites use drugs than their African-American counterparts. A recent study released by the Parents' Resource Institute for Drug Education, Inc. surveyed 350,000 high school students during the 1988-89 academic year. Although the poll was nonrandom, the survey covered teenagers in 958 schools in thirty-eight states. Sixty-five percent of white high school seniors admitted drinking liquor in the study compared to 37 percent of African-American seniors. Another 29 percent of white seniors admitted smoking marijuana while 7 percent used cocaine compared to 17 percent and 4 percent for African-Americans. The results prompted Dr. Marsha Keith Schuchard, a cofounder of the Institute, to remark "there is not enough money in the ghetto areas to sustain the multi-billion-dollar market for illegal drugs. The drug cartels depend mainly on middle-class and affluent white users to produce the profits."[5]

Dr. Schuchard has touched on an important element of the drug market. For the most part, the demand for drugs eminates from upper-middle-income suburbanites. Their demand provides the profit margin that underwrites the illegal drug trade.

The distribution system is highly complex, operating on at least two different levels. The importation and regional distribution of these drugs is controlled by well-run and sophisticated trafficking organizations such as the well- known Colombian cartels or the now infamous Los Angeles street gangs such as the Crips and the Bloods. The retail level, on the other hand, is highly decentralized and idiosynchratic. In some markets, street-level distribution is tightly controlled by well-established neighborhood gangs (e.g., in Los Angeles). In others, such as Washington, D.C., street-level dealers may free-lance or deal as members of smaller organizations.

This chapter begins to disentangle the economic development consequences of the drug trade by focusing on the labor supply decisions of young African-American men in the inner-cities.[6] Juvenile males are becoming prominent in the illicit drug trade. This participation is prompted directly by the trade's money-making potential. Compared to other inner-city alternatives, drug trafficking promises more money for less work. Unfortunately, as chapter 3 suggested, the values taught through drug trafficking work against the values needed to participate fully and productively in the legitimate economy.

African-American Youth and the Decline of the Central City

Cities in America have been grappling with the recent transformation of the national economy from a manufacturing to a services employment base. This shift to "advanced services" has dramatically altered the structure of labor demand in central cities. Low-skilled manufacturing jobs have either migrated to outlying suburban areas or have disappeared altogether. Cities have become more "human-centered," emphasizing traditionally white-collar occupations as well as management and information technology-based jobs. Increasingly, a dual labor market has appeared in central cities where low-skilled, low-educated city residents find their job opportunities constrained to unskilled minimum wage jobs with few opportunities for advancement.

For example, Baltimore's redevelopment has centered on corporate economic development and the promotion of service firms. The managerial jobs tend to go to middle-income suburbanites while the menial, minimum-wage jobs tend to go to inner-city residents. Thus, although Baltimore's economy has created thousands of jobs, the city has not replaced the high-paying manufacturing jobs that once provided a hedge against poverty and economic isolation for its urban residents.[7] Typically, the higher-paying jobs with career potential require more educated employees with the interpersonal skills needed in the information economy.

These structural changes have had important consequences for the labor market for inner-city youth. The demand for labor has shifted to unskilled service jobs with little or no opportunity for immediate advancement. Ever fewer jobs are available to inner-city youth, particularly minority teenagers. Teenage African-American males have experienced exceptionally high unemployment rates, often twice as high as white youth (table 5.1), rising from 24 percent in 1960 to 34 percent in 1987. In contrast, white youth unemployment hardly changed over this period (although unemployment rates experienced a precipitous increase in the late 1970s). Further, while white youth unemployment rates have been restored to their early 1960s levels, African-American youth unemployment has persisted well above historic levels. Clearly, for African-American men looking for work, the legal employment market in the 1980s appears less viable than in the 1960s.[8]

A more important trend, however, has been the dramatic decrease in the labor force participation rates among young African-American males. As chapter 1 detailed, the participation rates of African-American youth in the labor force exceeded white youth until the late 1960s. By 1987, their participation rates had dropped to only 43 percent. White youth, in contrast, experienced a slight increase in their labor force participation rates. Substantial portions of African-American youth have dropped out of the official labor force altogether, choosing not to work at all or participating in a growing underground economy.

The problems of young African-American males are reinforced by the concentration of African-Americans in central cities. In 1986, 81.6 percent of America's African- American population lived within metropolitan areas and over 16 million (57 percent) lived in central cities. In contrast, while 77.5 percent of the general U.S. population lives within a metropolitan area, only 30.9 percent live in central cities.[9] This geographic phenomenon has presented significant problems and challenges for the African-American community generally as well as for their youth.

TABLE 5.1
Unemployment and Labor Force Participation Rates for Teenagers, 1960 to 1987

| | Civilian Unemployment Rate | | Labor Force Participation Rate | |
| | Male Whites | Male Blacks | Male Whites | Male Blacks |
	(16-19 Yrs)		(16-19 Yrs)	
1960	14.0	24.0	55.9	57.6
1965	12.9	23.3	54.1	51.3
1970	13.7	25.0	57.5	47.4
1975	18.3	38.1	61.9	42.6
1980	16.2	37.5	63.7	43.2
1985	16.5	41.0	59.7	43.6
1987	14.2	34.4	59.0	43.6

Source: U.S. Department of Labor, Bureau of Labor Statistics. Reported in *Economic Report of the President* (Washington, D.C.: Government Printing Office, 1988), tables B-37, B-40. Data for 1960, 1965, and 1970 for black and others; data for 1975 and later for blacks only.

The economic progress of urban youth appears to have stagnated along with central cities. While long-term data show significant gains in real income for African-Americans, particularly among the middle class,[10] progress for those at the lower end of the income scale has slowed and may have reversed in recent years.[11] In 1986, 31.1 percent of the African-American population lived below the poverty level compared to 13.6 percent for the nation as a whole.[12] Further, current estimates show that over half of all African-American children are born into single-parent homes, most of which are located in central cities.

Thus, the out-migration of low-paying, low-skilled retail and service jobs to largely white suburban areas appears to have established a segmented labor market. Statistically, the labor market appears split into two groups: one employed and participating in the legal labor market, and the other unemployed or not participating in the legal labor market. The dramatic drop in labor force participation rates among teenage

African-American men strongly suggests that a relatively large extralegal employment market may exist in America's central cities. This suggestion is reinforced by the economic and demographic changes detailed in chapter 1. Employment opportunities for teenage African-Americans appear more promising in outlying suburban areas, while the demographic concentration of African-American youth persists in central cities.

The Labor Market for Inner-City Youth

The labor-market effects of national and economic trends are usually analyzed through either supply-side or demand-side approaches.[13] Supply-side approaches typically focus on the incentives facing economic agents who participate in the urban labor market.[14] Demand-side approaches often focus more exclusively on the desire for labor among firms in central cities.[15]

The difficulty faced by most formal analyses of central city employment markets is their failure to incorporate the informal (or illegal) sector into their general framework. Declining formal employment opportunities often mirror rising informal employment opportunities in urban economies. Since official statistics only capture economic activity in legal employment markets, extralegal employment is often ignored as an important element of a general framework for understanding labor market adjustments in central cities.

The declining fortunes of central cities reduced the demand for low-skilled teenage workers and may have, in fact, motivated "entrepreneurial" supply-side decisions by youth to enter into the extralegal employment: the informal economy (which includes illegal employment in the drug trade, prostitution, etc.) may have become a viable (and sometimes necessary) employment alternative for many young people in inner-city environments. Indeed, one observer of the informal economy speculated that the "high rates of unemployment and low rates of labor force participation among nonwhite teenage males in the United States suggests that this group may provide a substantial number of individuals who work full time in unrecorded [extralegal] activity."[16]

Entrepreneurship is usually defined within a heroic, Horatio Alger context or narrowly to include only the self-employed or sole proprietorships. Yet, these classifications are merely proxies for the behavioral traits of a class of market participants called "entrepreneurs." An alternative way to define *entrepreneurship* is to frame the discussion in terms of behavior in economic markets.[17]

Entrepreneurship defined behaviorally permits a broader application to real social and economic processes at work in America's central cities and is more appropriate for analyzing the behavior of youth in depressed inner-city areas as well. The entrepreneur is not necessarily the person who starts a business, although businesspeople are often entrepreneurs. Rather, the entrepreneur pursues objectives that maximize his or her welfare, responding to opportunities that may promote tangible rewards (money or physical objects such as cars) or less tangible rewards (respect, prestige, or personal power). Within the context of inner-city labor markets, the dramatic withdrawal of African-American youth from the labor force may in fact reflect a shift in youth employment from legal economic activities to extralegal economic activities.

The out-migration of firms and employment reduced labor demand for teenage workers in the central cities in legal employment markets, increasing unemployment among central city youth. Yet, urban teenagers were also faced with potential employment in the illegal employment market, which became more viable with the decline in legal employment opportunities. Since illegal employment carries a higher risk (e.g., possible arrest) and social stigma (e.g., disapproval of parents and friends), the equilibrium wage rate in the illegal market would be higher than in the legal market to compensate for these additional costs.

Substantial anecdotal evidence exists suggesting that employment in illegal activity, particularly the drug trade, carries a negative social stigma. For example, children are often employed as "lookouts" during drug deals and are paid hundreds of dollars.[18] If this employment were acceptable behavior, drug traffickers would not pay such high wages for relatively low-risk and short-term jobs (since they are also profit maximizers).

More systematically, Peter Reuter, Robert MacCoun, and Patrick Murphy surveyed 387 students in Washington, D.C. about their perceptions of drug dealing.[19] Eighty-two percent indicated that they did not admire a person who sold drugs. The only occupation receiving a lower approval rating was a pimp (92 percent said they did not admire a pimp). Moreover, although the study estimated that 25 percent of African-American men were engaged in drug trafficking at some point in their lives, only 10 percent of the students surveyed said they were at least somewhat likely to sell drugs after they finished school. Clearly, among the students surveyed in this study, drug trafficking is not considered socially acceptable.

In fact, wages can vary significantly depending on the drug being sold and the person selling the drugs. For example, a detailed survey of 201 heroin users[20] found that the "average heroin abuser" provided over $15,000 in services to the drug industry through sales, distribution, steering and locating customers, and transporting drugs and money. In return, the average drug abuser received less than $2,000 in cash from sales and other services rendered.[21] Heroin abusers are often a ready source of labor for drug distributors, however, since they often do not have a steady source of income. Moreover, the demands of a daily heroin habit induce the daily user to spend more time raising money to supply the habit, often through criminal activity.[22]

This relationship appears even stronger when the heroin abusers were subcategorized into three groups: daily users, regular users, and irregular users. Daily heroin users generated $26,126 in drug-business activity, while regular users generated another $13,875 and irregular users generated only $5,528. Yet, for every dollar generated in income by the daily and regular heroin abuser, he received only eleven cents in cash income. In contrast, the irregular heroin abuser received thirty-two cents on every dollar raised. Thus, the irregular user is likely to be paid a higher wage than the regular or daily abuser, who is more likely to provide human capital to the drug distribution business.

The differences in compensation can be seen even more dramatically by comparing the productivity of the heroin abuser with income generated from his activity (table 5.2). By far, the most productive group is the daily heroin user. On average, daily users generate income of $29.31 per transaction, almost one-third higher than irregular users and twice the income generated of regular users.

Nevertheless, daily users are paid substantially less than irregular users on a per transaction basis. The cash income derived from illegal drug transactions is less than half the income received by irregular users. Less frequent users, then, appear to be paid higher wages than frequent users, reflecting the availability of other sources of income.

Cash income is only one measure of income derived from the drug business. Another source is avoided expenditures on drugs from in-kind payments, drug thefts, and miscellaneous drug sales. These expenditures are reflected in the abuser's total drug income. Indeed, daily heroin users appear to derive most of their compensation through these routes. Cash income is only 36 percent of the daily heroin abuser's total drug income. In contrast, cash income is 96 percent of the irregular users total income derived from drug transactions. Thus, wages tend to be higher for those users who are less frequent participants, probably compensating for higher risks for less experienced dealers and the availability of alternative sources of income.

TABLE 5.2
Productivity and Compensation of Heroin Abusers, 1981

| | Heroin User Group | | | |
	Irregular	Regular	Daily	Average
Drug transactions per year	245	823	880	665
Value Distributed	$ 4,925	$13,260	$25,790	$14,596
Cash Income	1,556	1,402	2,752	1,868
Total Drug Income	1,634	4,209	7,653	4,489
Value Distributed per crime	$20.10	$16.11	$29.31	$21.95
Cash Income per crime	6.37	1.52	3.13	2.81
Total Drug Income per crime	6.67	5.11	8.69	6.75

Source: Calculated from Bruce D. Johnson, Paul J. Goldstein, Edward Preble, et al., *Taking Care of Business: The Economics of Crime by Heroin Abusers* (Lexington, Mass.: Lexington Books, 1985), table B-12.

Moreover, evidence collected by sociologists, discussed below, has found that many drug dealers view their employment as short-term and have left the "profession" by their mid- to late twenties. This behavior suggests that criminal activity still carries a social stigma (in the long run) that encourages participants to seek long-term employment in the legal sector.

If wage rates are sufficiently high in the extralegal market, labor will shift out of the legal market and into the extralegal sector. Declines in the supply of labor in the legal market will be reflected in lower labor force participation rates in official statistics. On the other hand, if the legal labor market remains competitive in wage and nonwage benefits, a legal market equilibrium could be maintained resulting in a labor shortage in the extralegal market.

The important implication of this approach for urban labor markets is that many teenagers do not leave the general labor force (only the official labor force). They are faced with a wide range of employment opportunities within as well as outside the legal system. The factor driving the model is the simple but plausible assumption that labor market participants engage in welfare maximizing behavior. Within the context of teenage youth, the apparent profits gleaned from extralegal employment, particularly the drug trade, are sufficiently high to compensate for the added risk of participating in illegal activity as well as for any additional moral objections.

Moreover, an active extralegal employment market suggests that labor force participation rates may significantly overestimate the degree of withdrawal from the labor force among teenagers, African-American teenagers in particular. To the extent that income statistics do not incorporate wages and profits made from extralegal employment, these statistics may be overstated as well.

Criminal Activity and Employability

Evidence supporting this approach to inner-city labor markets appears in several recent empirical studies on youth employment and criminal activity in central cities. For example, several recent studies found significant differences in expectations among white and African-American teenagers with respect to their "reservation wage" (the wage an employer would have to offer before the job would be accepted).[23] Surveys indicate that the reservation wages for white and African-American youth are approximately equal. In the early 1980s, for example, reservation wages were estimated at around $4.00 per hour for both African-American and white youth.

Yet, African-American youths were typically offered jobs paying below their reservation wage while white youths were offered jobs paying above their reservation wage. Harry J. Holzer, an economist at Michigan State University, analyzed data on reservation wages for over

2,500 white and African- American youths (ages fourteen to twenty-one) using the National Longitudinal Survey for 1979 and 1980.[24] The average reservation wage was $4.59 per hour for nonemployed white youth and $4.47 per hour for nonemployed African- American youth. The received wage from the most recent job, however, was $4.75 per hour for white youth and only $4.00 for African-American youth.

These discrepancies continued even when the youths were employed. Employed African-Americans reported an average reservation wage of $5.40 per hour but received only $4.26 in their most recent job. Employed white youth reported a reservation wage of $6.01 but received only $5.13 on average in their most recent job. Even though white youth received less than their reservation wage, young African-Americans received a smaller proportion of their reservation wage.

The problem, then, is not that African-American youth do not have the same aspirations as white youth. Rather, the problem is providing the means by which African-American youth can attain their aspirations. As Holzer notes, "young blacks seek jobs and wages that are comparable to those of young whites but that are at higher levels than the jobs and wages the young blacks ultimately obtain."[25]

The differences between reservation wages and actual wages faced by inner-city youth have important implications for their assessment of job prospects in the underground economy vis-a-vis the legal economy. Prospective workers experiencing large differences between their reservation wages and actual wages are more likely to become employed in the underground economy. If the worker's reservation wage is higher than that offered in the legal market, he or she is more likely to search for employment in informal labor markets. Reservation wages may serve as indirect signals of the likelihood that workers will shift their labor into informal industries such as the drug trade.

As the evidence presented in chapter 1 clearly indicated, the job opportunities for unskilled labor in high-paying jobs have declined significantly in central cities. The jobs unskilled and inexperienced teenage laborers are likely to fill are in the low-skilled service industries such as fast-food, retail, and light wholesale. Moroever, these jobs have few benefits and possibilities for advancement and are often part-time. As teenage reservation wages continue to exceed actual compensation in the work force, young workers will be tempted into the underground economy.

Increasingly, the income-earning aspirations of inner-city youth and young African-Americans are being met through illegal employment, particularly criminal activity. W. Kip Viscusi, an economist at Northwestern University used information from the National Bureau of Economic Research's (NBER) Survey of Inner-City Black Youth to assess the criminal opportunities, the apparent risks, and rewards.[26] The survey included 2,358 youths between seventeen and twenty-four years of age during 1981. This age group, according to FBI crime statistics, accounts for over 60 percent of all city arrests. During the last year, 15 percent of the youths responding to the NBER study reported committing a crime in the past month, while 19 percent said they had committed a crime in the past year.

Participation in criminal activity is pervasive within the inner city. Over 12 percent of the sample of inner-city youth admitted to participating in numbers running in the past year, the highest of any category (table 5.3). The second-largest category of admitted criminal activity was drug dealing. Of those committing crimes, however, 63 percent admitted to running numbers and another 37 percent admitted to dealing drugs.

Yet youths participating in drug dealing may be more pervasive than these numbers suggest. FBI data on arrests for the same year (1981) show that 18 percent of all arrests were for drug violations. The only category with a higher proportion of arrests was larceny and theft (39 percent). Moreover, 62 percent of the arrests for drug violations in 1981 were of youths fifteen to twenty-four years old.[27]

Moreover, the study on drug dealing in Washington, D.C., found that 25 percent of young African-American men would likely become drug dealers at some point in their careers.

More important, drug dealing is a relatively lucrative criminal activity (table 5.4). After adjusting for earnings per criminal offense, the youth in the NBER survey reported higher earnings for drug dealing than any other listed offense. A category termed "other" netted the highest annual income, suggesting that the incomes reported by youth for the specific crime categories may be understated.[28] Numbers running, the crime that experienced the greatest degree of participation, paid relatively poorly.

The high levels of criminal income may also suggest that drug dealing is a relatively specialized activity. Viscusi found that drug dealers have a "narrow crime pattern," participating in numbers running and illegal gambling but not other crimes.[29] Yet drug dealing had the highest amount of self-reported activity next to numbers running. This specialization suggests that it may be a mistake to treat drug dealers as criminals as we do burglars and those committing violent crimes. Indeed, as this book stresses, drug dealing reflects the economic realities of our inner cities and not simply the breakdown of a moral code.

TABLE 5.3
Past Year Criminal Activity for Inner-City Youth

Crime	Criminal Activity in Past Year	
	Percent of Sample	Percent of Criminals
Numbers running	12%	63%
Drug Dealing	7	37
Fencing Stolen Goods	3	19
Mugging	3	13
Robbery	3	16
Burglary	2	11

Source: National Bureau of Economic Research Survey of Inner-City Youth, reported in W. Kip Viscusi, "Market Incentives for Criminal Behavior," in *The Black Youth Employment Crisis*, ed. Richard B. Freeman and Harry J. Holzer (Chicago: University of Chicago Press, 1986), 332, table 8.12.

Despite the relatively high earnings for drug dealing compared to other crimes, youth earn relatively little money. In fact, compared to their expected earnings, the actual payoff is substantially lower. Expected illegal earnings for the entire sample of inner-city youth averaged $22,945 annually. For those who actually committed a crime, expected earnings were higher at $31,200 for the year. Actual income for the entire group, however, averaged around $1,500 (including the higher income from the "other" category). Thus, realized earnings were substantially lower than the youth anticipated although drug dealing appeared to have the highest payoff.

In fact, this reality persists even after a decade of growth in the drug industry, prompting former juvenile court judge Reggie Walton to note "[t]here is a myth out there that everyone involved in the drug trade . . . is making a lot of money and we know that's not the case. There are relatively few people who make the big bucks."[30]

TABLE 5.4
Average Income from Criminal Activity by Category

Crime	Average Annual Income ($)
Drug Dealing	994.54
Forgery	891.48
Burglary	760.78
Mugging	744.36
Fencing stolen goods	720.85
Robbery	624.39
Numbers	565.14
Shoplifting	373.17
Con games	337.67

Source: Viscusi, "Market Incentives," 332, table 8.12.

Yet despite lower actual payoffs from criminal activity, those expecting to make more money from crime than in the legal economy did (earning $714 annually compared to $167 annually). In fact, expectations about the money-earning potential of the formal employment sector versus the illegal employment sector was a "fundamental determinant of criminal income levels." Viscusi found that the "economic attractiveness of crime accounted for 26 percent of past- month crime income and 34 percent of past-year crime income."[31]

Those participating in criminal activity were those most likely to be left out of the system (table 5.5). Youth in school were the least likely to report annual income from crime and were also the least likely to participate in criminal activities. Employed youth earned substantially more in the legal employment market than they did through crime. In addition, these youths earned more annually than those who were not in school and did not work. Thus, the appeal of crime as an income generating source may be largely economic. This evidence supports the more general empirical work on reservation wages as well.

Another independent study using survey data reinforces these conclusions, finding that many youth view criminal employment as an income-substituting activity. The authors find that their "results suggest that if the increased expectations [of employment in the legal sector] are not realized, this increased difference between desired employment and actual employment will lead to increased criminal activity for blacks."[32] Thus, faced with declining employment opportunities for young, un-skilled, and relatively uneducated workers, central-city youth are more willing to take advantage of opportunities outside the traditional, legal employment market.

TABLE 5.5
Earnings from Legal Sources and Criminal Activity

	Annual Legal Earnings	Annual Criminal Earnings	Probability of Criminal Participation
Employed	$5,329	$ 177	.18
In school	610	80	.12
Not employed and not in school	487	505	.51

Source: Viscusi, "Market Incentives," 340, table 8.17.

Further, a study by Llad Phillips and Harold Votey has found that participants in criminal activity generally do not view their criminal activity as permanent employment, moving between the legal and illegal job market fairly frequently. They find that age is significantly correlated with participation in criminal activity. As participants become older, they are less inclined to participate in illegal activity.[33]

This result is also consistent with more general empirical labor market evidence. Labor force participation rates for 1987 calculated by the U.S. Department of Labor jump from only 43 percent among African-American youth sixteen to nineteen years old to over 74 percent for those over twenty years old. Further, this is only slightly lower than the 78 percent labor force participation rate among white men over twenty. Viewing the labor market as a continuum crossing legal and extralegal markets appears to be consistent with the actual behavior and attitudes of labor market participants.

The New Entrepreneurial Class

The perception that money can be made in the drug trade is drawing more and more youth at increasingly younger ages. The extent of the drug trade appears to have become much worse with the explosion of the cocaine market[34] and the emergence of crack in poor neighborhoods.

The extent of this "entrepreneurial" activity is evident in arrest rates among young African-Americans. In 1989, *USA Today* and Gannett News Service extensively analyzed previously unpublished and unanalyzed arrest data for drug offenses from 1984 to 1988. Their results revealed that African-Americans made up three-quarters of all juveniles arrested for cocaine and heroin dealing in 1988.[35]

Moreover, the percentage of African-Americans arrested for drug offenses increased from 30 percent in 1984 to 38 percent in 1988.[36] Thirty-eight percent of all arrests of African-American juveniles were for cocaine or heroin dealing, while only 25 percent of arrests among African- American adults were for the same crime. In contrast, only 9 percent of white juveniles and 13 percent of white adults were arrested for cocaine or heroin dealing.

A more important trend, however, for the purposes of this discussion, is that the arrest rate for African-Americans on drug offenses exceeds their rate of drug use. According to the National Institute of Drug Abuse, a 1988 survey revealed that African-Americans make up only 12 percent of drug users.[37] If jobs in the drug trade were randomly distributed among African-Americans and Caucasians, the proportion of African-Americans involved in trafficking should reflect their proportion of the general population. The evident concentration of African-Americans in drug-related activity, specifically trafficking, implies a decision that opportunities are "better" in the underground economy than in the legal economy.

The drug economy appears to have become even more lucrative in the 1990s. The RAND Corporation, a government-sponsored research organization, recently completed a study of 24,000 street-level drug dealers in Washington, D.C. Drug dealers, the report estimates, make up 4 percent of the population of the District. On average, the income derived from drug trafficking ranged from $24,000 to $43,000 per year.[38]

Moreover, most of these traffickers are part-time dealers. Less than half, 11,600, reported selling drugs on a daily basis, and 13,000 reported selling one day per week or less. In addition, over two-thirds of the traffickers held legitimate jobs, using drug dealing as an important supplemental income activity. These more recent trends reinforce results from research performed in the late 1970s. For example, a study of 902 Brooklyn male arrestees revealed that 40 percent of young African-

Americans participating in crimes also held other jobs.[39] Clearly, in addition to crime as an income-substituting activity, the drug trade is becoming an important income supplementing activity.

Unfortunately, to the less well educated and unskilled workers, most legitimate jobs in the inner city do not compare well financially to the promise of drug trafficking. In Washington, D.C., for example, the average hourly wage rate hovers near seven dollars per hour. Annually, this translates into gross income of about $14,000 per year if the employee works a full, forty-hour work week. Federal and city taxes accumulate to almost 30 percent of the gross income, leaving less than $12,000 per year in disposable income.

This contrasts with an hourly wage rate near thirty dollars per hour in drug trafficking according to the RAND study. Most of the drug traffickers held legal jobs, which were categorized as deliverymen, office clerks, cooks, and construction laborers. The limited hours of selling—usually between 6:00 P.M. and 10:00 P.M. Monday through Friday and weekends—limits their ability to work their jobs full-time.

Nevertheless, the caveats concerning realized earnings discussed earlier should be carefully considered. The average income data may mask substantial inequality. For example, if gross income for five workers equals $100,000, the average would be $20,000 per employee regardless of the distribution of income. For example, if one person earns $100,000 and the other four earn nothing, the average will still be $20,000 per employee.[40]

As mentioned earlier, substantial evidence exists suggesting that expected returns are much lower than realized income gains in the drug trade for most traffickers. Earnings usually peak in the late teens and early twenties, falling off substantially later. Thus, while a teenager may earn enough money to buy a gold chain or fancy pair of tennis shoes, very few drive Porsches or BMWs.

Still, the power and allure of high drug profits should not be underestimated. If drug dealing moves increasingly into an income-supplementing activity, drawing workers away from the drug trade will be difficult. As Peter Reuter, an economist who has written extensively on the drug trade, has noted, the "creation of considerably higher paying legitimate jobs probably wouldn't get us very far. Dealers would still have smaller total incomes than they can earn now by supplementing their regular wages with drug selling."[41]

The potential profits are dramatically illustrated by an anecdote from Colorado.[42] A thirteen-year-old boy tries marijuana and finds he enjoys it. Since the boy is broke, a friend suggests he sell part of his initial supply to new customers.

> Being more fond of money than marijuana, he often sold his whole supply instead of smoking it. This he found was extraordinarily lucrative. He concentrated on expanding his business. The action became so heavy that he started to fly to Los Angeles to buy wholesale. He would tell his parents that he was going skiing, or in warmer weather, camping on the weekends. On Friday evening he would fly to L.A. and return with his wares on Sunday.[43]

At the height of his business, this teenage dealer eventually was selling drugs to over two thousand students in the high school. As in any business, for those with ambition and drive, hard work can be financially rewarding.

Unfortunately, the incentives to engage in drug dealing center on absolute income levels. For many dealers in their teens and early twenties, decisions to traffic or engage in criminal activity are based on calculations of their opportunity costs associated with other employment. The reservation wages discussed earlier serve as examples of the opportunity costs of leisure compared to legitimate employment. Similarly, the opportunity costs of the drug trade should be viewed from the viewpoint of the potential trafficker.

The Case of Jim

For African-American men, the employment prospects in the legitimate market are bleak. Those who complete high school look forward to jobs in the low-paying service industry as short order cooks at fast-food restaurants, deliverymen, or clerks. As one former drug trafficker intoned bitterly, "Society is set up so that black people can't get ahead. I'm not supposed to have the American dream and all that. I'm supposed to be in jail."[44]

Jim, for instance, is an inner-city African-American high school junior in a major city.[45] His performance is school is good, although not exceptional. In fact, his performance is sufficient to make him competitive at several smaller private colleges if he had the money to pay the tuition. More likely, Jim will attend the local state university on a part-time basis.

Jim's future educational prospects are cloudy, however. Given his strong academic performance, Jim's teachers have encouraged him but devoted most of their time to the academically "gifted" students. In a high school where less than 10 percent of the graduates go on to college immediately after graduation, Jim's grades do not suggest to his teachers that he is a worthwhile prospect.

Jim's nonacademic activities revolve around the school's athletes and a small group of friends from his neighborhood. Only one of the dozen or so teenagers Jim "hangs" with is committed to going on to college. School athletics has always excited Jim, although he never had the ability to become a varsity player. After one year on the bench for the junior varsity basketball team, Jim "retired" to become the team's equipment manager and statistician. The athletes, for most of Jim's high school experience, have always formed the higher social strata of his graduating class.

When he graduates, Jim expects to find a job that will support him independently of his mother (his father does not live with his mother) and possibly go on to school. His mother works a full-time job as a clerk in a local retail store, earning about $15,000, which covers the basic necessities of living in an apartment with his younger brother and sister.

Most of the encouragement for going on to college comes from his mother. Although she claims she will find the money to send him to school somewhere, Jim is less optimistic.

Jim is well aware of his job prospects when he graduates. His high school diploma from the public school system will be valued minimally by local employers. After all, his school has a 40 percent dropout rate.

Jim is also aware that his race will place him at a serious disadvantage. Many of his friends on the basketball team who graduated last year are still unemployed. Some now earn money from crime although most perform temporary work and get paid "under the table." The jobs are in the suburbs, but they cannot afford to move. Even those who scraped up enough money to move found advertised apartments become unavailable when they showed up for the interview. The commuting costs were too high to make the suburban jobs cost-effective.

The local fast-food restaurant has had a "help wanted" sign out ever since it opened when Jim was in junior high. Jim estimates he could make $5.00 an hour and work 15 hours per week on average. Over the course of a year, Jim's gross income would be about $3,750, or $3,225 after social security taxes (his income would be too low to qualify for federal, state, and city income taxes).

Another possibility is an internship with a local radio station that caters to his neighborhood.[46] The station management was impressed with Jim's initiative when he was managing his high school's basketball team and looking for sponsors. Jim expressed an interest in radio and television during a casual conversation with the station manager. The manager told him that he would arrange an internship for Jim if he wanted some experience before he went off to college. The internship would be full-time during the summer but would be unpaid. Thus, the benefits of the internship would be intangible and not contribute to Jim's short-run financial condition.

The third employment possibility is selling drugs with his friends. They would provide him with some early training and an initial supply to get started. After a while, as long as Jim played the game and did not start trouble, he could develop a relatively small group of regular customers, supplemented by street-corner sales to strangers.

Jim's mother is pushing him to take the internship. The internship, she argues correctly, would prepare him for a career when he finishes his four-year degree at the university. The job would also teach him important job skills such as punctuality, organization, networking, and the importance of relating to people. Although the job would not pay money, Jim would be able to begin networking in a career area and learn the business on the inside. Even if Jim did not pursue communications as a career, he would make valuable contacts in the business world and be able to claim work experience on his resume. Moreover, the internship would increase his prospects of being accepted at a college or university.

Jim's girlfriend, on the other hand, wants him to get the job in the fast-food restaurant. She argues that he does not really know what he wants yet. Although his mother does not know it, Jim has not even decided whether he will go to college. He could get some work experience at the restaurant and earn some money as well. Jim's girlfriend is strongly against dealing drugs to earn money, noting the risk of being arrested or seriously hurt on the streets.

Jim's male friends are encouraging him to sell drugs. It only gets easier after the first arrest, they say. Not only that, the prospects of actually being arrested are very low. Further, as a juvenile, he would get probation at the most. Jim could always quit selling if he wanted to anyway. In any event, if he were successful Jim could finance his college education and even provide support for his family. Moreover, he could afford many of the material things his friends already take for granted, such as new coats, basketball shoes, radios, and jewelry. His friends even draw on their own experiences suggesting, incorrectly, that his girlfriend and mother would not be against his selling drugs once they realized how good he was at it and how much their life will be made easier financially. The bottom line, Jim's friends note, is the difference between twenty to thirty dollars per hour selling drugs, or five dollars per hour flipping hamburgers, or no money from working at the radio station.

With the exception of the internship, inner-city youth face these types of employment choices constantly during their school years. Some will try to mix all three options. More often, they will choose one or the other. The high profits in the drug trade are pulling youth into drug dealing at increasing rates. In fact, given the uncertainties of Jim's employment prospects even after he graduates from college, the third option—drug dealing—is a perfectly rational decision from the perspective of a seventeen year old.

Choices and Decisions in the Modern City

A crucial cog in the wheel of the drug economy is the supply of labor. Increasingly, the supply of street-level entrepreneurs is made up of juveniles. More specifically, inner-city African-American youth, ages eighteen through twenty-four, form the core of the drug distribution network that generates income for isolated, underclass neighborhoods in American cities.

Although many drug dealers are also drug users, drug use should not be equated with drug abuse or addiction. Although many addicts steal drugs, many people who are not addicts may be selling drugs. Even the recreational user, for example, may sell drugs on a part-time basis to underwrite recreational use. In essence, for many dealers the drug trade may be the equivalent of a second job to obtain a higher standard of living. In the same way some people take on second jobs to supplement their income to buy a new car or accumulate a down payment on their home, drug dealing represents a way to support another luxury of contemporary life.

In fact, some observers of the drug trade have noted that the drug dealers learn some very important skills. Robert Armstrong, the executive director of the Omaha Housing Authority and long-time opponent of the drug trade, admits:

> The gangs are offering opportunities to people who are being left out of the mainstream. These are young people whom society has decided are incorrigible, without the self-discipline or skills to work in a legitimate business. What the gangs have done is taken the same individuals, and shown them how to conduct business—how to buy wholesale, sell retail, do inventory and keep profit margins. They also teach discipline—how to pay your bills on time. The gangs are willing to do what no one else is: Train these kids.[47]

Many of the drug dealers are learning business skills at an earlier age and are forced to develop their business abilities to a fine art. The risks of not approaching the drug trade in a serious, businesslike manner could include arrest, financial losses, or even death.

Many of these young entrepreneurs are reluctant participants. The decision to enter into the drug trade is primarily economic. Faced with persistently high unemployment and depressed wages, many youth find the labor market for drug dealers more lucrative than alternative employment. Thus, the profits of drug trafficking are perceived by young inner-city residents as a means to bring themselves out of poverty, even if only temporarily. Criminal activity is a young person's occupation, and, based on arrest data, the dealers appear to be younger every year.

The trend away from criminal activity in later years can be explained to some extent by changes in occupational preferences. As workers get older, for example, they may prefer more stable jobs that are part of the legal employment market. Further, as employees gain work experience and are able to hold down jobs, they may find that formal jobs produce more long-term benefits such as unemployment insurance, health insurance, pensions, etc. These fringe benefits remain outside the scope of illegal employment and the drug trade. In addition, the hours for the drug dealer are limited. At the most, the drug dealer may be able to sell for four hours a night during the week plus weekend hours.

"People don't realize that hustling's [drug dealing] is [sic] hard work," notes one dealer. "You got your police, and our enemies, and kids trying to take your dope. You're tense every day."[48] Most agree and get out before its too late.

In the long run, drug trafficking is not as profitable as the short-term profits suggest. The implications for urban economic development are important, since the revealed preferences of drug traffickers, over the long haul, are for jobs in the legitimate sector. Thus, the occupational trend toward legitimate jobs reveal that the formal sector has a comparative advantage over the informal sector.

The nature of these advantages is important for development purposes. As discussed above, institutional change and the evolution of rules are important in sustaining communities over time. Only those institutions that encourage innovation and diversity through the protection of private property and civil liberties are likely to show real economic growth and social development. The evolution of these rules and institutions follows a version of natural selection in which the most "successful," or productive, rules emerge over time. The more destructive social arrangements eventually dissolve.

Similarly, the movement of laborers out of criminal activities into the legitimate employment sector implies that the rules that govern the formal sector may be more productive in the long run. The rules and institutions that govern economic activity in the drug economy eventually work against the drug trade's ability to be a productive subsector of the more general metropolitan economy. Thus, to the extent that public policy supports or encourages the drug economy, it also encourages the perseverance of institutions that will eventually destroy the very foundations of free and productive societies.

In sum, teenage drug traffickers are increasingly drawn into their trade for economic reasons. The drug addict is no longer the archtypical drug dealer. Instead, the young, marginal teenager with high expectations but few formal employment prospects is increasingly likely to become part of the multi-billion-dollar drug underworld. In many ways, this behavior is a rational response to the declining opportunities that form the core of his economic environment. The consequences of this shift, however, have dire implications for the future of economic development in American central cities.

Notes

1. Of particular importance has been the rise of an urban underclass. While several factors have contributed to the rise of the underclass, economic issues have appeared preeminent in the scholarly discussion surrounding causes and potential solutions. For a more thorough discussion of the underclass dilemma from diverging sides of the policy debate, see Charles Murray, *Losing Ground: American Social Policy, 1950—1980* (New York: Basic Books, 1984); William J. Wilson *The Truly Disadvantaged: The Inner-City, the Underclass, and Public Policy* (Chicago: University of Chicago Press, 1987); and Sam Staley, review of *The Truly Disadvantaged* by William J. Wilson, *Journal of Urban Affairs* 11, no. 3 (1989): 315-26.

2. William J. Wilson, *The Declining Significance* of Race, 2d ed. (Chicago: University of Chicago Press, 1982); Michael L. Wachter, "The Dimensions and Complexities of the Youth Employment Problem," in *Youth Employment and Public Policy*, ed., Bernard E. Anderson and Isabel Sawhill (Englewood Cliffs, N.J.: Prentice-Hall, 1980), 33-63.

3. The classic statement of the economic approach to crime is contained in Gary S. Becker, "Crime and Punishment: An Economic Approach," *Journal of Political Economy* 76, no. 2 (March/April 1968): 169-217. A survey of the literature evolving out of Becker's work can be found in Samuel Cameron, "The Economics of Crime Deterrence: A Survey of Theory and Evidence," *Kyklos* 41, no. 2 (1988): 301-323 and an application to the present problem in Maureen A. Pirog-Good, "Modeling Employment and Crime Relationships," *Social Science Quarterly* 67, no. 4 (December 1986): 767-784.

4. Anthony Downs, "The Future of Industrial Cities," in *The New Urban Reality*, ed., Paul E. Peterson (Washington, D.C.: Brookings Institution, 1985), 293.

5. Quoted in Bob Dart, "Survey Says White Male Most Typical High School Druggie," *Dayton Daily News*, 19 December 1989, sec. A, p. 4.

6. This does not necessarily imply that African-American youth dominate the drug trade, although this may be true for particular cities or neighborhoods. Dominican youth, for example, dominate much of the cocaine trade in New York City. See Terry Williams, *The Cocaine Kids: the Inside Story of a Teenage Drug Ring* (New York: Addison-Wesley, 1989), 51-53. Nevertheless, the analysis should apply to most youth in the inner city regardless of their race.

7. Mark V. Levine, "Downtown Redevelopment as an Urban Growth Strategy: A Critical Appraisal of the Baltimore Renaissance," *Journal of Urban Affairs* 9, no. 2, (1987): 103- 23.

8. See also Wilson, *The Truly Disadvantaged.*

9. U.S. Bureau of the Census, "Current Population Reports," *Money Income and Poverty Status of Families and Persons in the United States: 1986 (Advance Data From the March 1987 Current Population Survey)* ser. P-60, no. 157 (Washington, D.C.: Government Printing Office, 1987), table 18.

10. James P. Smith and Finis Welch, "Race and Poverty: A Forty-year Record," *American Economic Review* 77 (May 1987): 154-55; and "Black Economic Progress After Myrdal," *Journal of Economic Literature* 28, no. 2 (March 1989): 519-64.

11. Alphonso Pinkney, *The Myth of Black Progress* (New York: Cambridge University Press, 1984); Wilson, *The Truly Disadvantaged*, 46-62.

12. U.S. Bureau of the Census, "Current Population Reports," 5, table B.

13. Smith and Welch, "Black Economic Progress After Myrdal," 550-552.

14. For example, this is the approach taken by Murray, *Losing Ground.*

15. An example of this approach can be found in Wilson, *The Truly Disadvantaged.*

16. Anne D. Witte, "The Underground Economy in the United States and Western Europe," in *Examination of Basic Weaknesses of Income as the Major Federal Tax Base*, ed. Richard W. Lindhom (New York: Prager, 1986), 211. See also Williams, *The Cocaine Kids*, 8, 45.

17. Israel Kirzner, for example, notes that *entrepreneurship* can be defined as "alertness" to opportunities. Entrepreneurial behavior occurs when market participants (e.g., teenagers supplying labor) are triggered by price signals (e.g., wages) to invest resources in the activity of producing goods or services in markets for the "demanders" of those goods or services. The decision to supply labor, like the decision to produce a product, requires an entrepreneur to integrate large and complex amounts of knowledge acquired through personal experience. Much of this knowledge is

"tacit" and unknowable to others. The accumulation of tacit knowledge and the ability to translate this knowledge into profit-maximizing behavior (i.e., maximizing expected earnings or general welfare) can be classed broadly as entrepreneurial behavior. See Israel Kirzner, *Competition and Entrepreneurship* (Chicago: University of Chicago Press, 1973); Don Lavoie, *National Economic Planning: What is Left?* (Cambridge, Mass.: Ballinger Publishing Company, 1985); F.A. Hayek, "The Use of Knowledge in Society," *American Economic Review* 35, no. 4 (September 1945): 519-30.

18. See Laurel Adams, "Drug War's Lost Innocence: Preteens Used as Lookouts, Runners, Dealers," *USA Today* 20 December, 1989, sec. A, p. 2. 19. Peter Reuter, Robert MacCoun, and Patrick Murphy, *Money From Crime: A Study of the Economics of Drug Dealing in Washington, D.C.* (Santa Monica, Calif.: RAND Corporation, 1990), 82-83.

20. Bruce D. Johnson, Paul J. Godstein, Edward Preble et al., *Taking Care of Business: The Economics of Crime by Heroin Abusers* (Lexington, Mass.: Lexington Books, 1985).

21. Ibid., table B-12.

22. In fact, the criminal income averaged $11,854 per heroin abuser. Daily abusers tended to earn the most from crime, $18,710, followed by regular users, $11,086, and irregular users, $5,867. Nondrug crime income amounted to 36 percent of total income for daily users, 35 percent for regular users, and 25 percent for irregular users. Ibid., 99, table 10-1.

23. These issues are discussed extensively in Albert Rees, "An Essay on Youth Joblessness," *Journal of Economic Literature* 24, no. 2 (June 1986): 613-28; Harry J. Holzer, "Black Youth Nonemployment: Duration and Job Search," in *The Black Youth Employment Crisis*, ed., Richard B. Freeman and Harry J. Holzer (Chicago: University of Chicago Press, 1986), 23-70.

24. Holzer, "Black Youth Nonemployment," 34, table 1.1.

25. Ibid., 65.

26. W. Kip Viscusi, "Market Incentives for Criminal Behavior," in Freeman and Holzer, *Black Youth Employment Crisis*, 301-346.

27. U.S. Department of Justice, Federal Bureau of Investigation, *Uniform Crime Reports*, 1982, 196-87, 191.

28. Viscusi, "Market Incentives," 336.

29. Ibid.

30. Sam Meddis, "Street Life a Game 'Until the Ax Falls,'" *USA Today*, 20 December 1989, sec. A, p. 2.

31. Viscusi, "Market Incentives," 328.

32. David H. Good and Maureen A. Pirog-Good, "Employment, Crime, and Race," *Contemporary Policy Issues* 5 (October 1987): 102.

33. Llad Phillips and Harold L. Votey, Jr., "The Choice Between Legitimate and Illegitimate Work: Micro Study of Individual Behavior," *Contemporary Policy Issues* 5 (October 1987): 59-72

34. A detailed analysis of the cocaine trade can be found in Steven Wisotsky, *Beyond the War on Drugs: Overcoming a Failed Public Policy* (Buffalo, N.Y.: Prometheus Books, 1990), especially the preface to the 1990 edition.

35. Meddis, "Street Life," sec. A, p. 1.

36. Jack Kelley, "Cocaine, Other Hard Drugs Invade Rural Areas: Police Forced to Change Priorities," *USA Today*, 20 December 1989, sec. A, p. 11.

37. Sam Meddis, "Drug Arrest Rate Higher for Blacks," *USA Today*, 20 December 1989, sec. A, p. 11.
38. Reuter, MacCoun, and Murphy, *Money from Crime*, 62- 66.
39. James W. Thompson and James Cataldo, "Comment on Market Incentives for Criminal Behavior," in Freeman and Holzer, *Black Youth Employment Crisis*, 347.
40. The implications of the distribution of earnings in a public policy context are discussed more thoroughly in Richard E. Wagner, *To Promote the General Welfare: Market Processes Vs. Political Transfers* (San Francisco, Calif.: Pacific Research Institute for Public Policy, 1989).
41. Quoted in Joseph B. Treaster, "Study Finds Many Drug Dealers Hold Other Jobs," *New York Times*, 11 July 1990, sec. A, p. 12.
42. This anecdote was provided by Joseph Ganssle, President of the Religious Coalition for a Moral Drug Policy, in an unpublished article titled "The War On Drugs/War Against the Young."
43. Ibid., 1.
44. Jane Meyer, "In the War on Drugs, Toughest Foes May Be The Alienated Youth," *Wall Street Journal*, 8 September 1989, sec. A, p. 7.
45. This person represents a composite of several individuals taken from the personal observations of the author.
46. Some people may argue that an unpaid internship is not relevant within the decision framework of an inner-city African-American teenager. In fact, several unpaid internships are available if the individual is willing to pursue them and forgo the tangible benefits of paid employment. White teenagers will very often perform unpaid duties in businesses. In Washington, D.C., interns from a congressman's home district are routinely used for paperwork within the office. These interns often work long hours for unpaid work or a small enough wage that the money is largely irrelevant to their decision to work in the congressman's office. Generally, unpaid internships go to wealthier students who are supported by their parents. The opportunities, however, are still available to those interested in seeking them out.
47. Meyer, "In the War on Drugs," sec. A, p. 7.
48. Ibid.

6

The Organization of the Drug Economy

Illegal drug trafficking is a growth industry in many American cities. In some, the drug industry has become a stable business enterprise, while in others violent turf wars rip neighborhoods apart as new drug organizations vie for control over consumer markets.

The illicit drug trade in the United States represents a collection of individual firms rather than an economic monolith. Each firm organizes resources such as labor and equipment to produce and distribute its product in a broad range of regional and local markets. The drug industry is made up of a variety of organizations designed to efficiently accomplish this task, from vertically integrated international drug syndicates (or cartels) operating out of foreign countries to small entrepreneurial enterprises that control drug supplies in neighborhoods and small cities.

Drug trafficking organizations are set up to provide their products—illicit drugs—at minimum cost. Since selling drugs is illegal, the costs to the firm exceed simple costs of plant, equipment, and labor. In fact, growing and processing are small parts of the drug-supply network. The drug industry revolves principally around distribution, which is labor-intensive. Much of the cost of drug trafficking thus involves compensation for the risks of participating in the drug trade. These risks and compensations also reflect the opportunity costs of directing entrepreneurial behavior into a risky, uncertain, and dangerous enterprise rather than into employment in the legitimate sector.

The firm's cost structure must also include the costs associated with the uncertainty of the markets they serve. As discussed above, drug use

145

is susceptible to personal and social controls that, in turn, can affect the demand for drugs. If the costs of consuming these drugs are high, the vast majority of drug users will reduce their consumption of their drug of choice. For the most part, however, Americans have shown a relatively stable demand for psychoactive substances, and drug traffickers may be more concerned with which drugs the public wants rather than whether the demand exists for them.

Drug trafficking organizations are primarily wholesale and distributing organizations. Most cocaine processing, for example, is performed in Colombia, Peru, or Mexico. Most heroin processing occurs in Mexico, Pakistan, Afghanistan, Iran, India, Burma, Laos, or Thailand. The growers and processors then sell their produce to wholesalers who import the drugs into the United States for nationwide distribution.

With the exception of derivatives of cocaine (e.g., crack), heroin (e.g., black tar), amphetamines, or other synthetic drugs, illicit drug manufacturing appears to be a small part of the domestic industry's primary activities.[1]

Still, changes in narcotic control strategies by governments can alter the supply conditions and underlying cost structure of the industry. Increased international law enforcement efforts, for instance, will make processing less expensive closer to the street in American cities. Recent trends in cocaine processing and shifts in cocaine laboratories between the U.S., Mexico, and South America reflect changes in law enforcement strategies.[2]

Advantages of Cities to the Drug Industry

The domestic drug trade, then, focuses primarily on marketing, distribution and street-level sales. Recent structural transformations in urban economies have provided an environment supportive of large, decentralized, people-oriented industries. The rise of "advanced services" refocused the role of the central city on administration and distribution functions.[3] Combined with the illicit nature of the business, modern central cities are natural havens for drug traffickers. More specifically, modern central cities have four major advantages for illicit trafficking organizations: labor supply, centralized distribution, population density, and cultural diversity.

Labor Supply

First and foremost, central cities have a large supply of unemployed and under-employed workers, that can provide a large and lucrative labor pool for drug trafficking organizations. While social stigmas prevent most younger workers from becoming traffickers, as many as 25 percent of all young African-American men in some major cities may have sold drugs at least part-time. As long as urban economies fail to produce semiskilled jobs that pay well, an excess labor supply will continue to feed labor hungry drug trafficking organizations.[4]

These workers become the "day laborers" of the drug industry, performing whatever task is assigned to them within the broader drug-distribution network.[5] In addition to low-level dealing, laborers within the drug trade may be involved in steering customers to drug dealers ("steering"), locating new customers ("touting"), or transporting drugs and money from buyers to higher-level dealers ("copping"). Several other "jobs" may be available at irregular intervals, such as holding drugs for a dealer, guarding sellers, running large quantities of drugs from place to place, overseeing "shooting galleries," and testing drugs. Any of these activities provide a source of income for those involved in drug trafficking. One study of heroin abusers in New York City in the late 1970s found that over 75 percent of the income derived from selling drugs came from activities not directly related to dealing.[6]

Location

A second important attribute of central cities lies in their location. While legitimate businesses are moving to the suburbs, illicit businesses are taking over poor neighborhoods in central cities. Legal businesses do not have to worry about transporting their wares to other markets via highways or airports. They can, to a large extent, move to their customer base.

Drug traffickers, on the other hand, cannot afford that visibility. Drug wholesalers and retailers need to disperse their cache quickly among street-level salesmen and neighborhood warehouses. The longer drug inventories remain in one place, the more likely it is that the police will detect and seize them.

Nevertheless, traffickers need easy access to their clients. The central city provides easy access to a large suburban drug-using population while minimizing the risk to trafficking. Since customers must seek out the dealers, traffickers are not exposed to a potentially hostile clientele (unlike, for instance, a door-to-door salesman). Prospective buyers must come into the city to make purchases, reducing the exposure of retailers through transporting their merchandise to the client. Central cities also allow small, street-level dealers easy access to inner-city neighborhood supply networks to replenish their inventories.

The face-to-face contact between buyers and suppliers permits dealers to scrutinize their customers more thoroughly (to detect undercover police operations) while maximizing their sales volume. The very structure of the market requires centralized locations for retailing. Many of the same factors that make central cities attractive locations for finance, services, administration, government, and other advanced services support the service-oriented drug trade as well.

The heroin market provides a telling example of how important face-to-face contact is in the drug trade. The heroin-distribution system includes a multilevel network of laborers extending from the primary dealer to the buyer. The dealer relies on other people to locate customers or steer prospective customers to the right location. In addition, the dealer often will use runners or cop men to transport drugs and money. These procedures minimize the exposure of dealers to arrest, since they are not directly involved in illegal drug transactions with the buyer.

Personal contact between dealers and laborers also permits the employer to carefully monitor their workers' performance. The dealer offers the day laborer "piecework" until the worker proves himself. As the authors of a study on the New York heroin trade observe,

> If the heroin abuser routinely meets these commitments, his prospects for future employment rise dramatically. But if he *uses up* the drugs, or *messes up the money* . . . he will almost certainly be without work the following day, as well as risk being assaulted (emphasis in original.)[7]

The importance of face-to-face contact, of course, also places limits on economies of scale that can be gained from drug dealing. Since the dealer must always be careful of being arrested or attacked, and he must monitor closely the behavior of his workers, an expansion of the enterprise may be extremely difficult and cumbersome without a core group of trustworthy partners. If the dealer allows his organization to become too large, he risks losing control of the organization to rivals or being arrested.

Population Density

Another important characteristic of central cities lies in their high population densities. Large central cities are anonymous communities, where individuals fade into blocks, streets, or large apartment complexes. Major central cities support complicated economic and social structures that extend over hundreds of square miles of streets, alleys, and buildings. Their size provides a convenient hiding place for anyone seeking a low profile.

The structure of police departments in large cities may also aid the drug distribution system. Although the number of officers per one thousand people increases as population increases, the number of patrol cars per full-time officer declines. As a result, larger cities tend to allocate their patrol hours to two-man car patrols rather than one-man patrols. In cities with populations over one million, for example, 44 percent of the patrols included two men in a patrol car. In contrast, cities with populations between five hundred thousand and one million allocated only 27.9 percent of their patrols to two-man patrol cars.[8] Moreover, even in very large cities, less than 10 percent of the patrol hours were allocated to foot-patrol units. Thus, although large cities have large numbers of officers, their departments are not necessarily more flexible since more men are patrolling together and cover less ground.

Cultural Diversity

Finally, large cities are extremely diverse. In the largest cities, ethnic enclaves exist that permit members to assimilate into the urban environment. Thus, Colombian drug traffickers typically use other Colombians to transport cocaine, knowing they can disappear in large South American communities in New York, Los Angeles, Washington, D.C., or Miami.

Similarly, Mexican traffickers take advantage of the large, diverse Hispanic population along the Mexican-American border to transport their merchandise. Asian street gangs are able to marshal their heroin distribution networks in nascent immigrant communities from Southeast Asia as well. Cultural values, accents, and family backgrounds that may distinguish a trafficker in the suburbs disappear in the culturally diverse central city.

The rule structure governing city life is less strict and formal since individual behavior is hard to monitor. The out-migration of the middle-class and manufacturing jobs has resulted in the deterioration of neigh-borhoods, allowing survival rules to prevail as a normal part of community. Many residents will tolerate behavior considered socially unacceptable in a previous era simply because the behavior is now considered necessary for survival.

A hierarchy still exists among American cities with respect to traffick-ing patterns of specific drugs. Some cities become primary centers for illicit drug distribution for geographic reasons (e.g., Miami's proximity to South American export centers). Other cities rise in importance as law enforcement authorities attempt to close down other points of entry. The largest cities, such as New York and Los Angeles, will always be major centers for national drug-distribution networks on regional and wholesale levels.

Thus, central cities have a comparative advantage over smaller, more homogeneous cities and suburbs. These advantages make central cities natural habitats for underground and illegal activities. While each one of these factors individually would increase the likelihood of illegal drug trafficking in any particular city, urban areas that have all of these characteristics will most likely become drug trafficking havens.

The Markets for Heroin, Cocaine, and Marijuana

The illegal drug trade is a huge industry, with sales exceeding $150 billion by some estimates. Taken as a single firm, this sales volume would easily place the industry in the Fortune 500. This observation, however, is misleading.

The illicit drug industry, like any other industry, is a conglomeration of firms, some of which specialize in particular aspects of the industry. Competition in the domestic drug industry is fierce, often resulting in violent confrontations between rival suppliers on the retail level. The perception that the U.S. drug-distribution system is composed of one or two powerful organizations fails to acknowledge its complexity and sophistication.

As mentioned earlier, the domestic drug industry manifests itself primarily as a distribution and retail industry. Very little production or manufacturing of illicit drugs, particularly cocaine and heroin, occurs within the United States, although this aspect of the trade is changing for the more widely consumed drugs.

The Drug Enforcement Administration (DEA) estimates that domestic marijuana production has increased steadily since the early 1980s. In 1983, U.S. production accounted for only 14 percent of the total domestic supply of marijuana.[9] By 1988, domestic production accounted for 25 percent of the total.[10] Agricultural production of marijuana has become so pervasive, a recent report by the U.S. attorney general emphasized,

> marijuana cultivation activity in some rural areas is so intense that it distorts entire local economies through the influence of the drug monies it generates. . . . In some rural communities, marijuana has even become the primary cash crop, and an underground economy has developed, with the prices fixed to benefit everyone involved in its cultivation.[11]

Although the claim that prices are "fixed" by the marijuana growers is doubtful given the way the drug market works (prices are also influenced by consumer demand), the growing importance of marijuana as a principal cash crop is hard to refute.

The National Organization for the Reform of Marijuana Laws (NORML) periodically publishes estimates of the size of domestic marijuana crops by state. The most recent and complete figures are available for 1986 (table 6.1). Marijuana has clearly become an important cash crop in many states, and in five states, the value of the crop exceeds one billion dollars. NORML estimates the entire marijuana crop in 1986 could be valued at $26.7 billion, more than doubling the value of corn for grain ($10.77 billion), hay ($9.1 billion), soybeans ($9.0 billion), wheat ($4.8 billion), and cotton ($2.1 billion). The value of the domestic tobacco crop—a legal psychoactive drug—was only $1.79 billion.

Heroin and cocaine are imported from other countries. Almost three quarters of the domestic supply of processed cocaine comes from Colombia,[12] although Peru remains the largest producer of coca leaves.[13] Peruvian farmers cultivated over one hundred thousand hectares of coca and over 90 percent of this cultivation was illegal.[14] Similarly, Mexico produces about five metric tons of heroin destined for American markets. Southeast Asian countries (i.e., Burma, Thailand, Laos), on the other hand, were capable of producing over one hundred tons of heroin for international markets, although most of the opium is consumed domestically.[15] Similarly, Southwest Asian countries (i.e., Afghanistan, Iran, Pakistan) were capable of producing one hundred tons of heroin but, like the Southeast Asian countries, most opium was consumed in the source countries.[16]

Drug Distribution in the United States

The drug trade is often portrayed in the United States as a monopolistic, vertically integrated conglomerate with complete control over cultivation, processing, importing, distribution, and retailing. More informed approaches to the illicit drug industry picture the market in a slightly different way. The drug industry is viewed as a highly concentrated industry with a few large organizations controlling drug supplies. To these observers, the drug industry is viewed as exhibiting oligopolistic tendencies, in which a few large firms, acting independently or in concert as a cartel, operate to maximize their profits. Hence, the Colombian cocaine cartels operating out of Bogota, Cali, and Medellin are singled out as examples of how the industry converges toward a monopolistic market structure.

The reality, as this chapter will show, is very different. While a few large distribution organizations may control imports, particularly in the cocaine industry, the industry on the street and regional levels appears to be characterized as a "monopolistically competitive" market. A monopolistically competitive market exists when a large number of firms compete for customers by differentiating their product. Local dealers, for example, may establish their trade in a particular neighborhood or differentiate their organizations through the people they hire. Product differentiation allows producers to exert a limited degree of monopoly power over prices in drug markets and earn economic profits.

Drug markets, like other monopolistically competitive markets, are also characterized by easy entry and exit of new dealers. This suggests that the profits emerging from street-level trafficking may be smaller than often assumed (see chap. 5) or reflect the opportunity costs of drug dealing to traffickers. While the ease of entry and exit may vary from city to city or neighborhood to neighborhood, most would-be dealers can find "employment opportunities" if they play by the established rules of the street. In some cases, these rules may be relatively stringent and demanding, such as the necessity of joining a street gang in Los Angeles. In others, entry may be as easy as locating the local distributor and selling on commission.

TABLE 6.1
Estimated Value of Selected State Marijuana crops in 1986

State	Value (in millions of dollars)
California	3,102
Hawaii	1,722
Oregon	1,307
Kentucky	1,115
North California	1,025
Washington	913
Arkansas	934
Tennessee	873
Oklahoma	766
Georgia	760
Virginia	660
Missouri	655
Alabama	615
Florida	615
Mississippi	607
Texas	595
Michigan	595
Montana	587
Idaho	563
West Virginia	563
Kansas	547
Louisiana	530
South Carolina	530

Source: "Marijuana in America: NORML's 1986 Domestic Marijuana Crop," *Common Sense for America* 2, no. 1 (Spring 1987): 34.

The illicit drug industry is also a highly diversified market. Coca leaves are harvested on plantations as well as on smaller, individualized plots in South America. In some cases, coca leaf and marijuana production provides the major source of income for rural farmers, creating severe political problems in the source countries if coca production is terminated.[17]

The Structure of the Industry

A wide range of organizational structures is involved in supplying drugs to U.S. consumers. In the industry's most general form, it represents an hour-glass shape: large numbers of people are involved in the growing and retailing of the drugs, while fewer are involved in the processing, importing, exporting, and wholesaling (fig. 6.1).[18] The small number of firms involved in large-scale importing and exporting has captured the imaginations of the media and law enforcement officials. Yet, the true magnitude of the drug industry can only be captured by incorporating all elements of illicit drug production and distribution.

FIGURE 6.1
Drug Industry Structure

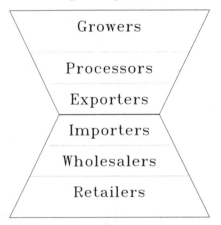

For example, large numbers of farmers and growers raise coca plants in Peru and Bolivia for processing in Colombia. In Colombia, the processed cocaine is exported to the United States (usually via one of the cocaine syndicates). The import-export organizations then sell their product to national and regional distributor's in the United States, such as the more traditional Mafia, Los Angeles street gangs, or other regional organizations (i.e., local drug "kingpins"). These distributors then supply thousands of small-time dealers who often run independent retailing operations.

The marijuana market exhibits similar general characteristics according to an extensive study of the marijuana industry by Mark Kleiman.[19] With well over 20 million users, 500,000 may be engaged in selling marijuana on the street level, usually dealing by the ounce. Another 50,000 may be involved in wholesaling units around one kilogram. About 5,000 middlemen serve the national marijuana-distribution market by supplying wholesalers with supplies of about fifty kilograms from around 420 large distributors (with primary sales units of about one ton). The importing and exporting elements of the U.S. marijuana market are becoming less important as larger and larger proportions of the supply of marijuana are grown domestically. The number of domestic growers clearly reaches well into the hundreds of thousands and spans all fifty states.

The growing and retail levels of the drug trade may be very competitive. Large numbers of farmers and independent retailers compete for business and are usually considered "price takers" since individual farmers are unable to affect the selling price of their crop. Similarly, street-level retailers are forced to sell their product for what the market will bear. Moreover, few retailers are big enough to significantly affect the market price outside their local market. Higher-level suppliers and wholesalers may have more discretion over prices.[20]

Nevertheless, the industry becomes less competitive as the industry becomes more specialized. Oligopolistic tendencies may exist at higher distribution levels where organizations are able to influence price by redirecting supply routes or restricting the supply of drugs into the country. Further, with smaller numbers of firms, cartels are more likely to form in order to fully capitalize on monopolistic behavior by acting as the sole source of drugs. "Because of the extraordinary amounts of money involved," notes nationally recognized drug policy analyst Steven Wisotsky, "the smuggling of cocaine into the United States has become too highly organized and too violent for amateurs and small-scale operators to survive very long."[21]

More recently, the War on Drugs may have aided the concentration of drug markets among fewer organizations by eliminating lower level dealers. As Mark Moore, a researcher at Harvard University recently observed,

> Aggressive law enforcement efforts directed at marginal trafficking organizations might well reduce the overall supply of drugs to illicit markets. But these efforts, by eliminating marginal traffickers, may increase the wealth and power of the drug trafficking organizations that remain by allowing them to gain effective control over the market.[22]

Thus, the Medellin Cartel operating from Medellin, Colombia, represents a loose confederation of several cocaine processors and exporters. At one extreme, the U.S. Department of Justice reports that the Medellin and Cali cocaine cartels "act as true cartels in the classic sense that they attempt, through collusion, to set prices and to eliminate any effective competition."[23] By colluding and forming a cartel, South American drug traffickers can act as a sole supplier of South American drugs and exert considerable influence over the supply of cocaine into the United States.

More recently, experts are tempering their allusions to the drug cartels, acknowledging their multifaceted organization. When one leading member of the Medellin Cartel (Rodriguez Gacha) was killed by Colombian police, for example, few thought the death would significantly affect cocaine supplies to the United States. "Only a few years ago," notes the report, "U.S. officials routinely depicted the Medellin cartel as a ruthless monolith. . . . Today, the Medellin group is viewed as a loose-knit and shifting coalition of drug traffickers. . . ."[24]

The cartel's behavior is kept in check by other exporting organizations operating out of Cali, Bogota, integrated trafficking organizations in Mexico, and the Suarez syndicate operating out of Bolivia. Suppliers from other areas of the continent are more than willing to step into the newly vacated positions within the international drug-distribution network.

These international organizations are extremely fluid and flexible. They adapt to new tactics used by law enforcement authorities. With increased narcotics enforcement in Miami, for example, drug traffickers have moved their importing operations to San Diego and San Francisco. In Arizona, drug arrests increased dramatically during the mid-1980s as Mexican trafficking organizations moved their operations from Miami to Tucson.[25] Heroin seizures on the border increased from 5.7 kilograms in 1985 to 7.1 kilograms in 1987. Cocaine increased from 31 kilograms in 1985 to 1,338 kilograms in 1987. In the first six months of 1988, drug enforcement officials seized almost 2,000 kilograms of cocaine. A principle reason for this increased activity was changing "routes and distribution patterns because of concentrated law enforcement efforts in South Florida."[26]

The illicit drug industry is also capable of supporting a variety of trafficking organizations, from highly integrated international networks to more diffuse and decentralized local firms. The South American cartels, for example, usually are not involved in retailing or wholesale distributing within the United States.[27] These functions are left to local organizations. On the other hand, Mexican heroin organizations are more fully integrated. One DEA report observed,

> In Mexico, organizations or confederations direct virtually all aspects of heroin trafficking: opium poppy cultivation, the refining process, and the transportation and distribution of heroin within Mexico. In most instances, these same organizations also control the smuggling of the heroin into the United States and its eventual sale at both the wholesale and retail levels.[28]

The organizational efficiency of the Mexican trafficking industries have contributed to their growing importance in the international distribution network along the U.S.-Mexican border.

The types of organizations involved in various aspects of the drug trade are also influenced by the particular markets they serve. The most used illicit substance in the Unnited States is marijuana, probably generating revenues of more than $30 billion in the larger drug economy. Cocaine, in contrast, is the most profitable drug used, generating well over $100 billion in revenues on a regular consumer base of 5 or 6 million. The heroin market may be one-fourth the size of the markets for cocaine and marijuana and is far more concentrated around 500,000 regular users.

Peter Reuter and Mark A.R. Kleiman, using 1982 data, estimated that the marijuana market employed over five hundred thousand dealers based on a user population of 20 million.[29] The cocaine market, with an estimated user population of 4.5 million, employed another one hundred eighty thousand while forty-five thousand dealers sold heroin to about four hundred and fifty thousand users.

The Heroin Market

Structurally, the heroin market may be the most concentrated.[30] The number of heroin users is relatively small and geographically concentrated (in New York State and New York City). The heroin market has also experienced some of the most intensive law enforcement efforts, during the 1960s and 1970s. In the 1970s, for example, New York govenor Nelson Rockefeller implemented some of the strictest drug laws in the country.[31] Several cities have also tried to implement focused street-level enforcement of drug laws. In Lynn, Massachusetts, for example, street-level enforcement of drug laws on the local heroin market reduced robberies by 18 percent and burglaries by 37 percent.[32] In Manhattan, a similar program reportedly reduced robberies by 40 percent and burglaries by 27 percent.

Despite the relatively small consumer market, the heroin industry remains competitive. At one point, in the 1960s and early 1970s, only ten or twelve major wholesale organizations were thought to service the domestic heroin market. Currently, most analysts consider the heroin distribution system highly competitive.[33] Economist Robert Michaels notes that heroin production and distribution does not require specialized production technologies or specialized labor.[34] Heroin can be produced in several different environments and countries and no significant barriers to entry exist. In fact, opium growing and use is a revered tradition in many Asian countries. The heroin market, therefore, appears to be a classic example of a competitive market in supply. Monopoly profits, or economic rents, must result from some source other than the natural characteristics of the heroin market per se.

The markets for marijuana and cocaine are much larger and, in some respects, even more competitive. Extensive law enforcement efforts to reduce the supply of cocaine in the United States have yielded few results. Federal and local law enforcement agencies have failed to reduce the supply. Several international sources for opium exist and distributors can be changed relatively easily. While some organizations can be infiltrated and supplies interrupted temporarily, the high profit margins in the drug industry ensure other entrepreneurs will fill the newly vacated positions.

Drug Trafficking in Cities

The large consumer markets for illicit drugs translates into a highly diversified distribution system within the United States. Drug distribution in some cities is tightly controlled by a handful of highly organized and specialized distribution organizations. Other cities are characterized by a highly diffused distribution system. As one recent federal report noted,

> There is no single pattern in the structure and operation of drug trafficking organizations. These organizations vary widely in size, sophistication, area of operation, clientele, and product. They have differing degrees of vertical and horizontal integration, differing propensities to violence, and differing patterns of interaction with other organizations. They vary in these and in a multitude of other characteristics.[35]

Among the numerous types of trafficking organizations are the South American drug cartels, the traditional mafia, motorcycle gangs, street gangs, and independents. The South American drug cartels have already been discussed. Their primary concern is in processing and importing rather than domestic street-level distribution. The two largest cartels, the Cali and Medellin cartels in Colombia, control approximately 80 percent of the cocaine distributed in the United States according to the U.S. Department of Justice.[36]

The Mafia

The Mafia, or La Cosa Nostra (LCN), consists of roughly twenty-five known "families" with over two thousand members.[37] Officially, American Mafia organizations banned drug trafficking in 1957, although the ban is not observed or enforced. Recent generations of Mafia members appear more amenable to drug trafficking than older generations and LCN members from nineteen families have been arrested on drug violations. Further, the Boston FBI estimates that 50 percent of LCN members "have had some form of involvement in illegal drug trafficking or personal abuse."[38] Moreover, several Mafia families have become middlemen in the drug-distribution network, developing close ties to South American drug cartels.

In the 1950s, some observers argue, the Mafia had a practical monopoly on heroin distribution in the United States. While LCN members still distribute substantial amounts of heroin, and their trafficking has expanded to include cocaine, the distribution system is much more competitive in the 1990s. As Peter Reuter and Mark Kleiman note, the Mafia no longer has significant influence within the New York Police Department (to protect their interests) or over the International Longshoreman's Association (to control the docks), and most heroin and cocaine producers are not located in Europe where ethnic ties enhanced the Mafia's ability to import illicit drugs.[39] Thus, the Mafia remains a major player, but probably does not dominate drug distribution.

Street Gangs

Street gangs may provide the single largest integrated distribution network in the country.[40] These gangs include Asian gangs on the West and East Coasts, Jamaican Posses, and the infamous Los Angeles street gangs. In Los Angeles County, California, alone, over six hundred and fifty gangs are active with between forty and fifty thousand members. Originally, these groups were established for protection from other gangs that would extort, rob, and terrorize neighborhoods and communities. The Los Angeles street gang the Bloods, for example was organized to protect the members from the larger organization of the Crips. Currently, the Crips and Bloods comprise a number of "sets" that are identified by street names and neighborhoods. Federal law enforcement agencies estimate that the Crips and the Bloods comprise over two hundred and fifty sets with a combined membership of twenty five thousand. Recently, these gangs have coalesced into large drug trafficking organizations that resemble major corporations rather than neighborhood protection groups.

The rise of gangs and gang-related violence is a direct result of the high profits generated from drug trafficking, primarily cocaine. These profits are also providing incentives for these gangs to expand into other states.

> The Cocaine trafficking of these gangs is the major reason for their expansion into other jurisdictions. It's simply the law of economics. Cocaine can be purchased in Los Angeles for about $300 per ounce and sold elsewhere for about $800 to $1500 per ounce. They have learned that for the price of a plane ticket they can dramatically increase their profits. The more money they make, the more they expand into other jurisdictions. This has also changed the philosophy of most gangs. At one time they were concerned with controlling a particular Los Angeles neighborhood, but now they are more concerned with making large amounts of money. They now equate money with power.[41]

Asian street gangs operate in concert with the more traditional Chinese Organized Crime Organizations and include over five thousand members nationwide. One international organization based in Taiwan, the United Bamboo Gang, may have as many as fifteen thousand members worldwide.[42] Ethnic connections to Southeast Asia have made these gangs potent forces in the heroin trade, particularly in New York City. "Chinese criminal organizations operate mainly as shippers and wholesalers," notes a recent federal report.[43] They process the raw product and import it for local retailers.

Jamaican posses are the third major type of gang involved in domestic drug trafficking and importing. About forty posses operate in the United States with over ten thousand members, according to the U.S. Department of Justice. Beginning as marijuana traffickers, Jamaican posses are now major distributors of crack cocaine, and several are capable of operating as many as fifty crack houses, which can bring in $9 million per month. Crack houses often double as distribution centers for a tightly controlled, vertically integrated international trafficking operation. Posses are well-known for their willingness to use violence as a routine element of their business.

Local Independents

Major local traffickers, or "kingpins," represent the fringe of the illicit drug distribution industry in most American cities. These organizations revolve around the personality of one or two people. These organizations have also become the focus of most federal efforts to curb the supply of drugs into the United States despite the expense required to investigate and prosecute them.

One of the most publicized examples of the drug kingpin was twenty-four-year-old Rayful Edmond III, in Washington, D.C. Federal authorities estimated Edmond's organization controlled 30 percent of the cocaine trade in Washington, D.C. through its connections with the Cali drug cartel. Edmond was convicted in 1989 of operating a continuing criminal enterprise and sentenced to life imprisonment without parole and assessed a $2 million fine under a federal "drug kingpin" law.

Yet, as Peter Reuter, Robert MacCoun, and Patrick Murphy recently observed, "The speed of Edmond's rise and fall points to the fragility of the new generation of drug-dealing organizations."[44] A high-profile organization attracts the attention of law enforcement officials. Large multi-million dollar firms—Edmond was importing over one hundred kilograms a month into Washington, D.C.—will be noticed on the street and by the police.

These organizations are likely to be replaced just as easily by other entrepreneurs who see trafficking as a vehicle for social mobility. Given the dismal legal employment opportunities faced by inner-city youth, drug trafficking appears lucrative and rewarding, at least in the short-term. "Cocaine distribution," write Reuter, MacCoun, and Murphy, "appears to be the first illegal market in which youth have opportunities to be the primary entrepreneurs, instead of merely occupying support roles for adult distributors."[45] Significantly, Rayful Edmond, considered by law enforcement officials as the key drug figure in Washington, D.C., was only twenty-four years old and a multimillionaire.

Major local distributor's have also been found in smaller cities. In one midsize city in the Midwest, a local drug distributor was arrested and charged with controlling an organization with "underbosses and a professional financial advisor."[46] Jay Aaron Shephard, a twenty-five-year-old man in Dayton, Ohio, recently surrendered to federal authorities and was charged with importing and distributing twenty kilograms of cocaine per month. His organization amassed known assets that included over ten cars and four houses.

The role of the independent distributor is fluid, depending on the circumstances. Independents are vulnerable to law enforcement officials as well as encroachments from other organizations within the drug trade. For example, the expanding influence of the Crips and the Bloods will have an impact on the ability of independent distributors to survive in the often violent world of drug trafficking. Shephard sparked gang-related violence when he attempted to shift suppliers from the Crips in Los Angeles to alternates in Detroit and Chicago. Between January and October 1989 seven members of Shephard's organization had been killed.

Nevertheless, the local independent is the organization within the U.S. distribution network that resembles the more traditional entrepreneurial model. As law enforcement authorities continue to arrest and convict the local drug kingpins, larger more organized groups are replacing them. Unfortunately, the high profits of the drug trade inspire the violence now commonplace in illegal markets.

Entrepreneurship in the Drug Industry

Despite the hierarchical nature of the international drug industry, where large organizations tend to dominate importing and distributing, substantial scope exists for entrepreneurial opportunity. In most American cities, this occurs at the retail level or regional wholesale level. The reasons for these entrepreneurial opportunities are varied but, for the most part, are directly tied to the legal status of the drug trade. The drug trade is a labor-intensive occupation in the United States and may be one of the largest service industries in the contemporary urban economy.

The Crime Tariff

The source of economic profits in drug trafficking derives directly from its illegal status. Artificial restrictions on drug supplies result in higher prices and profits than would exist in legal markets.[47] Drug laws, in this respect, have fundamentally different effects than those of other crimes. Typically, with property crimes the criminal must sell stolen property at significantly discounted prices. The effects of drug laws, in contrast, increase the value of items sold in the black market. This occurs because people do not want stolen property, but they do want illicit drugs.

Law professor Randy Barnett has noted that what distinguishes drug crimes from other crimes such as burglary and robbery is the role of the victim.[48] For most crimes involving persons and property, there is a clear "victim" in the sense that someone is forced to relinquish rights to ownership and control over their property, having liberties and rights guaranteed by law compromised. These crimes always produce a person who can claim a "harm" as a result of the actions of the burglar or robber.

Drug violations, on the other hand, do not have victims in the traditional sense. Drug laws are aimed at preventing people from using substances they desire and preventing voluntary transactions from occurring. Moreover, drug users consume the substance, capturing the benefits of their behavior immediately. Stolen property, on the other hand, must be stored and hidden as a result of the fear that it could be returned to the original owner.

Gross revenues (and profits) in the drug market are currently determined largely by the legal status of the drugs. If the demand for drugs remains constant, successful law enforcement policies will reduce their supply by disrupting existing production and distribution systems. A more important side effect of law enforcement will be to increase the costs of drug trafficking. These costs will be reflected in higher opportunity costs faced by prospective dealers, which, like the scarcity of drugs, are an artifact of drug prohibition.

By preventing peaceful means for resolving disputes and conflicts, drug traffickers are subjected to systematic violence, since they cannot rely on the legal system to protect them. Traffickers are also more likely to become victims of personal crimes (i.e., assault) or property crimes (i.e., burglary and robbery). The threat of arrest and incarceration further increases the opportunity costs of trafficking versus working in some other legal occupation.

FIGURE 6.2
The Crime Tariff

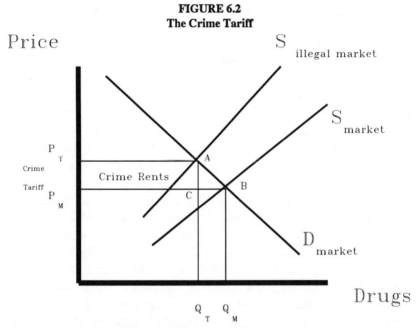

The legal status of drug trafficking produces a "crime tariff," or crime premium (fig. 6.2). Drug prohibition strategies that focus on reducing the supply of drugs or increasing the opportunity costs of working in the drug trade will shift the market supply curve to the left. This results in an increase in the price of illegal drugs on the market, since the costs to suppliers of placing these drugs on the market increase. Under a drug prohibition regime, for example, a supplier (dealer) must face the additional risks of being arrested, the confiscation of inventories, or personal injury in the drug trade. Without these risks to persons and property, the market would naturally support a larger number of dealers and a higher volume of drugs (Q_M) since the drug market would reflect natural market costs to suppliers.

At first glance, these effects appear beneficial. Prices rise and the volume of drugs declines on the market. Yet, as chapter 4 suggested, the social costs of drug use are primarily the costs of drug *abuse*. Drugs can be consumed recreationally and, in some cases, such as moderate alcohol consumption, may have beneficial physiological effects for some users. Nevertheless, the consumer must also calculate the potential costs of addiction in his decision to use drugs even on a recreational basis.

The demand curve represents the amount of psychoactive drugs consumers would be willing to buy at specific prices. Under normal market conditions, they would be willing to consume Q_M. The effects of prohibition allows them to consume only Q_T at the higher price of P_T. The result is what economists call a loss in consumer surplus (the amount people would be willing to pay but do not have to pay) equivalent to the triangle ABC. Drug users are clearly made worse off since they are unable to obtain a product they clearly would be willing to purchase at lower prices.

More important may be the increased opportunities to make money as a result of attempts to limit supply. As Randy Barnett recently observed,

> The actions of drug law enforcement create an artificial scarcity of a desired product. As a result sellers receive a higher price than they would without such laws. While it is true that drug prohibition makes it more costly to engage in the activity, this cost is partially or wholly offset by an increased return (higher prices) and by attracting individuals to the activity who are less risk-averse (criminals)—that is individuals who are less likely to discount their realized cash receipts by their risk of being caught.[49]

The result of the scarcity induced by drug policies is the rectangle P_TACP_M in figure 6.2. These are the "rents" or economic profits earned by criminals engaging in the drug trade. These profits would not exist if the market were allowed to operate naturally.

A hypothetical numerical example illustrates these effects more concretely. While the example is not based on an accurate empirical test— cocaine, marijuana, and heroin have not been legal in the United States for over seventy-five years—it approximates the effects of the current enforcement strategy and "best estimates" of cocaine use and prices.

For example, in a market where cocaine is traded legally, S_{market} in figure 6.2 represents the cocaine industry's supply curve. Consumers demand Q_M, or, for our purposes, 150 tons of cocaine per year. The legal market price might be fifty dollars per gram. (This is a conservative estimate: the actual price would probably be lower.) Total revenues from the cocaine market in this case would equal $7.5 billion dollars.

In an illegal market, successful law enforcement efforts reduce the supply of drugs on the market through interdiction, domestic drug seizures and the arrest of street-level distributors and major distributors. This shifts the supply curve for cocaine to S$_{illegal market}$ in figure 6.2, or, in our numerical illustration, to eighty tons (at Q$_t$).

The demand for cocaine has not been affected by the supply-side drug enforcement efforts. Thus, the demand curve remains the same. This, in turn, puts upward pressure on prices since the same number of people wanting to purchase 150 tons of cocaine can now only buy 80 tons. A successful enforcement effort may at least double the price of a gram of cocaine on the illegal market. Based on data from the DEA, a gram of cocaine costs a cocaine user around $100 on the street level. Thus, total revenues in the black market will be $8 billion.

While enforcement efforts have reduced the amount of cocaine available on the market, *they have also increased profits in the cocaine distribution industry by $500 million.* The actual results of U.S. drug enforcement efforts may be even more dramatic. As mentioned earlier, some estimate that the cocaine industry alone generates *over* $100 billion per year. Thus, the results of this simple exercise could be reasonably magnified by ten times.

The existence of these profits, or rents, provides the incentives for young inner-city men to sell drugs and for South American drug cartels to attempt to monopolize cocaine importing and exporting. These rents appear to be extremely large and the competitive retail market provides plentiful opportunities for the young, ambitious entrepreneur interested in making money despite the risks.

The extent that current drug policy affects the price of drugs can be seen in reported prices for drugs at different stages of the production and distribution process. The data presented in figures 6.3 and 6.4 were derived from 1988 prices for marijuana and cocaine reported by the DEA.[50] The prices in the figures represent the midpoint of ranges of prices reported by undercover law enforcement personnel.

Marijuana prices increase dramatically at each stage of the production and distribution process. Although the domestic marijuana market does not have a "broker" stage—brokers negotiate shipments across international borders—prices received by U.S. growers are substantially higher than in the foreign source countries. In Mexico, one pound of marijuana costs only $75 when purchased from the grower. By the time the same pound reaches the U.S. wholesale level, the price has risen to $487. The steepest jump in prices occurs in marijuana coming from Thailand. At the border point, one pound will cost $22, but the price rises to over $1,000 by the time it reaches the wholesale level.

FIGURE 6.3
Selling Price of One Pound of Marijuana by Source (Commercial Grade)

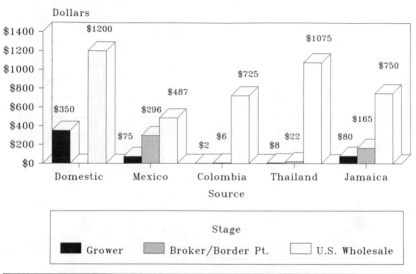

Source: DEA, "From the Source to the Street," *Intelligence Trends* 14, 3 (1987):2–5.

Prices for cocaine increase significantly at each stage of the process and rise dramatically the closer it gets to the final product, usually cocaine hydrochloride, or HCL. Cocaine is usually imported into the United States as cocaine base or cocaine HCL since it is easier to smuggle. At the wholesale level, the DEA estimates that one kilogram of cocaine HCL in Miami with about 90 percent purity will sell for $13,000 to $20,000 on the street, a jump of more than four times the price in the source country.[51]

These jumps in price provide the primary incentive for budding entrepreneurs to enter the market. While larger organizations will attempt to monopolize or control large segments of the drug industry, the huge rents that can be gained from trafficking provide substantial incentives for others to enter the business. As chapter 5 detailed, most inner-city residents are faced with jobs earning thirty tax free dollars per hour in the drug trade or seven taxable dollars per hour in the legal sector. Given these factors alone, widespread participation in the drug trade would be expected as individual dealers attempt to capture a portion of the rents created by prohibition.

FIGURE 6.4
Selling Price of One Kilogram of Cocaine by Source

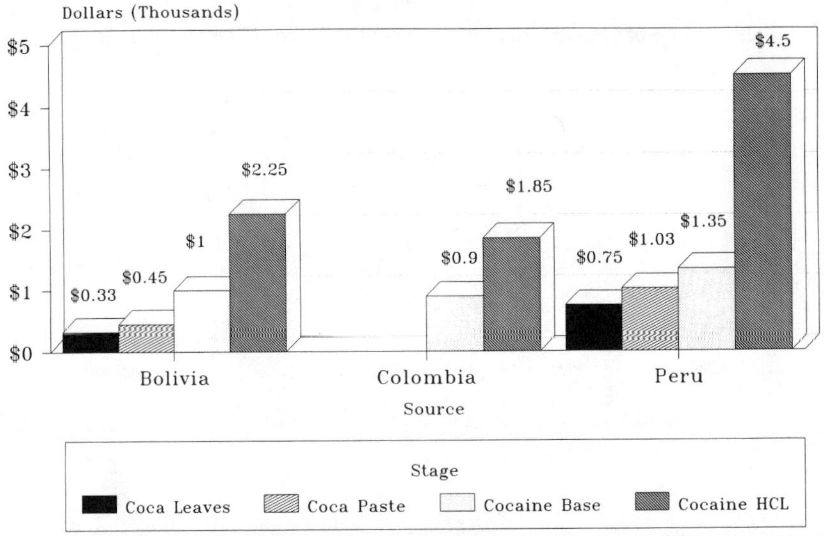

Dollars (Thousands)

Source: DEA, "From the Source to the Street,"pp. 6–7.

Routine Risks of the Drug Trade

Offsetting the extremely high profits of the drug trade, of course, are the risks inherent in the occupation. Given the importance of human capital in the drug-distribution system, these risks are essential for understanding the drug-trafficking process. The risks are an important part of the opportunity costs associated with employment in the drug trade. Most of these costs are nonpecuniary or have indirect effects but place inherent limits on the returns gained from drug trafficking.

The Risk of Incarceration

One of the most obvious costs to drug trafficking is the probability of being arrested. These probabilities vary significantly according to the type of drug. For example, using data from 1984, Peter Reuter and Mark Kleiman estimated that the probability a heroin trafficker would spend time in prison was 0.14.[52] The probability that a cocaine trafficker would spend time in prison was significantly less at 0.035, while the marijuana trafficker faced the smallest probability (0.001).

Similarly, they found that, on average, the heroin trafficker could expect to spend 131 days incarcerated. The cocaine trafficker could expect to spend only thirty-three days per year, while the marijuana dealer would spend slightly more than four days.

The more often someone deals drugs, the more likely they will get caught. A recent survey of inner-city youth in custody in Washington, D.C., found that those trafficking in drugs more than once per week were more likely to be arrested. Only 23 percent of the respondents selling drugs less than once per week were arrested, while 31 percent selling drugs daily were arrested.[53]

The Risk of Injury

A more important risk associated with drug trafficking is the probability of physical injury. These risks were calculated in a recent RAND Corporation study of drug trafficking in Washington, D.C. (Table 6.2).[54] The authors estimated that the twenty-four thousand sellers in Washington, D.C., faced a 1.4 percent chance of death, a 7 percent chance of serious injury, and an expected prison term of four months. Given these probabilities, the average year-round drug dealer would have to earn $20,000 per year to be compensated for the risks inherent in the drug trade. The average drug dealer in Washington earned roughly $24,000 per year, suggesting that 80 percent of the dealer's earnings may be attributed to "risk compensation."

While these data are extremely imprecise, they clearly show that drug dealing is a very risky enterprise. The importance of these risks figures prominently as a structural characteristic of inner-city drug markets. This risk compensation may also be a proxy for the opportunity costs inner-city residents face when deciding between unemployment, legitimate employment, and drug trafficking.

Chapter 5 discussed the labor supply decision of many inner-city youth. High profits were seen as the primary inducement to entering the drug trade. The prospective drug dealer makes a tradeoff between the stability of a legitimate job and the risks of the drug economy. Given the data in Table 6.2, the prospective dealer should be asking herself if drug dealing is worth $4,000 in economic profits since the remainder must be used to compensate the "costs" associated with the risks of serious injury, death, or incarceration. These tradeoffs may explain why even larger proportions of the inner-city population are not involved in drug trafficking.

The Risk of Addiction

A third risk to drug traffickers often ignored in the literature is the risk of addiction. While increasing evidence suggests that younger dealers are trafficking drugs for monetary reasons, the risk of addiction increases as the dealer becomes more involved in the trade. In fact, the nature of the drug trade encourages drug use, increasing the probability of addiction.

For example, many heroin dealers will "test" prospective customers by having them sample the drug. If the customer is an undercover cop, he or she will not take the drug. The dealer will also work with addicts on a routine basis and, over time, may begin to adopt the values of his client base. Since drug profits cannot be invested readily, the small businessman will also be tempted to use his excess profits on drugs as a perk of the trade. Indeed, substantial evidence suggests that most dealers are also drug users. The study of traffickers in Washington, D.C. found that all respondents had used a drug, although the drug and frequency varied considerably: 77 percent reported using marijuana, 72 percent reported using cocaine, 54 percent reported using PCP, and 52 percent reported using crack.[55]

Seventy-nine percent had used a drug in the "target period" (the preceding six months) although the proportions dropped significantly for individual drugs. Forty-eight percent reported they had used cocaine in the target period and 42 percent said they had used marijuana. Twenty-eight percent said they had used PCP and 31 percent reported using crack.

Of those using drugs daily, crack was used most frequently (table 6.3). Both cocaine and marijuana were used relatively infrequently. Over half of the heroin users used their drug two or three times per day. In contrast, 45 percent of the marijuana users used their drug only once.

TABLE 6.2
Risks and Compensations per Year for Drug Trafficking in Washington, D.C.

Hazard	Number	Risk (%)	Estimated Required Compensation ($)
Death	200	1.4	10,500
Injury	1,000	7	2,100
Incarceration (avg. 18 months)	3,000	22	9,000

Source: Reuter, MacCoun, and Murphy, *Money From Crime*, 104, table 6.1.

The statistics reported for Washington, D.C., are indicative of more general trends tracked in the literature. A case study of a New York City drug ring found that all participants in the organization were also users.[56] A survey of state prison inmates conducted by the U.S. Department of Justice in 1986 found that 42.7 percent of the inmates surveyed had used a drug daily in the month before their arrest.[57] Fifty-one percent of the inmates convicted of drug offenses reported daily usage the previous month, higher than those for property offenses, violent offenses, and public order offenses. Moreover, the survey revealed that inmates convicted of trafficking were more likely than those convicted of possession to have used drugs the previous month. Similarly, other studies of heroin trafficking have found that heroin users are heavily involved in drug trafficking, often to support their own habits.[58]

Despite these risks, most entering the drug trade sell cocaine or crack. Again, according to the RAND Corporation study of Washington, D.C., dealers tended to concentrate their efforts on the highly lucrative crack and cocaine markets (table 6.4). These drugs were a major source of income for over one-third of the traffickers surveyed in the study.

The number of sales increased with the potential earnings. Crack registered the highest number of sales per day (16) and the highest number of customers (15). Similarly, the crack dealer's earnings were higher than for cocaine, heroin, or marijuana. Marijuana dealers were the most likely to sell on a less-than-daily basis, with fewer customers and fewer sales. Annualized, the median earnings for these dealers ranged from about \$36,000 for crack dealers to about \$26,000 for cocaine and heroin dealers, to only about \$16,000 for marijuana dealers.

TABLE 6.3
Drug Consumption by Traffickers in Washington, D.C.

Drug	N	Uses Per Day (%)		
		Once	2 to 3	Over 3
Crack	59	33	27	40
Cocaine	84	37	31	32
Marijuana	65	45	37	18
Heroin	33	29	53	18

Source: Reuter, MacCoun, and Murphy, *Money from Crime*, 74, table 4.16.

Some escape the cocaine trade. Sociologist Terry Williams tracked a teenage drug ring in New York City during the mid- to late-1980s. The leader of the drug ring eventually left the cocaine trade and opened a legitimate business: "the realization that he could make money within the law, without risk, helped convinced [sic] him to leave the cocaine trade."[59] Of the eight teenagers that formed the core of the drug ring, one was shot (and eventually died in a swimming accident), one returned to the Dominican Republic, one is in college, three are employed in legitimate jobs, and only one continues to sell drugs. Ultimately, the drug trade is too unstable, insecure, and dangerous to become a long-term career option.

Public Policy and Drug Trafficking

The role of public policy in shaping the structure and rules of the game in the drug economy is indelible. The drug-distribution network is set up to evade legal institutions. The market structure of the drug industry is thus a product (or unintended consequence) of a prohibitionist policy toward illicit drugs. Americans have a persistent but limited demand for psychoactive substances, most notably marijuana, cocaine, and heroin. To some extent, the supplyside of the drug industry will reflect these factors. For example, one study on the demand for heroin by addicts suggests the elasticity of demand may be very elastic and close to -1.

"Heroin takes such a large share of the total budget of many regular users, and they have to be so active criminally to maintain their consumption, that price increases may lead to almost proportional reductions in their intake."[60]

TABLE 6.4.
Trafficking Activity in Washington, D.C

Characteristic	All	Type of Drug Sold			
		Crack	Cocaine	Marijuana	Heroin
Frequency (in percent):					
Daily	37	41	39	21	38
Several days/wk	40	39	41	43	31
1 day/wk. or less	23	20	20	36	31
Median hours spent selling	3	4	4	1	4
Median # sales	13	16	15	4	14
Median # customers	12	15	12	3	10
Median weekly income	N/AV	$700	$500	$310	$500
Drug major source of income (in percent)		34	32	9	9

Source: Adapted from Reuter, MacCoun, and Murphy, *Money from Crime*, 75, 61, tables 4.5, 4.6.

Notes: Hours spent selling, median number of sales, and median customers are for the last day dealing. Median weekly income is gross income among persons earning income from each drug.

This suggests, contrary to popular opinion, that movements in the price of heroin may have large effects on the quantity demanded. If the percentage change in the quantity of illicit drugs is met by a similar percentage change in their price, the effect on total revenue will be neutral. By implication, demand constrains the pricing policies of drug dealers regardless of their size and control over the supply network. Drug traffickers, even if they are monopolists, cannot force people to buy drugs and their pricing policies will influence consumer behavior.

The persistence of consumer demand ensures that a market for illicit substances will always exist. Whether or not the drugs will be supplied rests on the potential profits gained through the drug trade. In essence, the monopoly profits earned by drug traffickers are largely an artifact of existing public policy, which attempts to prohibit consumption of the drugs for recreational purposes.

More important, perhaps, existing policy allows the most devious and violent organizations to thrive and prosper. In the drug industry, "Might makes Right" is the rule by which laws are made and systematically broken. The rules of the game are rigged so that only the strongest (most violent and ruthless) are able to enforce contracts and ensure compliance on their terms. Rule and law become arbitrary, hinging on the wishes and desires of the organization (or organizations) that dominate the trade. Rights to property and markets are granted or denied based on the values of the controlling organization rather than on abstract principles.

Breaking the rules could end a career. The case of Jay Aaron Shephard's drug-distribution ring in Dayton, Ohio, is illustrative of this point. Shephard nurtured his organization into a multi-million-dollar enterprise over several years, employing dozens of others in his operations. While not the largest trafficking organization in the midsize Midwestern city, Shephard was a significant distributor. Yet, when he attempted to change suppliers—a move that would be protected by law if his business were legal—a rival gang (the Crips) moved in to punish Shephard and his organization for their indiscretion. Shephard surrendered to local authorities after seven members of his organization had been murdered, believing his life chances were better in prison than on the streets.

Shephard's case exemplifies how violence survives and is nurtured in black-market environments. Shephard's organization was large relative to the city of Dayton with a metropolitan population near 1 million and a central city population of 180,000. His organization was small compared to the power and numbers of the Crips with a membership estimated into the thousands extending into most states in the country. Profits in the drug economy are collected by those who survive. Without recourse to a commonly accepted legal system based on abstract principles such as private property rights and the sanctity of human life, weaker organizations inevitably fall prey to larger and more violent members.

How Public Policy Creates Monopoly Rents

Public policy encourages the growth of violence and market concentration by successfully restricting supply or raising the opportunity costs of employment (e.g., requiring high incomes to compensate the risks of injury or incarceration). Crime rents, or monopoly rents, are created if one of four factors are present.

Specialized knowledge. The production technology is characterized by specialized knowledge. If the processing of coca leaves into cocaine HCL were difficult, only a few people would have the technological know-how to process the drug. In fact, the technology for processing cocaine is widespread and easily obtainable with minimum capital outlays. Cocaine processing takes place in South America only because the laboratories are easier to hide in the jungles than in American cities.

Similarly, marijuana is easy to grow and does not require processing. Opium is also abundant worldwide and requires little specialized knowledge to process into heroin. The production technology for manufacturing illicit drugs does not inhibit the entry of new firms or entrepreneurs. Most producers cannot even claim significant property rights to new inventions. Crack was a technical innovation intended to lower price sufficiently to tap into poor, inner-city neighborhoods. Once crack made it to the streets, however, any cocaine distributor could adapt the technology sufficiently to distribute it in any market in the country.

Control over resources. Resources may be geographically constrained. Coca leaves and opium, however, can be grown in most humid environments. Coca has adapted particularly well to the environment of the Andes in South America. Similarly, marijuana thrives in a variety of environments, which explains its growing importance as a domestic agricultural crop in states as diverse as North Carolina, Oklahoma, and Washington. The fact that domestic marijuana production now comprises at least 25 percent of the total suggests that production technologies are easily transferable across continents. Clearly, control over natural resources does not provide the source for the profits reaped in the drug market.

Economies of scale. Economies of scale in production may limit the ability of other firms to enter into the market. If a firm could expand output continuously while incurring a cost advantage over any other firm entering the market, the market would result in one firm dominating its competitors. This would allow the firm to earn economic profits by restricting output.

As the previous discussion emphasized, economies of scale are not sufficient along the relevant production ranges to result in a cost advantage of one firm over another. The price data in this chapter suggests that the profits are made on the distribution end of the network, not the production end. New firms could reduce their production costs relatively early in the production process and, given current street prices, make profits.

Barriers to entry. Significant barriers to entry may also prohibit the entry of new firms and allow existing firms to earn monopoly profits. These barriers could include legal prohibitions on firm entry as well as other factors such as high start-up costs. Legal prohibitions on competition are the most common form of prohibiting entry into new industries. In many cases, such as local public utilities or cable companies, governments give firms an exclusive franchise to provide a service or good to the community. The discussions in this chapter and chapter 5 have shown that entry into the drug industry is open.

Nevertheless, the prohibitionist policies of federal, state, and local governments have erected barriers to entry into the drug industry by crippling the growth of competitors. Rather than granting monopolies, government policies have focused on eliminating any dealer, distributor, or manufacturer. As a result, the most inexperienced and smallest traffickers have born the brunt of most law enforcement efforts. By eliminating small competitors who could expand and rival established firms, the government has facilitated a transfer of monopoly power to larger organizations and abetted the concentration of market power among a few large distributors and importers. Thus, reducing the number of local-level dealers has encouraged the establishment of oligopolistic market structures.

Moreover, by reducing the number of competitors and ensuring that the most well-organized and violent firms survive, the public policy has created an environment conducive to collusive behavior. Cartels are difficult to organize if large numbers for firms are involved or pricing strategies difficult to negotiate. The drug firms' interest in avoiding arrest or inventory seizures provides common ground on which the organizations can coalesce into a larger coordinated structure.

Public Policy, Market Structure, and Institutions

A prohibitionist policy thus reinforces the values and rules that inevitably destroy the institutional foundations of successful expansion and economic development. The drug industry is a large and growing component of the inner-city economy. Yet, its structure and internal organization are a by-product of public policy that determines which rules will be supported and which will be discouraged. The black market, by operating outside the boundaries and institutional constraints of the legitimate market economy, operates according to rules that are arbitrary and, in the long run, self-destructive.

These effects are directly attributable to the legal status of the industry that has emerged to satisfy domestic demand for psychoactive substances such as marijuana, cocaine, and heroin. The profits of the drug industry result from above-competitive market prices generated by government attempts to restrict supply and raise the opportunity costs of drug trafficking. The result is the creation of a lucrative black market which, combined with the poor economic performance of urban economies, make employment in the drug economy acceptable and rational.

Unfortunately, the lessons learned in the drug trade are that law is harmful, violence is necessary, individual life is expendable, and distrust is essential for survival. These lessons contradict the rules on which contemporary, industrial economies are built.

Notes

1. A more detailed description of manufacturing facilities in foreign source countries can be found in National Narcotics Intelligence Consumers Committee, *The Supply of Illicit Drugs to the United States* (Washington, D.C.: NNICC, April 1988), 29-30, 66. See also Drug Enforcement Administration (DEA), "From the Source to the Street: Current Prices for Cannabis, Cocaine, and Heroin," *Intelligence Trends* 16, no.2 (1989): 6-9.
2. NNICC, *The Supply of Illicit Drugs*, 30.
3. The term *advanced services* was formally introduced to the growing literature on the urban transformations in T. Noyelle and T.M. Stanbach, *The Economic Transformation of American Cities* (Totowa, N.J.: Rowman & Allenheld, 1985). See also T. Noyelle, "The Rise of Advanced Services: Some Implications for Economic Development in U.S. Cities," *Journal of the American Planning Association* 49, no. 3 (1983):280-290.
4. This was an important implication of a RAND Corporation study on drug trafficking in Washington, D.C. See Peter Reuter, Robert MacCoun, and Patrick Murphy, *Money from Crime: A Study of the Economics of Drug Dealing in Washington, D.C.* (Santa Monica, Calif.: RAND Corporation, 1990), 75-77.
5. This analogy was developed in Bruce D. Johnson, Paul J. Goldstein, Edward Preble et al. *Taking Care of Business: The Economics of Crime by Heroin Abusers* (Lexington, Mass.: Lexington Books/D.C. Heath, 1985), 61-72.
6. Ibid., 234.

7. Ibid., 72.
8. Brian A. Reaves, "Police Departments in Large Cities, 1987," *Bureau of Justice Statistics Special Report* (Washington, D.C.: U.S. Department of Justice, Bureau of Justice Statistics, 1989), 3, Table 5.
9. DEA, *Illicit Drug Situation in the United States and Canada, 1984-86* (Washington, D.C.: U.S. Department of Justice, 1987), 4.
10. U.S. Department of Justice, *Drug Trafficking: A Report to The President of the United States* (Washington, D.C.: Office of the Attorney General, 1989), 11.
11. Ibid., 12.
12. DEA, *Illicit Drug Situation*, 4.
13. NNICC, *The Supply of Illicit Drugs*, 31.
14. Ibid.
15. Ibid., 63-64.
16. Ibid., 70-73.
17. The full implications of this phenomenon is the subject of considerable dispute in the literature. See the extensive discussions in Jose Blanes Jimenez, "Cocaine, Informality, and the Urban Economy in La Paz, Bolivia," in *The Informal Economy: Studies in Advanced and Less Developed Countries*, ed. Alejandro Portes, Manuel Castells, and Lauren A. Benton, (Baltimore, Md.: Johns Hopkins University Press, 1989), 135-49; Roberto Junguito and Carlos Caballero, "Illegal Trade Transactions and the Underground Economy of Colombia," in *The Underground Economy in the United States and Abroad*, ed. Vito Tanzi, (Lexington, Mass.: Lexington Books/D.C. Heath, 1982), 285-313; Steven Wisotsky, *Beyond the War on Drugs: Overcoming a Failed Public Policy* (Buffalo, NY: Prometheus Books, 1990), 49-60; Ethan A. Nadelmann, "U.S. Drug Policy: A Bad Export," *Foreign Policy* 71 (Summer 1988): 85-91.
18. A more detailed examination of the structure of the cocaine industry can be found in Wisotsky, *Beyond the War on Drugs*, 41-46. See also Peter Reuter and Mark A.R. Kleiman, "Risks and Prices: An Economic Analysis of Drug Enforcement," in *Crime and Justice: An Annual Review of Research*, vol. 7, ed. Michael Tonry and Norval Morris (Chicago: University of Chicago Press, 1986), 292-96.
19. The numerical breakdown uses 1982 data and is taken from Mark A.R. Kleiman, *Marijuana: Costs of Abuse, Costs of Control* (New York: Greenwood Press, 1989), 83-85.
20. See the discussion in Terry Williams, *The Cocaine Kids: The Inside Story of a Teenage Drug Ring* (Reading, Mass.: Addison-Wesley, 1989), 34-39.
21. Wisotsky, *Beyond the War on Drugs*, 43. For further discussion along these themes, see Paul Eddy, Hugo Sabogal, and Sara Walden, *The Cocaine Wars* (New York: Bantam Books, 1988).
22. Mark H. Moore, *Drug Trafficking* (Washington, D.C.: U.S. Department of Justice, National Institute of Justice, 1988), 2. This effect has also been noted in Kleiman, *Marijuana*, 58-65, 107-21.
23. U.S. Department of Justice, *Drug Trafficking*, 18. A more accurate analysis would emphasize that the cartel attempts to influence price by manipulating the supply of drugs available on the market. Prices are determined by the *interaction* of supply and demand, not solely supply considerations as the attorney general suggests. While the cartels can control certain elements of the supplyside of the distribution system, they cannot control demand (see also the discussion in chapter 4 on addiction).

24. "Drug Kingpin's Death Won't Stop Cocaine Flow," *Dayton Daily News*, 18 December, 1989, sec. A, p. 7 (report from the Washington Post).

25. DEA, "Drug Trafficking and Availability in the State of Arizona," *Intelligence Trends* 16, no. 1 (1989): 16-24.

26. Ibid., 16.

27. A recent report by the U.S. Department of Justice, however, contends that South American cartels are involved in virtually every level of drug trafficking in the United States and in South America. See U.S. Department of Justice, *Drug Trafficking*, 17.

28. DEA, "From the Source to the Street: Current Prices for Cannabis, Cocaine, and Heroin," *Intelligence Trends* 16, no. 2 (1989): 7.

29. See Reuter and Kleiman, "Risks and Prices," 292-94.

30. A thorough review of the market for heroin can be found in James F. Holahan, "The Economics of Heroin," in *Dealing with Drug Abuse: A Report to the Ford Foundation* (New York: Praeger Publishers, 1972), 255-99.

31. The laws were widely considered a failure. See the discussion in Arnold Trebach, *The Heroin Solution* (New Haven, Conn.: Yale University Press, 1982), 251-253.

32. See the discussion in Moore, *Drug Trafficking*.

33. See Holohan, "The Economics of Heroin," 269-75.

34. Robert Michaels, "The Market for Heroin Before and After Legalization," in Ronald Hamowy, ed., *Dealing With Drugs: Consequences of Government Control* (Lexington, Mass.: Lexington Books/D.C. Heath, 1987), 295-304.

35. U.S. Department of Justice, *Drug Trafficking*, 16.

36. Ibid., 18.

37. This discussion draws heavily on U.S. Department of Justice, *Drug Trafficking*, 22-24.

38. Ibid., 23.

39. Reuter and Kleiman, "Risks and Prices," 300-1.

40. Motorcycle gangs are also heavily involved in the distribution of illicit drugs. They are not as heavily involved in the distribution of heroin, cocaine, or marijuana although they dominate the production and distribution of methamphetimines. The exception may be the Outlaws and the Hells Angels, which appear to engage heavily in cocaine trafficking along with other drugs. See the discussion in U.S. Department of Justice, *Drug Trafficking*, 30-33.

41. DEA, "Crips and Bloods," *Intelligence Trends* 16, no. 1 (1989): 12.

42. U.S. Department of Justice, *Drug Trafficking*, 24-27.

43. Ibid., 26.

44. Reuter, MacCoun, and Murphy, *Money from Crime*, 24.

45. Ibid., 88.

46. Wes Hills and Mizzell Stewart III, "Man Called Drug King Surrenders Throne: Suspect Gets to Feds Before Enemies Get to Him," *Dayton Daily News* 2 October 1989, sec. A, 1, 4.

47. Some have argued that the prices might not decline if the drug trade were legalized. As the earlier discussion in chapters 4 and 5 indicated, current prices are substantially above the marginal cost of production. In a legal and more competitive marketplace, prices would converge toward marginal costs. Most observers and scholars familiar with the drug trade concede that prices would moderate. The extent of the fall, however, is unclear since the U.S. has not experienced a legalized drug regime in the modern era.

48. Randy Barnett, "Curing the Drug-Law Addiction: the Harmful Side Effects of Legal Prohibition," in Hamowy, *Dealing with Drugs*, 73-102.
49. Ibid., 96.
50. Data taken from the DEA, "From the Source to the Street." Also see the discussion in Wisotsky, *Beyond the War on Drugs*, 37-47.
51. DEA, "From the Source to the Street," 6.
52. Reuter and Kleiman, "Risks and Prices," 332, table 8.
53. Reuter, MacCoun, and Murphy, *Money from Crime*, 63, table 4.7.
54. See the discussion in Reuter, MacCoun, and Murphy, Ibid., 102-7.
55. Ibid., 73, table 4.15.
56. See Williams, *The Cocaine Kids.*
57. Christopher A. Innes, "Drug Use and Crime: State Prison Inmate Survey, 1986," *Bureau of Justice Statistics Special Report* (Washington, D.C.: U.S. Department of Justice, Bureau of Justice Statistics, 1988), 3, table 3.
58. See Johnson et al., *Taking Care of Business*; John Kaplan, *The Hardest Drug: Heroin and Public Policy* (Chicago: University of Chicago Press, 1983), 25-32; Richard H. Blum, "Drug Pushers: A Collective Portrait," in *Drugs and Politics*, ed. Paul E. Rock, (New Brunswick, N.J.: Transaction Publishers, 1977), 223-32.
59. Williams, *The Cocaine Kids*, 122.
60. Reuter and Kleiman, "Risks and Prices," 300.

PART III

PUBLIC POLICY
AND THE DRUG ECONOMY

7

The Drug War
and the Growth of the Drug Economy

Governments on all levels have mounted an impressive campaign against illicit drugs for decades. Earlier enforcement efforts, however, paled in comparison to that mounted in the 1980s. In 1982, the federal government allocated a mere $3 billion to the War. By 1990, federal expenditures had ballooned to over $10 billion. To help finance state,local, and federal drug law enforcement efforts, over $1 billion in assets were seized by law enforcement personnel from 1985 to 1990. These efforts represent the most recent version of the nation's commitment to the War on Drugs.

Many recent reports suggest that the drug war is working. Statistics reported in June 1990 by the U.S. Drug Enforcement Administration (DEA) found that coca prices were plummeting in South America and wholesale cocaine prices were soaring in the United States.[1] Wholesale prices in Los Angeles doubled in 1989 while average purity declined from 90 percent to 74 percent. In some cases, coca farmers were losing money on their crops and switching to oranges, bananas and macadamia nuts. A DEA official testifying before the Senate Foreign Relations Committee's Western Hemisphere Subcommittee and Subcommittee on Terrorism, Narcotics, and International Operations credited a ten-month crackdown by Colombian law enforcement personnel, a "change in attitude" in Peru concerning coca leaf production, and intensified enforcement in Mexico aimed at slowing exports of cocaine into the United States for these dramatic results.

Meanwhile, another DEA official, this time testifying before the Senate Judiciary Committee, warned that the "exact cause" of the supply shortage was unknown.[2] While crediting enforcement efforts with much of the reduced supply, the official also warned that distributors and dealers may be stockpiling cocaine to increase prices before flooding the U.S. market. Disruptions in flights from Bolivia and Peru to Colombia, where coca is processed, may have also forced Latin American farmers to dump their product on the market before the coca leaves became unusable.[3] As coca crops become less profitable (prices per one hundred pounds of leaf dropped from sixty-two dollars to ten dollars in eight months), fewer crops were harvested. Despite intensified drug enforcement efforts in the early and mid-1980s, the market for cocaine experienced a "glut" as wholesale and retail cocaine prices declined to record lows.

The "war" continues unabated in other areas as prosecutors and other law enforcement personnel seek increasingly broader powers. State law enforcement organizations are pushing for tougher arrest, seizure, and forfeiture laws. The National Conference of Commissioners on Uniform State Laws finalized revisions of a proposed law that, as a principle component, shifts the burden of proof on asset forfeitures from law enforcement to suspects.[4] Currently, forfeiture proceedings cannot be initiated against innocent property owners. If the new law were adopted, property owners would have to prove that they were unaware that their property was being used in a drug-related crime.

Law enforcement personnel are also encouraging children to report their parents for drug law violations in efforts to penetrate the most intimate sanctuaries of personal behavior. Some West Virginia newspapers have begun publishing "coupons" that allow readers to provide anonymous tips on suspected drug dealers. In the six months since the program's inception, 700 coupons had been returned to the state police.[5] In Boston, Massachusetts, a Dorchester woman started a program for residents to telephone anonymous tips through a "Drop-A-Dime/Report Crime" program.[6] Through these programs and hundreds of others instituted in communities across the country, awareness of crime and drugs has reached the highest levels in years.

The War on Drugs has brought the issue of drug abuse and distribution to the forefront of public discussion and debate. For all the successes of the current drug war, however, they are likely to be temporary and fleeting. Existing strategies for combatting illicit drugs ignore many of the most salient causes of the more general problem. In virtually every aspect of federal drug enforcement strategies, public policy concentrates on the symptoms rather than the causes.

To date, the results of the War on Drugs have been far from satisfactory, despite the recent claims of law enforcement officials before congressional subcommittees. There are inherent structural problems associated with domestic and international drug control that may be insurmountable in the the long run. Thus, despite apparent successes such as the recent crackdown on coca production and processing in Latin America, current policies will simply shift these functions of the international drug industry to other locations that may compound the problem even further.

The War on Drugs

The federal government has been financing a "war" on drugs since the early twentieth century. The first drug control laws were instituted on the local level, beginning with regulations on opium smoking in San Francisco in 1875. These laws were not directed at opium dens as much as at the Chinese immigrants who frequented them.[7] The federal government's first major foray into narcotics control came with the passage of the Harrison Narcotic Act of 1914. Originally intended only to regulate the dispensation of narcotics through licensing, the law quickly became the principal instrument for drug prohibition.[8] Since the passage of the Harrison Act, laws have become more stringent and penalties more harsh.

One of the most important aspects of U.S. drug policy is its political nature. "American concern with narcotics," observes David Musto, one of the most respected historians of domestic drug issues, "is more than a medical or legal problem—it is in the fullest sense a political problem."[9] Indeed, the most impassioned arguments for drug control have come from special interests, such as the Women's Christian Temperance Union, which argued for alcohol prohibition in the first decades of this century, or the American Medical Association (AMA), which argued for narcotic control to help solidify its influence over the dispensation and regulation of medicine in the late nineteenth century.

Calls for drug regulation have also been accompanied by arguments focusing on the effects of drugs on particular minority groups. Musto effectively chronicles the social perceptions that provided the context for the regulation and ultimate prohibition of various drugs during the twentieth century.[10] Arguments for the prohibition of cocaine were based on beliefs in the late nineteenth century that cocaine provided blacks with superhuman strength such as the ability to withstand bullets. Opium laws were promoted at the turn of the century because of widespread belief that smoking the drug promoted sexual contact between Chinese and white American women. Marijuana was claimed to incite violence among Hispanic Americans and Mexican immigrants in the 1930s, eventually leading to its prohibition through the Marijuana Tax Act of 1937. In more recent decades, heroin was supposed to incite violent and reckless behavior among the youth. In each case, the regulation of the drug corresponded with some social problem or crisis requiring a political response.

The events leading up to the passage of the Marijuana Tax Act of 1937 illustrates the relationship between politics and drug policy. Despite medical evidence that marijuana is one of the least harmful drugs available, public policy has followed a consistent prohibitionist course since the 1930s. Political and social pressures were building toward prohibition well before the Marijuana Tax Act was finally passed in the mid-1930s.

Pressure for the national prohibition of marijuana, however, was not based on medical evidence. In fact, commissions created to evaluate drug policy with respect to marijuana have consistently concluded the drug should be decriminalized or at least considered a less severe problem than other hard drugs.[11] Thus, the push for marijuana prohibition came largely from politicians and law enforcement agencies responding to a perceived social "crisis" in the Southwest during the 1930s. Marijuana was called the "most insidious" of the "narcotics" used at the time and prohibitionists claimed its spread was a direct result of Mexican immigration.[12] Harry J. Anslinger, the first commissioner of the Federal Bureau of Narcotics, vigorously promoted marijuana prohibition throughout the 1930s, drawing more on his experience as an assistant commissioner of prohibition than medical evidence.

During the congressional hearings called to evaluate the propriety of the Marijuana Tax Act, evidence minimizing the negative effects of marijuana was ignored to present a "solid front" for prohibition before Congress.[13] Officially, the AMA opposed marijuana prohibition, even running an editorial in its professional journal opposing the Marijuana Tax Act.[14] Only one person, William C. Woodward (representing the AMA), offered opposing testimony and his opinions were met with hostility by the committee. In the end, while ignoring the testimony of the medical profession, Congress recognized only the legitimate needs of the birdseed manufacturers "who complained that canaries would not sing as well, or might stop singing altogether, if marijuana seeds were eliminated from their diet."[15]

The political elements of drug policy were also clearly demonstrated in inequities in sentencing for violations of marijuana prohibition. Enforcement was targeted mainly toward Mexican and Hispanic Americans. Wealthy and powerful white violators rarely received sentences as long or as stringent as the poor.[16]

Another, more current example of how politics is intertwined with drug policy is taken from the failure of the Compassionate Pain Relief Act (CPRA) of 1984. Heroin is widely acknowledged as an effective painkiller within the medical profession. The CPRA would have allowed heroin to be used by 20,000 to 40,000 terminally ill patients in the United States after other treatments proved to be ineffective. The act would have affected only 5 to 10 percent of all terminally ill patients in the U.S. If all the patients covered by the act used heroin as a painkiller, the quantity consumed would have amounted to only 5.6 percent of the amount currently consumed on the black market.[17]

Opponents of the bill quickly claimed that the effect of the act would be to legalize heroin in an effort to "scare off" supporters. Arguments used to defeat the legislation included claims that the passage of the bill would send signals to America's youth that heroin was "O.K.," that it would open the door for wholesale legalization, that the heroin might be diverted to the street and end up in criminal hands, and that the legislation would legitimize heroin and eventually lead to its legalization.[18] Thus, even though experts, including some doctors testifying against the legislation, admitted that heroin could have had substantial medical value as a painkiller in the limited application to terminally ill patients, political considerations dominated the debate over the bill. In the end, legislators who would have testified in favor of the bill quietly admitted they backed down from the bill to avoid being labeled "heroin pushers" in an election year.[19]

"The history of drug laws in the United States," notes Musto, "shows that the degree to which the drug has been outlawed or curbed has no direct relation to its inherent danger."[20] This was clearly the case with respect to marijuana prohibition and heroin during the events surrounding the defeat of the CPRA. Interestingly, alcohol, widely acknowledged by medical experts as more harmful than virtually all currently illicit substances, required a constitutional amendment before national prohibition could be implemented in the early decades of the twentieth century. Other drugs such as cocaine, marijuana, and opium were simply prohibited by statute. The constitutional amendment was necessary, Musto speculates, because there was widespread agreement on the "evils" of drugs such as cocaine, opium, and marijuana, while substantial disagreement existed over the social and moral costs of alcohol.[21]

American drug laws have gone through successive periods of strict and lax enforcement. Musto observes that American public opinion seems to vacillate from tolerance of drug use to intolerance. The 1960s experienced dramatic growth in drug use, followed by a severe law enforcement crackdown during the Nixon presidency. Nixon pursued an aggressive antidrug campaign that saw expenditures jump from $86 million in 1969 to almost $800 million in 1974. Nevertheless, the country continued to move in a direction of drug use toleration until the early 1980s. With the election of Ronald Reagan, the United States was poised for a renewed attempt to institute ever-harsher penalties on drug users and traffickers.

By the end of 1989, every state in the union and the District of Columbia had laws restricting the possession, manufacture, delivery and sale of illegal drugs.[22] Twenty-seven percent had laws prohibiting or restricting drug use while 27 percent also had laws specifically designed to address drug trafficking. Similarly, all states and the District of Columbia have laws allowing for asset forfeiture for drug-law violations and 68 percent have enhanced penalties under their state's provisions.

President Reagan declared "war" on drug use and abuse in America in 1982. Since then, virtually every indicator of drug-law enforcement bears testimony to federal efforts to enforce drug prohibition (table 7.1). Federal arrests for drug law violations increased 83 percent from 1984 to 1988 according the data collected by the DEA. These arrests did not always translate into convictions. While arrests rose to almost twenty-four thousand in 1988, convictions represented only 56 percent of the total. In 1984, in contrast, 82 percent of the people arrested for drug law violations were convicted.

These trends mirror arrests for drug offenses more generally. In 1979, 394,632 arrests for drug abuse violations were reported to the FBI by law enforcement agencies. By 1988, arrests for drug violations increased 90 percent to 749,468.[23] Moreover, cities accounted for 84.7 percent of all arrests for drug abuse violations.[24]

TABLE 7.1
The War on Drugs, 1984 to 1988: The Federal Effort

	1984	1988	Percent Change
Arrests	13,126	23,991	83%
Convictions	10,809	13,455	24
Domestic drug removals			
Heroin (kilograms)	346	826	142%
Cocaine (kilograms)	11,742	56,980	385
Marijuana (metric tons)	1,400	537	- 62
Asset removals			
Total ($1,000)	$150,975	$661,820	338%
DEA ($1,000)	92,545	477,550	416
Interagency ($1,000)	58,431	184,270	215

Source: Drug Enforcement Administration.

Seizures of illicit drugs increased dramatically for heroin and cocaine. Cocaine seizures alone almost quadrupled, reflecting intensive enforcement and interdiction efforts throughout the decade. During this period, the demand for cocaine in the United States swelled from under 50 metric tons to over 100 tons in 1990. Thus, by 1988, the DEA was seizing cocaine equivalent to the estimated demand for cocaine in the early- to mid-1980s. Similarly, seizures of heroin more than doubled to almost a metric ton. Clandestine laboratories used for manufacturing designer drugs, methamphetamines, and cocaine increased dramatically. The value of assets seized rose 338 percent during the four-year period.

Drug-Law Arrests and Convictions

From 1980 to 1989, the number of defendants convicted in U.S. district courts of drug offenses increased 198 percent from 4,749 to 14,139.[25] This increase was substantially higher than for nondrug offenses, which increased 25 percent from 1980 to 1987.[26] Drug-law violators thus became an increasingly larger percentage of all defendants convicted in federal courts, rising from only 17.1 percent in 1980 to 30.2 percent in 1987.[27]

FIGURE 7.1
Federal Defendants Convicted for Drug Offenses, 1980 to 1986

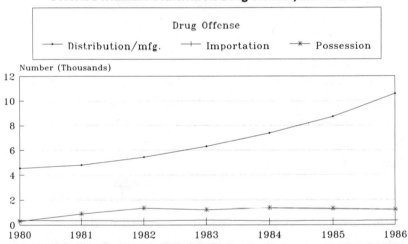

Source: U.S. Department of Justice, "Drug Law Violators, 1980-1986," *Bureau of Justice Statistics Special Report* (Washington, D.C.: Bureau of Justice Statistics, 1988)p.2.

This increase in federal defendants convicted for drug charges resulted from increased emphasis on drug trafficking arrests (fig. 7.1). The number of defendants convicted for drug distribution and manufacturing increased 133 percent from 1980 to 1986, rising from 4,537 to 10,564. The percentage of all defendants in federal court convicted of drug distribution and manufacturing increased from 15 percent of 24 percent.

Surprisingly, convictions for the importation of drugs remained relatively constant. In 1980, 367 people were convicted for drug importation. Only 358 persons were convicted for importation in 1986, declining from a high of only 376 in 1983. Convictions for possession increased dramatically early in the war—from 874 in 1981 to 1,353 in 1982—but have remained relatively constant since the mid-1980s.

These trends are largely an artifact of the sample being used. In 1986, for example, state and local law enforcement agencies arrested over 600,000 people for drug-law violations. In contrast, the DEA and FBI arrested only 21,000. A survey of inmates in local jails revealed that 40 percent of the total increase in the jail population resulted from arrests for drug-law offenses.[28] Overall, the percentage of the local jail population incarcerated for drug violations increased from only 9.3 percent in 1983 to 23 percent in 1989. Yet, among state prison inmates, only 8.6 percent were incarcerated for drug offenses in 1986. This represented a small increase over 1979 (6.4 percent).

Local authorities are also more likely to make arrests for possession. In New York City, for example, possession offenses represented two-thirds of all drug arrests for 1988.[29] Among felony drug arrests, on the other hand, sale offenses represented 63 percent of the total. According to the FBI, arrests per 100,000 for the sale or the manufacture of drugs increased from 57.9 to 103.6 between 1980 and 1987. Arrests for possession increased from 198.1 per 100,000 to 297.2 per 100,000. Thus, possession arrests increased but started from a much higher base than arrests for drug manufacturing or distribution.

Nevertheless, a general trend appears to be moving toward targeting drug distributing and manufacturing in the urban drug war. Overall, the FBI reports that arrests for sales and manufacturing as a proportion of total drug-law violations increased from slightly more than 20 percent to 27 percent from 1981 to 1988.[30] Arrests for the drug sales and manufacturing increased from 12 percent of all drug arrests in 1983 to 42 percent in 1986 for Milwaukee County, Wisconsin.[31] New York City reports that 43 percent of all drug arrests were for felony drug arrests, and most of these offenses were for felony sale.[32] In Chicago, arrests for sale comprised over 90 percent of all arrests for cocaine in 1988.[33] According to data from the U.S. Department of Justice, 40 percent of all arrests in the 75 largest counties in the United States were for drug sales or trafficking in 1988.[34]

Washington, D.C. exemplifies many of these trends in local law enforcement (figs. 7.2 and 7.3). According to data from the Office of Criminal Justice Plans and Analysis in the District of Columbia, adult arrests for drug offenses blossomed from 6,408 in 1981 to 11,066 in 1987. Arrests for possession, on the other hand, remained relatively stable, declining from 6,000 in 1981 to 4,729 in 1984, and then rising to 7,000 in 1986 before declining to 5,769 in 1987. As a proportion of total drug arrests, adult arrests for drug distribution increased from 6 percent to 48 percent. Of the total persons (rather than arrests) charged with drug offenses from 1985 to 1987, 60 percent were charged with distribution offenses.[35] Thus, the emphasis of recent law enforcement efforts have concentrated primarily on drugs sales.

FIGURE 7.2
Adult Arrests for Drug Offenses Washington, D.C.: 1981 to 1987

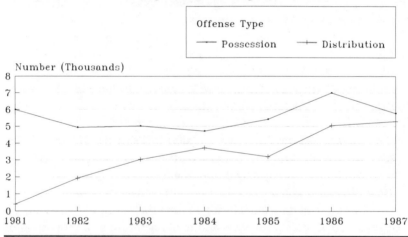

Source: Peter Reuter, Robert MacCoun, and Patrick Murphy, *Money From Crime* (Santa Monica, Calif.: the RAND Corporation, 1990), p. 29.

Similar trends are also evident among juvenile arrestees in the District of Columbia (fig. 7.4). Arrests for possession remained relatively constant from 1981 to 1987, with the exception of 1986 when 943 juveniles were arrested. In contrast, arrests for distribution have increased steadily, experiencing a dramatic increase in 1987. In fact, arrests for drug distribution were significantly less as a proportion of total drug arrests until this time. As chapter 3 noted, arrests for possession plummeted as a proportion of total arrests from 83 percent in 1981 to 18 percent in 1987.

Arrests for distribution were still only 23 percent of all drug arrests in 1986, clearly indicating a shift in emphasis on drug enforcement by District police.

FIGURE 7.3
Adult Arrests for Drug Offenses in Washington, D.C.: 1981 and 1987

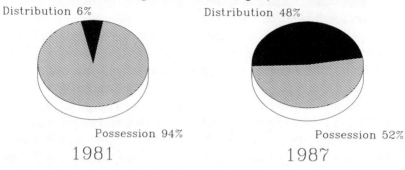

Source: Reuter, MacCoun, and Murphy, *Money from Crime*, 29.

FIGURE 7.4
Juvenile Arrests for Drug Offenses Washington, D.C., 1981 to 1987

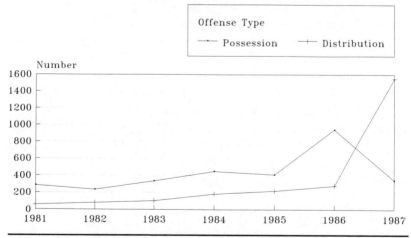

Source: Reuter, MacCoun, and Murphy, *Money from Crime*, 29.

Most major cities are experiencing dramatic increases in the amount of drug-related crime. In Philadelphia, Pennsylvania, arrests for narcotics offenses increased 89.4 percent from 1980 to 1987. From 1987 to 1988 alone, the city experienced a 44.9 percent increase. "Not only is the increase expected to continue into the future," warns the Pennsylvania Commission on Crime and Deliquency, "but based upon the level of demand and supply in the streets, it is estimated that Philadelphia could reach an annual drug arrest figure of 12,000-16,000 by the end of 1990."[36] The commission expected to experience an 80 percent increase in juvenile cases for drug offenses in 1988.

The character of the drug trade changed dramatically during the 1980s as well. The proportion of all drug arrests made for the possession, sale, or manufacture of heroin or cocaine increased from only 12 percent in 1981 to 65 percent in 1988 according to the FBI. Arrests for the sale and manufacture of cocaine or heroin increased from 18 percent of all arrests to 26 percent from 1980 to 1987. Arrests for the sale or manufacture of heroin or cocaine increased from 4 percent to 14 percent while arrests for possession increased from 8 percent to 32 percent. In contrast, arrests for marijuana violations declined from 61 percent to 33 percent of all drug arrests.

These trends are aptly described in figure 7.5. A survey of federal drug-law violators found that convictions for offenses involving cocaine and heroin increased dramatically during the 1980s. The number of convictions for marijuana offenses increased from 1,267 in 1980 to 3,285 in 1984, remaining relatively stable through 1986 (3,221). This represented a 154 percent increase from 1980 to 1986.

The number of convictions for cocaine and heroin offenses soared from 2,677 in 1980 to 7,769 in 1986, a 190 percent increase. The number of convictions involving cocaine and heroin increased dramatically after 1983 as the official War on Drugs began in earnest. Convictions of heroin and cocaine offenses increased to 63 percent of all convictions in 1980, up from 51 percent in 1980. As a percentage of total drug law convictions, the proportion involving cocaine or heroin declined from 1980 to 1983.

Marijuana offenders made-up 40 percent of all convictions in 1982 and 1983 but declined to only 26 percent by 1986.

Drug Seizures and Interdiction

Other tools used by police include intercepting drugs intended for sale in the U.S. and confiscating drugs already circulating in domestic markets. Thus detailed data reported by the U.S. Customs Service and the

DEA provide another perspective on how the War on Drugs escalated during the 1980s.

FIGURE 7.5
Federal Drug Law Violators by Drug Type, 1980 to 1986

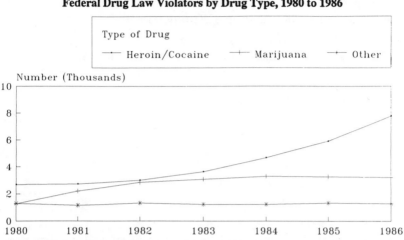

Source: U.S. Department of Justice, "Drug Law Violators," p.2.

Although aggregate drug seizures increased dramatically during the 1980s, the mix of drugs being confiscated changed significantly. Before the 1980s, as the arrest and conviction data presented in the previous section indicated, drug enforcement efforts were directed more toward marijuana than cocaine. During the 1980s, cocaine became the major focus of government interdiction and drug removal efforts.

Drug seizures and removals of marijuana declined from 1978 to 1989, mirroring the declines in arrests and convictions for marijuana offenses (fig. 7.6). In 1978, the DEA and Customs Service confiscated 2,867 net tons (3,159 metric tons) of marijuana. By 1989, marijuana confiscations had declined to only 697 net tons (768 metric tons). Yet, marijuana drug seizures and removals increased during the early 1980s, when the DEA and Customs service seized or removed over 3,000 net tons in 1981, 1982 and 1984.

The DEA has also pursued an aggressive domestic marijuana crop eradication program since the early 1980s to counter increased production within the United States. In 1982, 2,590,388 plants were eradicated, resulting in 2,512 arrests.[37] By 1989, 130 million plants were eradicated, culminating in 5,767 arrests, and the number of states participating in marijuana crop eradication programs had increased from twenty-five (in 1982) to forty-nine. Funding for the program had leveled off to $3.8 million per year. Over $29 million in assets were seized from marijuana producers during 1989, up from $13 million in 1987.

FIGURE 7.6
Marijuana Seizures by U.S. Customs and Drug Enforcement Administration

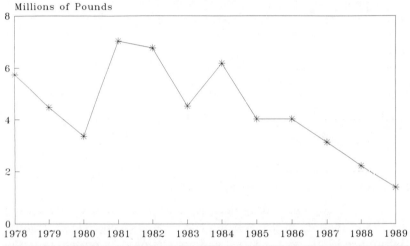

Millions of Pounds

Source: Timothy J. Flanagan and Kathleen Maguire, eds., *Sourcebook of Criminal Justice Statistics, 1989* (Washington, D.C., U.S. Department of Justice, Govt. Printing Office, 1990), 466-68.

The DEA further claims that half of the cultivated domestic marijuana crop is being destroyed. Over 5.6 million cultivated plants, weighing 2,548 metric tons were eradicated during 1989, although this was down from 7.4 million in 1987. Interestingly, the vast majority of plants destroyed—124 million in 1989—were growing wild. While every state reported eradication of cultivated marijuana plants, thirty states did not report eradicating one wild plant.

Thus, of the plants eradicated, less than 5 percent were cultivated plants. Clearly, the size of the domestic marijuana crop is very large. Cultivated and wild marijuana may easily exceed the national demand for marijuana, which is estimated at over 10,000 metric tons (or 9 standard net tons).

Nevertheless, the cannabis eradication programs are a substantial part of the DEA's war against marijuana. In 1988, for example, the DEA estimated that it alone removed about 685 metric tons of marijuana from the domestic market. Meanwhile, the eradication program combined resources on the state, local, and federal levels to remove over 2,000 tons of cultivated marijuana.

Despite these efforts, marijuana prices remained stable through most of the 1980s.[38] A survey of nineteen DEA divisional offices was conducted in 1987 to assess the impact of the DEA's efforts on the availability of marijuana. Only one divisional office indicated that the availability of marijuana had decreased in the fourth quarter of 1987.[39]

While marijuana seizures by federal agencies were dropping during the 1980s, seizures and removals of cocaine skyrocketed (fig. 7.7). The DEA and Customs Service confiscated over 85 net tons (93.8 metric tons) of cocaine in 1987 compared to 1.21 tons (1.46 metric tons) in 1978. Seizures of cocaine increased dramatically after 1982, rising from 11.8 tons in 1982 to 26.4 tons in 1984 and to 56.1 tons in 1986 to 155.0 tons in 1989.

FIGURE 7.7

Cocaine Seizures by U.S. Customs Service and Drug Enforcement Administration

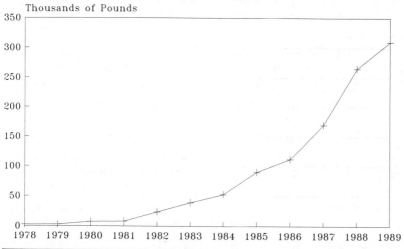

Thousands of Pounds

Source: Flanagan and Maguire, *Sourcebook,* 466-68.

Estimates of the demand for cocaine in the late 1980s hovered around 100 tons (110 metric tons) annually. Thus, total seizures appeared to approximate total domestic demand until 1988. Moreover, statistics compiled by the National Narcotics Consumers Intelligence Committee (NNICC) estimated that world cocaine production capacity in 1987 was between 322 and 418 metric tons.[40] From these data, seizures by federal authorities account for between 37 and 48 percent of the world's production of cocaine.

The DEA has also stepped up programs geared toward eliminating domestic cocaine processing. In 1989, federal officials closed down 852 clandestine drug laboratories.[41] While 95 percent of the laboratories are for processing PCP, methamphetamines, and amphetamines, an increasing number are for cocaine processing. Federal agents have closed 140 cocaine labs from 1975 to 1989, seizing 29 in 1985 and 23 in 1986.[42]

Still, cocaine prices remained stable throughout this period and, in most cities, declined. Wholesale prices declined from $40 to $50 per gram in 1984 to $12 to $40 per gram in 1987.[43] By 1988, prices had fallen even further to $13 to $20 per gram on the wholesale cocaine market.[44] These events began leading many experts and law enforcement officials to suspect the market for cocaine is larger than earlier estimates.[45]

Given current interdiction rates, price behavior and domestic consumption, cocaine producers suffer from excess capacity. If U.S. consumption were 110 metric tons and law enforcement officials were able to confiscate another 100 metric tons, world capacity would still more than equal the domestic U.S. demand for cocaine. Thus, in principle, even if law enforcement authorities were able to double their effectiveness (a highly unlikely scenario), cocaine producers in Latin America would still be more than capable of supplying the existing demand for cocaine in the United States.

Heroin seizures have never amounted to significant proportions of domestic consumption and world production although they increased significantly during the 1980s (fig. 7.8). Heroin seizures remained well below 1 ton (between 10 and 20 percent of the domestic market) until 1988 and 1989. The DEA reports that heroin removals from the domestic market increased to 1,828 pounds in 1988 (the largest amount to date) although this amount is still significantly less than domestic consumption which is estimated at between 5 and 10 metric tons.

Even if heroin seizures increased dramatically, the likelihood of the heroin supply being reduced are minimal. Heroin is produced from opium, which is used widely throughout the world. Indeed, most opium is consumed within the source countries. If the price were high enough, domestic consumption in foreign countries could be diverted to exports to the U.S. heroin market very easily.

The official reports of drug seizures and production suggest that law enforcement personnel are capable of interdicting substantial quantities of drugs. In fact, most experts concur that federal interdiction efforts intercept between 10 and 30 percent of all drugs bound for the United States, although opinions can diverge significantly. Law Professor Steven Wisotsky, for example, reports that federal authorities are able to interdict about 10 percent of total cocaine shipments into the U.S.[46] Edward M. Brecher has suggested that only 5 percent of the heroin smuggled into the United States was intercepted by authorities.[47] On the other end of the spectrum, Peter Reuter and Mark Kleiman, using data from 1984, estimated that interdiction rates ranged from 22.3 to 29.8 percent for cocaine and 10.9 to 22.2 percent for marijuana.[48] "Although the range of results indicates some uncertainties," they note, "it is clear that federal interdiction efforts currently impose significant costs on drug importers."[49]

FIGURE 7.8

Heroin Seizures by U.S. Customs Service and Drug Enforcement Administration

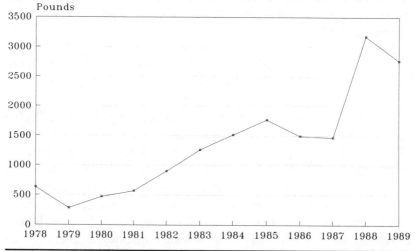

Source: Flanagan and Maguire, Sourcebook, 466-68.

Nevertheless, even Reuter and Kleiman note that interdiction was unlikely to affect consumption significantly, since higher prices for drugs and the subsequent profits go to domestic intermediaries. If, for example, drug enforcement officials were able to double the interdiction rate from 30 percent to 60 percent, the effect on the final retail price would be only 6 percent. Similarly, Reuter and Kleiman estimate that a doubling of interdiction rates for marijuana from 22 percent to 44 percent would raise its retail price by only 13 percent. In either case, the price rise associated with increased interdiction would be minimal.

Unfortunately, interdiction rates are likely to remain low. The cost of a comprehensive shutdown for drug imports is simply prohibitive even if authorities had the resources to stop and search every person coming over the border. In 1969, for instance, the Nixon administration implemented Operation Intercept to close the 2,700 mile border between Mexico and the United States to stop the in-flow of illegal drugs.[50] During the first week, almost two thousand body searches were performed, yielding only thirty-three arrests. Even though authorities used over two thousand agents and customs inspectors, almost 2 million people crossed the border without being searched. The operation was abandoned three weeks after it began after businessmen on the border, Mexican officials, and Latin American officials protested in face of the severe economic consequences for the legitimate economy. In the end, the operation netted the same amount of marijuana per day (about 150 pounds per day) as before the initiative.

Moreover, even if authorities were able to intercept substantial amounts of drugs in the short run, suppliers and producers could easily adjust their trafficking and production patterns to avoid detection. The city of Miami served as a primary center for importing cocaine throughout much of the 1980s. Increased enforcement efforts in South Florida merely shifted trafficking activities to other parts of the country. The state of Arizona, for instance, experienced a substantial increase in trafficking activity, particularly in the Tucson area.[51] Arizona has a 370-mile border with Mexico consisting of wide, open ranges ideal for overland smuggling. The state also has seven unmanned border crossings, abandoned airstrips and mines, desolate country roads, and sparse habitation, further increasing the states "vulnerability" to drug trafficking. Combined with several overlapping government jurisdictional boundaries that include state and national parks; Indian reservations; wildlife refuges; military installations; and more traditional state, local, and federal law enforcement agencies, Arizona has become a primary staging area for drug smuggling by Mexican and Colombian organizations.

Drug smugglers and traffickers could also move their operations to other, lesser-known ports of entry. New Orleans, for instance, has experienced a substantial increase in drug trafficking.[52] The Louisiana State Police reports that the state currently ranks third in marine and sixth in air drug smuggling. The state has over four hundred miles of coastline on the Gulf of Mexico, another seven thousand miles of shoreline, and hundreds of miles of navigable waterways. New Orleans is one of the busiest ports in the United States and is only one hundred miles from the mouth of the Mississippi River. Twenty-nine percent of the cocaine (twenty kilograms) seized in Louisiana and 31 percent of local drug arrests (4,892) already come from within the city of New Orleans. As an indicator of illegal drug activity, New Orleans police claim over 60 percent of their murders are drug-related.

Changing points of entry for drugs requires reestablishing local distribution networks. An alternative strategy might include simply altering the mode for smuggling illegal drugs. While marijuana is imported mainly on noncommercial vessels because of its bulk,[53] cocaine and heroin can be transported on a variety of vessels and in varied shipment sizes to remain profitable. During the 1980s, cocaine was usually imported in units of twenty-five kilograms or larger (about fifty-five pounds). Heroin, on the other hand, was usually transported in small shipments of less than 2.5 kilograms (about three pounds). Cocaine importers can simply adopt the heroin method of importation and remain profitable.[54]

Drug importers have shown a remarkable ability to shift modes of transportation from year to year, depending on the potential for interdiction. Drug seizures again provide an indication of how smugglers will change methods in this way. Cocaine seizures from general aviation aircraft declined from 48 percent to 36 percent from 1986 to 1987 based on the most recent estimates provided by the NNICC (fig. 7.9).[55] This was a decline from 56 percent seized from general aviation aircraft in 1985. Seizures from commercial vessels have increased dramatically from only 11 percent in 1986 to 22 percent in 1987. In 1985, seizures from commercial vessels comprised only 4 percent of total cocaine confiscated by drug enforcement authorities.

FIGURE 7.9
Cocaine Seizures by Form of Transportation, 1986 and 1987

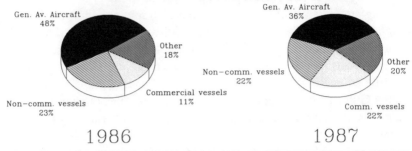

Source: National Narcotics Intelligence Consumers Committee, *The Supply of Illicit Drugs in the United States*, April, 1988, p. 9.

Heroin smuggling has changed even more dramatically according to drug seizure data (fig. 7.10). In 1986, almost 90 percent of all heroin seized by law enforcement agencies was from commercial air passengers. By 1987, commercial air passengers accounted for only 64 percent. Land transportation increased as a proportion of total heroin trafficking, increasing from 8 percent to 18 percent while commercial vessels increased from 5 percent to 15 percent during the same year. If these data reflect actual trafficking trends, heroin traffickers are capable of changing the mode of importation relatively easily.

FIGURE 7.10
Heroin Seizures by Form of Transportation, 1986 and 1987

Source: NNICC, *Supply of Illicit Drugs*, 59-60.

On the other extreme, marijuana trafficking is much easier to detect, and the product is far more bulky. Since marijuana profit margins are lower between border points and retail level than for cocaine or heroin, interdiction is likely to have a larger effect. Traffickers can still reduce their exposure by downsizing the scale of their shipments. "Instead of bringing up 'mother' ships from Colombia with fifty tons of marijuana and then off-loading to smaller coastal vessels, much marijuana is now smuggled in small, very fast oceangoing boats, known as 'cigarettes.'"[56] In addition, marijuana traffickers are just as likely to move their importing operations to other areas (e.g., from South Florida to Arizona, Texas, or Louisiana).

An inherent obstacle to any serious effort to reduce the supply of drugs in the United States through interdiction is the potential for domestic cultivation. Domestic marijuana growing is already widespread and becoming more sophisticated. The number of sinsemilla plants—a more potent form of marijuana—has increased steadily from slightly under 1 million in 1983 to over 2 million in 1989.[57] Sinsemilla plants now account for 40 percent of the cultivated marijuana plants destroyed by law enforcement personnel (up from 26 percent in 1983). The number of indoor cultivation operations seized increased from only 649 in 1984 to 1,398 in 1989. More important, domestic marijuana growers are becoming more sophisticated in their technology to make their crops more productive and powerful.[58] These trends are likely to continue even more rapidly as crop eradication programs become more important in South America.[59]

As interdiction and foreign sources for illicit drugs reduce the supply of drugs into the United States, the profits from domestic cultivation will increase as well. Edward Brecher, for example, notes that while coca plants are now cultivated almost exclusively in the Andean Mountains of Latin America, "there is no botanical reason why, if imports are successfully curtailed hereafter, the bushes cannot also be cultivated in the Rocky Mountains and the Appalachians."[60]

Even opium could be grown commercially in the United States. A Massachusetts study published in 1871 found that

> opium has recently been made from white poppies, cultivated for the purpose, in Vermont, New Hampshire, and Connecticut, the annual production being estimated in hundreds of pounds. . . . Opium has also been brought here from Florida and Louisiana, while comparatively large quantities are regularly sent east from California and Arizona, where its cultivation is becoming an important branch of industry, ten acres or poppies being said to yield, in Arizona, 1,200 pounds of opium.[61]

Moreover, some estimate that the entire demand for heroin in the United States could be satisfied through the cultivation of twenty-five acres of opium. Clearly, domestic cultivators could find enough secluded acreage to profitably grow opium poppies if the profits were high enough.

The Effects of the War on Drugs

The dramatic increases in expenditures in the War on Drugs during the 1980s resulted in higher arrest rates for drug-law violators and more drug seizures of imports and domestic supplies. Newspaper and television journalists across the country report larger and larger caches of drugs seized by local and federal authorities on a weekly and sometimes nightly basis. In Los Angeles in 1989, police discovered a warehouse storing 21.4 tons of cocaine destined for domestic retail markets. One week earlier, 5.5 tons of cocaine were discovered in one raid in Queens, New York, the largest discovery until that time.

Another important element of the War on Drugs has been the seizure of drug trafficking assets. The U.S. Customs Service alone seized over $1.1 billion in assets in 1989.[62] Assets seized through the cannabis eradication program increased to $29.5 million in 1989.[63] Many of these assets are subsequently turned over to local drug enforcement teams to finance further efforts in the War on Drugs.

Viewed from the perspective of drug availability, the war is being lost by law enforcement agencies. While the police can win a battle with each new discovery of a large cache of drugs, arrest of a drug dealer, or arrest of a drug user, their cumulative affect is negligible.

Historically, drug availability is at an all-time high in the United States. Cocaine, heroin, and marijuana are available to anyone willing to pay in most major American cities. Crack has spread to most of the largest cities, although its spread appears to have abated in recent years. Declines in drug use have resulted principally from changes in attitudes among potential users rather than declines in availability or accessibility.[64]

Law enforcement efforts are experiencing some success in some South American countries such as Colombia, but the long-term consequences are likely to be minimal. Even if coca and marijuana plants were completely eliminated from the Andean Mountains and interdiction capable of stopping all drug importation, domestic producers would soon supply recreational drug markets. Drug users have also been willing to substitute drugs according to their availability (e.g., marijuana to heroin among soldiers in Vietnam). Supply-side efforts to curb drug use may force temporary supply shocks to the drug using population, but the long-term prospects for eliminating the market for illicit drugs are extremely low.

A Negative Sum Game

Unfortunately, the effects of the War on Drugs are not neutral. Many consider efforts to enforce drug prohibition as a zero sum game, where any reduction in the supply of drugs should be considered a social benefit weighed only against the resources spent to control drug use and distribution. Attempts to arrest users and traffickers may be, in reality, a negative sum game.

If the demand for drugs continues unabated, restrictions on supply will simply increase the profits to entrepreneurs willing to take the risks necessary to produce and supply drugs on the black market. As the previous chapter indicated, the higher the potential profits are, the more likely drug markets will become violent and socially disruptive. Of course higher profits also represent the increased risks associated with the drug trade, but this simply suggests that the suppliers are less risk-averse than previous participants.

The cost of crime as a consequence of America's drug problem is well-known although misinterpreted. The standard approach is that drug users commit crimes and, therefore, drug users cause crime. Bernard A. Gropper, an experimental psychologist and specialist on the relationship between drug use and crime, recently concluded a review of research on crime and drug abuse by observing,

> perhaps the foremost finding is that heroin abusers, especially daily users, commit an extraordinary amount of crime. These studies reveal a lifestyle that is enveloped in drug use and crime. The major impetus for most of their criminal behavior is the need to obtain heroin or opiates.[65]

In fact, there is a wide body of literature linking trends in drug use and the amount of crime committed. As drug users move into an addictive stage in their life, they tend to commit more crime.[66] Further, daily users and addicts tend to earn the vast majority of their income through crime to sustain their habit.

Yet, as chapter 4 pointed out, the correlation between drug use and crime does not establish causality. There is an important intermediate stage in the analysis that is left out of the standard perspective. If the drug user is capable of sustaining his or her habit through a legitimate income source, participation in illegal activities is restricted to those required to purchase illegal drugs (not the commission of non-drug-related crime). The root of the criminal activity stemming from drug use flows from users' inability to afford their habit.

Ironically, the War on Drugs, which is aimed at reducing the supply of illicit drugs, will if successful drive up prices and increase crime by drug users. According to data compiled by scholars at the Research Triangle Institute in North Carolina, the costs of drug abuse in the United States amounted to $60 billion in 1983, although $33.3 billion was attributed to marijuana. While the data is outdated, the breakdown of costs is useful for understanding the importance of crime as an inherent part of America's drug problem.

FIGURE 7.11
Discounted Costs of Drug Abuse

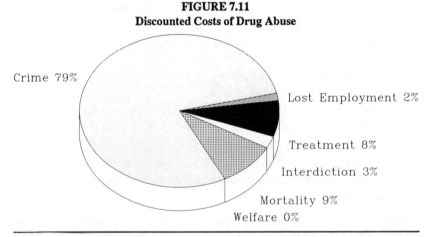

Source: James Ostrowski, "Thinking About Drug Legalization," *Policy Analysis No. 121* (Washington, D.C.: Cato Institute, May 1989, p. 20.

James Ostrowski revised the costs of drug abuse in the research triangle study, excluding the costs for marijuana for methodological reasons.[67] Based on total costs of drug abuse of $26.4 billion in 1983, almost 80 percent of the discounted costs are attributable to crime alone (fig. 7.11). All other categories pale in comparison to the importance of crime in understanding the drug problem in the United States. The emphasis of law enforcement personnel on arresting and incarcerating criminals is understandable in this context. But, to the extent current policy artificially raises prices, making the acquisition of illicit drugs expensive, criminality is an artifact of drug prohibition rather than drug use.

Attempts to reduce the supply of illicit drugs may also be contributing to the demandside of the drug problem. A survey of 13,711 inmates in state prisons conducted in 1986 by the U.S. Bureau of Justice Statistics found that most had first used a major drug *after* their first arrest (fig. 7.12).[68] While only 9 percent reported first use of a major drug in the year preceding and succeeding their arrest, 43 percent reported their first drug use one or more years after their first arrest. Incarceration may be associated with increased drug use rather than reduced drug use.[69]

FIGURE 7.12
First Use of a Major Drug Compared to First Arrest for State Inmates, 1986

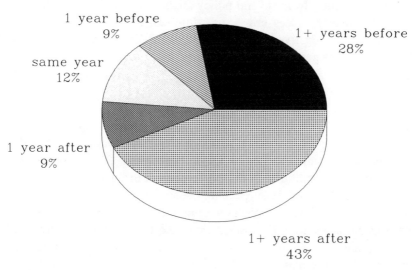

Source: C.A. Innes, "Drug Use and Crime," *Bureau of Justice Statistics Special Report* (Washington, D.C.: U.S. Department of Justice, July 1988), 5.

Moreover, the War on Drugs appears to have had little effect on drug availability. According to the National Institute on Drug Abuse's ongoing survey of high school seniors, the availability of all major drugs increased throughout the 1980s. The proportion of high school students indicating cocaine was "very easy" or "fairly easy" to obtain increased from 47.9 percent in 1980 to 58.7 percent in 1989. Crack, a late arrival to the drug scene, also increased in availability: 40 percent of seniors polled in 1987 found easy access to crack compared to 47 percent in 1989.[70]

Not only does the criminal justice system run the risk of increasing drug use, the current strategy is undermining the institutional foundations for peaceful and progressive community development. By encouraging the breakdown of the rule of law and the respect for private property rights, current drug policy may promote poverty by increasing drug-related crime. Most inner cities suffer because their residents are victims of crime. Most people, for example, are killed or victimized by people within their own neighborhood ("predatory street criminals").[71] Crime prevents investment in inner-city neighborhoods by threatening property values, endangering lives, and increasing the costs of doing business in the city. The role crime plays in creating poverty has received substantial attention recently from several policy analysts attempting to determine whether poverty causes crime, or crime causes poverty.[72] This book argues that the negative effects of crime on urban development can also be traced to the general weakening of private property rights discussed in chapter 3.

Economics, Drugs and Public Policy

The data present in this and previous chapters strongly suggests that current drug control strategies are not working. Despite substantial increases in expenditures on drug enforcement through the 1980s, little headway has been made in reducing the supply or demand for drugs in the United States. Any decreases in drug use have occurred as a result of general shifts in attitudes toward drug use rather than the effects of targeted antidrug programs sponsored by federal, state, and local law enforcement programs.

Dissent and Consensus on Drug Policy

This chapter has presented evidence indicating that supply-side strategies aimed at cutting off the inflow of drugs into domestic markets are, ultimately, doomed to failure. In essence, there are too many alternatives available to importers and traffickers to significantly affect long-run availability. Large-scale crackdowns on drug production and distribution are difficult to sustain over long periods of time. As one DEA agent observed about the recent crackdown in Colombia, "unless the pressure is continuous, there will be no long-term impact."[73] U.S. experience should confirm that long-term commitments to programs are virtually impossible to maintain.

Moreover, consensus does not exist on the proper drug control strategy on any level of government. While most people are convinced that drugs are inherently "bad" and should not be encouraged, large numbers of Americans routinely use them. In the case of alcohol, consumption is so ingrained in American culture that few argue for alcohol prohibition.

Several different drug control strategies are possible. The current strategy focuses on complete prohibition of select drugs for recreational use. These drugs are determined, for the most part, politically, with little concern for medical opinion on their mentally or physically damaging qualities. As this book has demonstrated, a policy of prohibition is virtually impossible to implement successfully.

The prohibition policy is even harder to maintain given the lack of consensus among the public and the law enforcement agencies responsible for drug law enforcement on the overall importance of the drug problem. A recent survey of 100 police chiefs across the nation revealed some surprising differences between law enforcement personnel and the general public when they ranked the importance of eighty separate crimes, including several drug crimes.[74]

The police chiefs ranked selling heroin as the seventeenth most serious crime, while an earlier survey of the general public in Baltimore (using the same list of crimes) ranked selling heroin first. Manufacturing and selling drugs known to be harmful to users was ranked twenty-first among police chiefs compared to thirteenth for the general public. Using heroin was ranked thirty-second among police chiefs compared to the ranking of fifteenth for the public. Generally speaking, drug offenses were considered less serious among police chiefs compared to the general public. On the other hand, police chiefs considered drug crimes a more serious offense than prosecutors, public defenders, probation officers, and criminal trial judges.

On most other offenses, the studies showed remarkable consensus among the survey populations. Thus, the authors conclude,

Our findings indicate that in their responses, the nation's police chiefs appear to be very much in accord with a previous sampling of public opinion in Baltimore almost a decade ago, as well as with a more recent study of criminal justice bureaucrats in a large midwestern city. The strongest variation between public and professional opinion about the seriousness of offenses concerned the sale and use of heroin, a matter which may reflect either growing tolerance, or tactical surrender, in regard to such behavior.[75]

The views of law enforcement personnel are weakening on the importance of drugs on other levels as well. A survey of police attitudes in Montgomery and Prince Georges counties in Maryland revealed that about 30 percent of their police officers favored decriminalization of marijuana.[76] Seventy-five percent of the officers surveyed said they felt laws for the possession of less than one ounce of marijuana were not actively enforced. Only 45 percent indicated that laws for possession of more than one ounce were actively enforced.

Notes on Public Policy and Alcohol Consumption

Some insights from the experience of national and state-level alcohol policy may help provide insight in determining the proper role of public policy. The most extreme policy option, prohibition, was attempted briefly in the 1920s and repealed in 1933. Alcohol prohibition was repealed, however, not because public policy was unable to affect consumption or the alcoholic beverage industry. Alcohol prohibition was repealed because the effects of a prohibitionist policy outweighed the costs of allowing alcohol to be consumed through a regulated policy framework.

Indeed, a recent analysis of alcohol consumption before, during, and after Prohibition reveals that legalization did not significantly increase consumption levels.[77] While the initial effect of Prohibition was to reduce alcohol consumption by two-thirds, consumption levels rose to betweeen 60 and 70 percent of pre-Prohibition levels throughout the 1920s. Consumption rose to 65 percent of pre-Prohibition levels by 1925 and to 71 percent by 1929. A comparison with alcohol consumption in the 1920s to the period 1937 to 1940 reveals that alcohol consumption levels remained approximately equal. Thus, Prohibition had an immediate, but not enduring impact, on the level of alcohol consumption.

Another twenty-five year study of alcoholic beverage restrictions on the state level between 1955 and 1980 reveals more important information with respect to the role of public policy.[78] The researchers found that the price of the beverage had the strongest impact on consumption during the period studied. They also found that certain regulatory variables such as the number of outlets and the method of licensing could impact consumption levels within states. More traditional variables such as advertising, hours of the day, and the drinking age had little or no effect.

This evidence shows that prohibition may not work if the goal is to eliminate drug use altogether. While proponents of alcohol prohibition may point to the *relative* success of the laws in their first years, the long-term effect was substantially weaker. *Public policy was unable to eliminate the market for alcohol.* Similarly, public policy has been unable to eliminate the market for illicit substance such as heroin, cocaine, and marijuana. Moreover, public policy was able to influence consumption largely through its impact on price.

The lesson from this era is not that public policy is ineffective. On the contrary, public policy has a significant impact on black markets for illegal products. Prohibition allowed alcohol distribution to become more concentrated in the hands of organized crime and allowed distilleries to avoid careful regulation of their product's quality.

Thus, what is important is *the way* public policy influences the market for illegal products. Policy has important implications for determining the structure and characteristics of an industry. A prohibitionist policy explicitly rejects any regulatory role for the industry even though a regulatory strategy appears to have the most profound impact on the consumption and structure of the industry.

The Contemporary Drug Policy Strategy

The proper role of public policy in addressing the nation's drug problem is difficult and complex. Proposals offered by the Bush administration included a $10.5 billion effort to stem drugs.[79] Forty-two percent of the money ($4.3 billion) would be allocated to domestic law enforcement, another 29 percent (about $3.7 billion) would be earmarked for interdiction and international drug control efforts, and 29 percent (about $3 billion) was to be allocated for education, treatment, and research. The proposed plan would significantly increase penalties for drug violations (including a death-penalty provision for drug kingpins) and expand prison capacity by at least six thousand new beds.

Mayors, on the other hand, want to see more money spent on drug treatment, opting for a plan presented by Senator Joseph Biden (D-Delaware). Biden's plan proposes spending of $14.6 billion, concentrating on treating addicts, education, and assisting foreign government drug eradication programs. The plan calls for the addition of 400,000 new places in drug treatment programs with a concentration on pregnant addicts and children.

Drug prohibition, however, is unlikely to solve what now constitutes the nation's drug problem. The drug problem is no longer simply the costs of drug addiction and resulting behavior. Rather the costs associated with the trappings of prohibition—crime and violence—have eclipsed drug addiction as the central problem with drug use in the nation. As a result, continued efforts to use law enforcement to stop the flow and distribution of drugs into domestic markets and reduce demand for drugs by arresting users is likely to compound the problem rather than solve it.

This does not mean that drug prohibition will not reduce the aggregate consumption of illicit substances. Indeed, current law enforcement programs may be able to increase the cost of using drugs sufficiently to deter some from experimenting with drugs.[80] The consequences of these policies, however, are to raise the prices to addicts and nonaddicts willing to pay the price for recreational drug use.

The result, as the events of the 1980s have demonstrated, is a highly profitable and violent drug trade. "Drug-related crime" has become the single largest result of the War on Drugs. As the next chapter will attempt to demonstrate, eliminating drug crime will only be accomplished by pursuing policies that are more sensitive to the problems of the drug user rather than to the entrepreneurial desires of drug traffickers.

Notes

1. Data taken from Frank Greve, "Cocaine Prices Show Success of Drug War, U.S. says," *Dayton Daily News*, 29 June 1990, sec. A, p. 5. See also Guy Gugliotta, "Drug Wars—Hey, We're Winning," *Washington Post*, 11 February 1990, sec. C, p. C1.
2. Sharyn Wizda, "Wholesale Price Up, Purity Down for Cocaine, Official Says," *Dayton Daily News*, 18 July, 1990, sec. D, p. 14.
3. Greve, "Cocaine Prices," 5.
4. Michael deCourcy Hinds, "States Are Seeking Tougher Laws on Seizing Property in Drug Cases," *New York Times* 16 July 1990, sec. C, p. 10.
5. "Citizens Can Tell on Drug Suspects by Filling Out W. Virginia Coupons," *Dayton Daily News* 18 July 1990, sec. D, p. 14.
6. "2 Warriors Fight Urban Drug War: Despite Bounty, Hot Line Founder Seeks 'Merry' Life," *USA Today* 19 December 1989, sec. A, p. 2.
7. In fact, the consensus among historians of narcotics control laws places heavy emphasis on the racial overtones of early regulations. See Edward M. Brecher,

"Drug Laws and Drug Law Enforcement: A Review and Evaluation Based on 111 Years of Experience," in *Perspectives on Drug Use in the United States*, ed. Bernard Segal (New York: Haworth Press, 1986), 1-27; David F. Musto, *The American Disease: Origins of Narcotic Control*, exp. ed. (New York: Oxford University Press, 1987).

8. Brecher, "Drug Laws," 5.
9. Musto, *The American Disease*, 244.
10. Ibid., 244-45.
11. An excellent review of the various marijuana commissions from the Indian Hemp Drugs Commission Report in 1894 to the LaGuardia Committee Report in 1944 to the National Commission on Marijuana and Drug Abuse is contained in Edward M. Brecher et al., *Licit and Illicit Drugs* (Boston: Little, Brown & Company, 1972), 451-72.
12. Musto, *The American Disease*, 220. Technically, however, marijuana is not a narcotic. It was classified as a narcotic for purely political reasons.
13. Ibid., p. 223.
14. Brecher et al., *Licit and Illicit Drugs*, 416-18.
15. Ibid., 418.
16. Ibid., 419-21.
17. The calculations were made by Arnold S. Trebach, an internationally recognized expert on heroin policy and someone heavily involved in the debate over the CPRA. A review of the events surrounding this legislation can be found in Arnold S. Trebach, *The Great Drug War* (New York: Macmillan, 1986), 295-97.
18. Ibid.
19. Ibid., 297.
20. Musto, *The American Disease*, 260.
21. Ibid., 247.
22. Timothy J. Flanagan and Kathleen Maguire, eds., *Sourcebook of Criminal Justice Statistics 1989* (Washington, D.C.: U.S. Department of Justice, Bureau of Justice Statistices, Government Printing Office, 1990), 118-19, tables 1.101-1.102.
23. Ibid., 425, table 4.5.
24. Ibid., 433, table 4.10.
25. Ibid., 492-93, table 5.17.
26. Ibid., 502, table 5.23.
27. Ibid., 503, table 5.24.
28. Allen J. Beck, "Profile of Jail Inmates, 1989," *Bureau of Justice Statistics Special Report* (Washington, D.C.: U.S. Department of Justice, Bureau of Justice Statistics, 1991), 4.
29. *New York State Drug Strategy*, report prepared for the Drug Control and System Improvement Formula Grant Program, U.S. Department of Justice, p. 12.
30. Flanagan and Maguire, *Sourcebook*, 456-57, table 4.32.
31. Wisconsin Statistical Analysis Center, Milwaukee, Wisconsin, report prepared for the Drug Control and System Improvement Forumula Grant Program, U.S. Department of Justice, n.p.
32. *New York State Drug Strategy*, p. 12.
33. *State of Illinois Application and Statewide Strategy to Control Drug and Violent Crime*, report prepared for the Drug Control and System Improvement Formula Grant Program, U.S. Department of Justice, January 1990.
34. Flanagan and Maguire, *Sourcebook*, 445, table 4.16.

35. Peter Reuter, Robert MacCoun, and Patrick Murphy, *Money From Crime: A Study of the Economics of Drug Trafficking in Washington, D.C.* (Santa Monica, Calif.: RAND Corporation, 1990), 30.
36. Pennsylvania Commission on Crime and Delinquency, *Pennsylvania Statewide Drug Control and Systems Improvement Strategy: Federal Fiscal Year 1990*, report prepared for the Drug Control and System Improvement Formula Grant Program, U.S. Department of Justice, p. 46.
37. Data taken from DEA, *1989 Domestic Cannabis Eradication/Supression Program* (Washington, D.C.: U.S. Department of Justice, 1990), 7.
38. The price of marijuana, however, has varied more significantly through the 1980s. In 1984, a pound of marijuana on the wholesale market cost between $400 and $600. By 1989, reported prices ranged from $350 to $2,000. Similarly, retail prices for an ounce had moved from $50 to $100 in 1985 to $20 to $225 in 1989. See DEA, *1989 Domestic Cannabis*; National Narcotics Intelligence Consumers Committee (NNICC), *The Supply of Illicit Drugs in the United States*, April 1988, p. 9.
39. The survey was conducted after a 1986 survey revealed that marijuana availability had declined in the last quarter of the year according to fourteen of the nineteen divisional offices. See the discussion in DEA, *1987 Domestic Cannabis Eradication/Suppression Program* (Washington, D.C.: U.S. Department of Justice, 1987), 20.
40. NNICC, *Supply of Illicit Drugs*, 33.
41. Joint Federal Task Force of the DEA, EPA, and Coast Guard, *Guidelines for the Cleanup of Clandestine Drug Laboratories*, March 1990, p. 1.
42. Data are from the DEA reported in Flanagan and Maguire, *Sourcebook*, 470.
43. NNICC, *Supply of Illicit Drugs*, 26.
44. DEA, "From the Source to the Street: Current Prices for Cannabis, Cocaine, and Heroin," *Intelligence Trends* 16, no. 2 (1989): 6.
45. A journalistic review of these events and issues can be found in Thomas McCarroll, "The Supply-Side Scourge: Cocaine is So Abundant that Interdiction Fails to Affect Prices," *Time*, 13 November 1989, p. 81.
46. Steven Wisotsky, *Beyond the War on Drugs: Overcoming a Failed Public Policy* (Buffalo, N.Y.: Prometheus Books, 1990), 65.
47. Brecher, "Drug Laws," 11; See also Brecher et al.
48. Peter Reuter and Mark Kleiman, "Risks and Prices: An Economic Analysis of Drug Enforcement," in *Crime and Justice: An Annual Review of Research*, vol. 7, ed., Michael Tonry and Norval Morris (Chicago: University of Chicago Press, 1986), 317, table 6.
49. Ibid., 317.
50. Brecher et al., *Licit and Illicit Drugs*, 434-50.
51. DEA, "Drug Trafficking and Availability in the State of Arizona," *Intelligence Trends* 16, no. 1 (1989): 16; see also Arizona Criminal Justice Commission, *Arizona Drug Enforcement Strategy 1990*, report submitted to the U.S. Department of Justice's Drug Control and System Improvement Formula Grant Program.
52. Louisiana Commission on Law Enforcement and Administration of Criminal Justice, *Louisiana Strategy and Program Application, January 1990*, report submitted to Drug Control and System Improvement Formula Grant Program, U.S. Department of Justice.
53. Reuter and Kleiman, "Risks and Prices," 320-21.
54. See NNICC, *The Supply of Illicit Drugs to the United States from Foreign and Domestic Sources in 1985 and 1986*, June 1987, pp. 9-10.

55. NNICC Report, *The Supply of Illicit Drugs in the United States, 1988.*
56. Reuter and Kleiman, "Risks and Prices," 321. See also the discussion of drug smuggling in Paul Eddy, Hugo Sabogal, and Sara Walden, *The Cocaine Wars* (New York: Bantam Books, 1988), 97-114.
57. DEA, *1989 Domestic Cannabis*, p. 7.
58. NNICC, *The Supply of Illicit Drugs in the United States, 1988*, p. 11.
59. According to the DEA, Colombia has eradicated as much as 65 percent of its domestic marijuana crop. This made the United States the world's second largest producer of marijuana behind Mexico. DEA, *1989 Domestic Cannabis*, p. 4.
60. Brecher, "Drug Laws," p. 24.
61. Quoted in ibid., p. 23.
62. Flanagan and Maguire, *Sourcebook*, 523.
63. DEA, *1989 Domestic Cannabis*, p. 16.
64. Trends and attitudes about drug use and availability were discussed more thoroughly in chapter 4. See Lloyd D. Johnston, Patrick M. O'Malley, and Jerald G. Bachman, *National Trends in Drug Use and Related Factors Among American High School Students and Young Adults, 1975-1986* (Washington, D.C.: National Institute on Drug Abuse, 1987), 118-53.
65. Bernard A. Gropper, "Probing the Links Between Drugs and Crime," *National Institute of Justice Research in Brief* (Washington, D.C.: U.S. Department of Justice, 1985), 5.
66. Examples of some of these studies include Bruce D. Johnson, Paul J. Goldstein, Edward Preble et. al., *Taking Care of Business: The Economics of Crime by Heroin Abusers* (Lexington, Mass.: Lexington Books/D.C. Heath, 1983); David N. Nurco, John W. Shaffer, John C. Ball, and Timothy W. Kinlock, "Trends in the Commission of Crime Among Narcotics Addicts over Successive Periods of Addiction and Nonaddiction," *American Journal of Drug and Alcohol Abuse* 10, no. 4 (1984): 481-89; David N. Nurco, John D. Ball, John W. Shaffer et al., "A Comparison of Race/Ethnicity of Narcotic Addict Crime Rates in Baltimore, New York, and Philadelphia," *American Journal of Drug and Alcohol Abuse* 12, no. 4 (1986): 297-307.
67. These data omit the $33.3 billion in costs associated with marijuana. See James Ostrowski, "Thinking About Drug Legalization," *Policy Analysis No. 121* (Washington, D.C.: Cato Institute, 1989), 18-20.
68. Major drugs were defined as cocaine, heroin, PCP, LSD or methadone. Other drugs were marijuana, amphetamines, barbituates, methaqualone or other drugs. Data taken from Christopher A. Innes, "Drug Use and Crime," *Bureau of Justice Statistics Special Report* (Washington, D.C.: U.S. Department of Justice, Bureau of Justice Statistics, 1988), 4-6.
69. Incarceration may contribute to a convict's life-style, which is associated with drug use. Recent research has indicated that a drug user's lifestyle may have important consequences for the types of the drugs they use and the intensity of their use. See Eugenie Walsh Flaherty, Lynne Kotranski, and Elaine Fox, "Frequency of Heroin Use and Drug Users' Life-style," *American Journal of Drug and Alcohol Abuse* 10, no. 2 (1984): 285-314.
70. Flanagan and Maguire, *Sourcebook*, 193, table 2.72.
71. John Iulio, Jr., "The Impact of Inner-city Crime," *The Public Interest* 96 (Summer 1989): 28-46.
72. See James K. Stewart, "The Urban Strangler: How Crime Causes Poverty in the Inner City," *Policy Review* no. 37 (Summer 1986): 6-10; Carl F. Horowitz, "An

Empowerment Strategy for Eliminating Neighborhood Crime," Heritage Foundation *State Backgrounder*, no. 814 (25 March 1991).
73. Quoted in Judy Keen, "Cocaine War Fallout Hits U.S. Borders," *USA Today* 29 August 1989, sec. A, p. 1.
74. Henry N. Pontell, Daniel Granite, Constance Keenan, and Gilbert Geis, "Seriousness of Crimes: A Survey of the Nation's Chiefs of Police," *Journal of Criminal Justice* 13, no. 1 (1985): 1-13.
75. Ibid., 12.
76. Kenneth H. Beck and Terry G. Summons, "Police Officer Attitudes Toward Marijuana: A Replication and Confirmation," *American Journal of Drug and Alcohol Abuse* 10, no. 3 (1984): 519-28.
77. Jeffrey A. Miron and Jeffrey Zwiebel, "Alcohol Consumption During Prohibition," *American Economic Review* 81, no. 2 (May 1991): 242-47.
78. Joan F. Hoadley, Beth C. Fuchs, and Harold D. Holder, "The Effect of Alcohol Beverage Restrictions on Consumption: A 25-Year longitudinal Analysis," *American Journal of Drug and Alcohol Abuse* 10, no. 3 (1984): 375-401.
79. Data and program breakdowns taken from the Cox News Service reported in Julia Malone and Mike Christensen, "Bush Targets Traffickers; Mayors Focus on Treatment," *Dayton Daily News* 6 January 1990, sec A, pp. 1, 4.
80. An early and influential article by Mark Moore argued that the "optimal" public policy would discourage new drug users while not punishing existing addicts who would be unresponsive to price changes. See Mark H. Moore, "Policies to Achieve Discrimination on the Effective Price of Heroin," *American Economic Review* 63, no. 2 (May 1973): 270-77.

8

The Decriminalization Alternative

The previous chapters have focused largely on the results of a prohibitionist policy concerning the most popular illicit drugs: marijuana,
cocaine, and heroin. Despite billions of dollars spent in reducing the
supply of drugs and incarcerating millions of drug users, public policy
has been unable to reduce accessibility to these drugs over the long run.

In the meantime, the illicit drug industry has become a growth industry
in American cities. High profits, induced by a supply-side oriented drug
policy, have attracted tens of thousands of low-skilled, undereducated,
youth into a violent industry that threatens to rip apart the social fabric
of inner-city neighborhoods. The widespread use of force and rejection
of the rule of law is undermining the very institutions necessary to sustain
long-term economic growth.

Moreover, trends in contemporary urban policy reenforce this breakdown of institutions by encouraging the breakdown of the rule of law in
the legitimate economy. While the aboveground economy lacks the
violent characteristics of the drug trade, personal politics is becoming
more important than the adherence to basic rules that protect people and
businesses from the arbitrary will of politics. The rising authority of the
local state is contributing to a parallel degeneration of the institutions
necessary for promoting economic growth.

Public policy plays a vital role in providing an environment capable
of nurturing economic development. Current drug policy is inconsistent
with obtaining more far-reaching goals such as establishing a framework
that allows cities to prosper. Rather than reduce the threat of the drug

217

economy to America's central cities, current drug policy enhances it. Ultimately, the only solution will be to significantly reduce the influence of a violent drug trade in the social and economic environment of the city.

Toward a Demand-Oriented Drug Policy

While the United States is far from a "nation of addicts," it has certainly become a nation of drug users. Over 100 million people use alcohol (the most abused drug) and over 50 million use tobacco. In addition, almost 30 million use marijuana, 6 million use cocaine, and almost 1 million use heroin. These categories, of course, are not strictly additive. Almost all of those who use illicit substances also drink and smoke. These numbers, then, may actually overstate drug use since they ignore the proportion of multiple drug users (people who smoke and drink, or use cocaine and drink, etc.). Moreover, as previous chapters have emphasized, drug use does not imply drug addiction, nor drug abuse.

American drug policy has concentrated almost completely on the supply-side, focusing on interdiction, crop reduction strategies in foreign countries, and the incarceration of drug traffickers. On the local level, law enforcement agencies have emphasized drug trafficking and intra-state interdiction.

Demand-side strategies have almost exclusively been directed at incarcerating users for possession. In the early days of the drug war, these efforts relied on a "buy and bust" strategy. More recently, private and public agency drug testing programs have been implemented to increase the personal risks of drug use. Testing positive for drug use can lead to unemployment or, in some cases, jail.

Virtually every observer of the drug war acknowledges that an exclusively supply-side strategy will not work. In fact, most contemporary observers acknowledge current drug control strategies are largely ineffective. Part II of this book has been devoted to detailing the failures and consequences of this strategy.

In this chapter, the data and arguments of previous sections will be marshaled to propose an alternative strategy: decriminalization. Decriminalization is not advanced as a panacea for the drug problem, nor as an apology for drug addicts. On the contrary, decriminalization is proposed as a fundamental shift in strategy from a supply-side approach to a demand-side approach more consistent with the political, economic, and cultural traditions of the United States. The shift, the argument goes, will provide a better foundation for public policy as a first step toward a solution.

Both proponents and opponents of decriminalization have raised important issues with respect to the consequences of this strategic shift in public policy. The following discussion will delineate the major issues and controversies using the discussions of previous chapters to evaluate them. While this analysis supports decriminalization, the issues and points raised by both sides suggests a deep philosophical schism that will significantly influence their policy recommendations and negate the possibility of a "middle ground."

Decriminalization as a Policy Option

The prospects for significant decriminalization appears slim in the early 1990s. Yet, a "legalization debate" sprouted during the late 1980s that has legitimized serious discussion of the topic. The effects of drug trafficking emerged as one of the preeminent concerns in public opinion and public policy. As the War on Drugs failed to produce significant results (e.g., decreases in crime rates, supplies of drugs, etc.), dissenters from the current prohibitionist strategy emerged in the public debate.

Conservative icon William F. Buckley endorsed legalization in 1985, beginning what seems to be a steadily rising tide in favor of the movement. By the 1990s, "thinking the unthinkable" became standard fare in drug policy debates.[1] Other "legalizers" include San Jose police chief Joseph McNamara, Baltimore mayor Kurt Schmoke, former secretary of state George Shultz, Arnold Trebach of the Drug Policy Foundation, and federal judge Robert Sweet, although numerous others have endorsed a national debate on the topic.

The legalization movement is distinctive, gaining notoriety through support from nonliberal sectors of the political landscape. Political conservatives have joined with civil libertarians in the growing call for decriminalization of major drugs. Buckley, for example, switched his original position favoring drug prohibition (for heroin in the 1970s) to comprehensive legalization in the 1980s. Economists Milton Friedman, Thomas Sowell, and the influential *Economist* magazine have also taken public positions in favor of legalization. The Cato Institute, a rising star among Washington public policy "think tanks," has developed an active policy research agenda exploring the decriminalization of drugs.

Of course, legalization advocates have been around for decades. Milton Friedman has been advocating drug legalization since the early 1970s, when a widespread movement surfaced to decriminalize marijuana. In 1975, the state of Alaska effectively legalized small amounts of marijuana by interpreting the state's constitutional protection of privacy to include the cultivation and use of marijuana for personal use. Currently, eleven states have decriminalized the possession and use of marijuana by reducing punishment and sentencing. Even predating this movement, however, libertarians have argued that the decision to use drugs was personal and should not be a concern of government.

The biggest boost for the legalization movement may have come in 1988, when Baltimore mayor Kurt Schmoke advocated decriminalization. A former prosecutor, Schmoke argued that decriminalization should at least be part of a national debate on the future of drug policy. The weight of a big-city mayor, grappling with the drug problems in the "trenches" of America's inner cities, placed enough pressure on Congress that hearings were held on drug legalization in 1988.

Intellectually, legalization received a boost from a young academic at Princeton University. Ethan Nadelmann wrote several influential articles in the periodicals *Foreign Policy, Science, The Public Interest,* and *The New Republic* that significantly improved the respectability of pro-legalization advocates. As the legalization movement gained grudging popular acceptance, early advocates of decriminalization such as Arnold Trebach (a moderate by contemporary standards) found an increasingly receptive audience.

Despite its high media profile, decriminalization represents an ad hoc collection of proposals. Some proponents intend to legalize only the use and sale of marijuana. Others advocate the comprehensive legalization of all psychoactive substances. Still other variations of decriminalization argue for the legalization of use and possession, but not trafficking in large amounts of drugs. Indeed, a significant weakness of the "legalization movement" according to its opponents, has been its lack of consensus concerning a practical policy position.

None of the advocates of drug decriminalization suggest that their approach will "solve" the drug problem. Rather, they advocate legalization as a first step toward a better and more effective public policy. In addition, few advocates propose legalization in desperation. On the contrary, most proponents have arrived at their position after careful reflection on the problem and the role of public policy. Decriminalization represents an approach to looking at the drug problem rather than a schedule of specific policy recommendations. As Ethan Nadelmann observes,

> In its broadest sense . . . legalization incorporates the many arguments and growing sentiment for de-emphasizing our traditional reliance on criminal justice resources to deal with drug abuse and for emphasizing instead drug abuse, prevention, treatment, and education, as well as noncriminal restrictions on the availability and use of psychoactive substances and positive inducements to abstain from drug abuse.[2]

Thus, decriminalization represents a *strategic shift* in drug policy away from treating drug abuse as a law enforcement problem to treating drug abuse as a behavioral problem. In this sense, decriminalization represents a *policy shift* from the supply-side strategy dominating the War on Drugs to a demand-side strategy emphasizing the human and social consequences of drug abuse.

Ultimately, use becomes a social problem when drugs are abused, becoming privately and socially disruptive. Like alcohol, the major drugs—marijuana, cocaine, and heroin—can be used without this use inevitably leading to addiction or socially disruptive behavior. Ultimately, the causes of drug abuse, as chapter 4 detailed, are far more complex than the legal system is capable of addressing. Decriminalization proposes a more realistic foundation and informed attitude toward drug use, focusing on the harms of abuse (rather than mere use) and addiction.

A move toward decriminalization requires that public policy toward illicit drugs be reconstituted on a fundamentally different foundation. Rather than focusing on which drugs would be legalized and how they would be regulated, the decriminalization alternative focuses on how drug abuse is viewed and interpreted through the legal system and public policy. Drug decriminalization acknowledges that addicts cannot be cured by throwing them in jail. The current law enforcement system virtually ignores the complexities of addiction and other behavioral aspects of drug use, such as the psychological and social profile of the individual and the family context.

On the supply side, the decriminalization alternative acknowledges that the "drug trade" is an economic development issue and problem. The drug trade like much black-market activity, flourishes in poverty and economic deprivation. By removing the profits from the drug trade, American cities can more effectively address inner-city development problems, particularly in minority communities.

Arguments for Decriminalization

Arguments for the decriminalization of drug use in the United States claim several origins. This, in part, reflects the diversity of backgrounds from which legalizers and decriminalizers have emerged. Some, such as Arnold Trebach, have extensive clinical and academic experience in drug treatment and policy analysis. Others, such as Ira Glasser of the American Civil Liberties Union and Steven Wisotsky of the NOVA Law School in Florida, approach the subject from a civil libertarian and legal background. Still others, such as Mayor Kurt Schmoke, Judge Robert Sweet, and Police Chief Joseph MacNamara, have come to their position after long, bitter experience fighting the War on Drugs in the streets and courts. Although the individuals cannot be lumped together as if they have the same interests and backgrounds, decriminalization arguments can be broken down into at least four broad categories: libertarian, cost-benefit, public health, and economic development.

Many legalizers base their position on a combination of these positions. Many libertarians, for example, will also use a cost-benefit framework for advancing their position. Similarly, public health concerns also implicitly reflect a cost-benefit calculus or consideration for the consequences for economic development. While these categories describe a typology of positions advocating legalization, they do not necessarily represent (accurately) the positions of individual proponents.

A potential fifth category (a popular target among legalization opponents) has been omitted. This category includes those turning to legalization because "nothing else has worked." The desperation argument, in the opinion of this author, does not add significantly to the policy discussion since it ignores the importance of basing public policy on sound principles and an understanding of the phenomenon being addressed. In addition, the desperation argument is a very small part of the larger decriminalization movement, although it appears to be converting larger numbers of people as drug prohibition continues to fall far short of its promises.

The Libertarian Position

One of the oldest arguments favoring decriminalization has come from civil libertarians such as psychiatrist Thomas Szasz[3] who focus on the role government plays in the lives of individual citizens. Constitutionally, every citizen has a right to privacy and the absence of the arbitrary intrusion of government into their personal lives. The War on Drugs directly intervenes into personal life by attempting to control voluntary, noncoercive behavior among citizens even when their behavior does not injure others. Indeed, as other parts of this book have emphasized, drug enforcement is especially difficult precisely because drug trafficking is a voluntary activity and drug use occurs in private.

Ultimately, drug use should remain the province of individual values and the family. Attorney Michael Monson, writing in the libertarian magazine *Reason* notes after reviewing the history of American drug laws,

> The basis for America's labyrinth of drug laws is, in short, the idea that some of us may force our neighbors not to engage in noncoercive acts that we deem harmful to them or that do not accord with our view of how citizens should live. It is a doctrine of force, a doctrine of intolerance.[4]

Despite the perceived harmfulness by prohibitionists, drug use is a voluntary activity and unlikely to inflict injury on an uninvolved third party. For libertarians, the only time a role for the state can be justified is when drug use jeopardizes the health and welfare of others (e.g., driving under the influence, assault under the influence, drug use during pregnancy, etc.).

Broadly interpreted, the libertarian argument often parallels more traditional objections to the separation of Church and state embedded in the First Amendment. Issues of morality and religion should not be a concern of the government. As long as drug use is considered a moral issue, the government does not have standing in regulating its use.

The War on Drugs is also leading to the wholesale scrapping of important legal restraints on the powers of the state. Steven Wisotsky, in a detailed and thoroughly researched critique of drug prohibition, concludes that the War on Drugs cannot be won without undermining the principles and traditions forming the core of the American legal system.[5] Already, restraints on the types of evidence permitted in trials, the weakening of the rights of the accused, and the ability of law enforcement personnel to circumvent civil liberties is undermining constitutional guarantees to a fair and proper trial.

Government agencies are liberalizing statutes regulating the power of law enforcement personnel to seize private property, even when the property cannot be directly linked to the commission of a crime. In some cases, the requirement that criminal punishment can be imposed only after someone is proven guilty "beyond reasonable doubt" is retreating to "probable cause." Libertarians further argue that the War on Drugs threatens the civil liberties that provide a stable foundation for democratic government. In the long run, democratic societies cannot afford to wage such a socially destructive (and ultimately divisive) war.

In an open letter to Drug Czar William Bennett, economist and Nobel Laureate Milton Friedman may have summarized the libertarian's worst fears of the end result of the War on Drugs. Writing in the *Wall Street Journal*, Friedman implores,

> Every friend of freedom ... must be as revolted as I am by the prospect of turning the United States into an armed camp, by the vision of jails filled with casual drug users and of an army of enforcers empowered to invade the liberty of citizens on slight evidence. A country in which shooting down unidentified planes "on suspicion" can be seriously considered as a drug-war tactic is not the kind of United States that either you [Bill Bennett] or I want to hand on to future generations.[6]

Given the risks to democratic government, in practice the War on Drugs is a counterproductive exercise of government coercion.

To maintain consistency, libertarians argue that, all psychoactive substances would have to be banned, not just politically unpopular drugs. The prohibition on marijuana, cocaine, and heroin is hypocritical given the widespread acceptance of alcohol and tobacco in American culture. Indeed, the health consequences of alcohol and tobacco loom far larger than currently illicit substances. Since the cultural restrictions on the use of marijuana, cocaine, and heroin are much more severe than for tobacco and alcohol, many libertarians perceive drug prohibition as an attempt to enforce a narrow set of values rather than serious concern over the harms of drug use.

One of the most significant obstacles faced by libertarians is their small numbers. As a voting bloc, libertarians remain a smaller proportion of the American electorate than conservatives (who agree with state intervention on moral issues) and populists (who agree with state intervention on both moral and economic issues) according to recent estimates by pollsters and political scientists. A study of 1980 election results found that libertarians represented less than 20 percent of the voting electorate, although their numbers were growing.[7] Most libertarians tend to be educated, wealthy, and upwardly mobile members of the baby-boom generation. Another study of the California public found that only 14 percent of the voting public could be classified as libertarian.[8]

Cost-Benefit Analysis

The libertarian argument is the oldest argument in favor of decriminalization. The argument that may have had the most impact on current public opinion is the cost-benefit perspective. Many of the most visible advocates of drug decriminalization fall (publically) into this category. In essence, the cost-benefit argument claims that the costs of waging a drug war are simply too high to continue. While these costs may include the abridgement of civil liberties (civil libertarians will also use cost-benefit arguments), they also include the crime and violence associated with drug prohibition, the health-care crisis resulting from contaminated drugs (as a result of poor quality control), the effects on U.S. foreign policy, and the vast sums of money expended on law enforcement.

Among the most prominent cost-benefit decriminalizers might be David Boaz, the executive vice president of the Cato Institute in Washington, D.C.; James Ostrowski, a lawyer in Buffalo, New York; Ethan Nadelman, a professor of public policy at Princeton University; William F. Buckley, Jr., conservative columnist and prominent author; and federal judge Robert Sweet of New York.

William F. Buckley, writing in 1985, may have summed up the attitudes of most legalizers when he noted (as a personal observation),

> It is hardly a novel suggestion to legalize dope. Shrewd observers of the scene have recommended it for years. I am on record as having opposed it in the matter of heroin. The accumulated evidence draws me away from my own opposition, on the purely empirical grounds that what we have now is a drug problem plus a crime problem plus a problem of huge export of capital to the dope-producing countries.[9]

Cost-benefit arguments emphasize the impracticalities of a drug prohibition policy given the physical limitations on jails, prisons, and courts and the geographic limitations on successfully controlling the supply of drugs. Decriminalizers conclude that, ultimately, public expenditures on drug prohibition strategies are a "black hole" for government spending. The only people who gain are employees of law enforcement agencies (if they survive) and the drug traffickers. Richard Cowan, a frequent writer for the conservative political magazine *National Review*, argues that the "narcocracy" is the primary reason drug prohibition persists despite widespread empirical evidence that the policy is a failure.[10]

Ultimately, the costs to society do not warrant the continuation of drug prohibition given the potential benefits of a legalization strategy. David Boaz of the Cato Institute enlists the cost-benefit position as an important supplement to a more general libertarian argument,

> We can either escalate the war on drugs, which would have dire implications for civil liberties and the right to privacy, or find a way to gracefully withdraw. Withdrawal should not be viewed as an endorsement of drug use; it would simply be an acknowledgement that the cost of this war — billions of dollars, runaway crime rates and restrictions on personal freedom — is too high.[11]

Similarly, in a public forum sponsored by the Cato Institute, New York lawyer James Ostrowski suggested that the government study whether prohibition works. Currently, the federal government is spending billions of dollars despite the paucity of evidence that there is any "return" on its investment.[12]

While decriminalizers do not argue that legalizing drugs would solve the problems of drug abuse, they do argue society would reap important benefits by reducing crime and black-market profits and avoiding the wholesale scrapping of the Bill of Rights.

Public Health

A third general category of arguments among the decriminalizers involves public health. The most vocal advocates of this position may be Baltimore mayor Kurt Schmoke and Arnold Trebach. Trebach, founder of the Institute on Drugs, Crime and Justice at American University with offices in Washington, D.C. and London, favors effective decriminalization for drug use and possession. Rather than consider users of illicit drugs "enemies of the state," a more rational approach is to treat addicts and drug abusers.[13] Education and treatment, Trebach believes, is far more effective than making the "drug problem" a "criminal problem" where resources are squandered on ineffective and inhumane supply-side strategies (e.g., interdiction, crop eradication, and arresting small-time dealers).

Baltimore mayor Kurt Schmoke also criticizes the current drug prohibition strategy for treating drug abuse as a criminal problem rather than a health problem. Calling for a drug war led by the surgeon general rather than the attorney general, Schmoke argues that drug abuse will be curtailed only when drug users recognize the dangers of the substances they ingest. Further, throwing addicts in jail will not provide the treatment they need to "kick" their habit. In fact, based on some of the evidence presented in the previous chapter, prison may increase exposure to major drugs.

At a public forum at the Cato Institute in 1989, Schmoke argued that drug abuse should be treated through health and education programs.[14] Tobacco use has declined precipitously because of efforts to educate users on the dangers of smoking. The same approach should be used with currently illicit substances. Schmoke also advocates clean needle exchanges to help prevent the spread of AIDS in inner cities. Most recently, writing in the *American Oxonian*, Mayor Schmoke has called for a drug policy focusing on the "medicalization" of currently illicit substances, which would place decisions over drug use in the hands of the public health system. The public health system would be responsible for regulating the sale and use of drugs based on medical definitions of the drugs "dangerousness."

The most compelling public health argument, however, may be associated with the reduction in crime that would result from decriminalization.[15] Drug prohibition feeds a criminal element that fears itself more than the criminal justice system. The profits gleaned from illicit drug trafficking sparks violence and crime that could be largely eliminated by adopting a comprehensive decriminalization policy.

At its core, the public health approach calls for a comprehensive reorientation of drug policy away from treating abuse and addiction as a legal problem to an education and treatment problem. The current policy, through its focus on criminal justice solutions, ignores the human dimensions of addiction, abuse, and crime.

Economic Development

The final argument for decriminalization emphasizes the economic development consequences of the current drug strategy. With the exception of the present book, this approach to the drug problem has received little systematic attention. Newspapers, television, and some economists have focused on the economics of the drug trade, detailing its multifaceted distribution system, but few have delved deeply into the potential consequences for economic development in cities. This book has attempted to fill that gap and explicate more fully the implications of a thriving illicit drug trade for economic development. The implications of drug prohibition extend far beyond their impact on users and the narrow world of the drug trafficker. They influence the way of life in American inner cities.

Through drug prohibition, public policy has created a vast black market for illicit substances, fueling violence and disrespect for law and human life. These values become an essential element of survival in economically devastated urban areas that offer few legitimate opportunities for employment. When those opportunities exist, as the case of Washington, D.C. clearly illustrates, they are far less attractive (financially) than the potential gains from drug trafficking.

The economic development perspective focuses on the implications of a system that trains young workers in an industry marked by violence and deceit, and transfers them (usually in their mid to late twenties) into the legitimate economy. While many have learned some skills (e.g., accounting, inventory control, supervision), the values are less consistent with the requirements of normal business activity in the legitimate economy.

Moreover, these values are reinforced by a political system that appears increasingly arbitrary as civil liberties and the respect for property are sacrificed for political expediency. Through the abrogation of personal freedoms and liberties engendered by the War on Drugs, the victims of drug prohibition learn that the arbitrary imposition of values and punishment is acceptable and encouraged. The rules governing behavior in the licit and illicit sectors of the economy become a technical, legal differentiation rather than an indication of substantive differences in conduct and behavior.

Drug prohibition works against the best interests of the community by dampening the incentives for its citizens to pursue economically productive and prosperous employment in the legitimate sector. Drug prohibition encourages new entrants into the labor force to emphasize short-term gains through drug trafficking rather than the long-term gains from legitimate employment and occupational training. Ultimately, the current policy is pushing the inner city even further toward economic destruction by weakening the institutional foundations necessary for a productive and prosperous society.

Arguments Opposing Legalization

The decriminalization alternative remains unpopular among most leading scholars and policymakers. Drug Czar William Bennett publicly called the idea "stupid" and suggested that many of its advocates are racist.[16] Others, such as Congresswoman Patricia Schroader (D-Colorado), oppose decriminalization because they fear the United States will become a "nation of addicts."[17] Others, basing their recommendations on more scholarly assessments of the drug problem, oppose legalization because they feel the increase in the number of addicts would not justify the benefits of legalized use.[18]

Like the arguments for decriminalization, general themes are detectable in their opposition. Prohibition proponents argue that the decriminalizers ignore the public health consequences of increased drug use, that legalization will feed the criminal element, and, perhaps most important, society cannot appear to condone or encourage drug use. Each of these propositions will be evaluated through the remainder of this section. Again, these themes represent a conglomeration of individual opinions.

Public Health Consequences of Legalization

Most prohibition proponents emphasize that prohibition works from a public health perspective. Any reduction in the price, either through criminal sanctions or the price system, will increase the number of drug users. The higher levels of drug use inevitably place more burdens on the health care system. Moreover, prohibition proponents note that during alcohol prohibition, diseases associated with alcohol consumption actually declined.

A decriminalization strategy will doom society as the number of addicts increases dramatically. Senator Alfonse D'Amato (R-New York), for example, is quoted as saying legalization would lead to "a society of drug-related zombies."[19] A.M. Rosenthal, a columnist for *The New York*

Times, claims that advocating the legalization of drugs is the same as advocating slavery.[20] By reducing the price of drugs, legalization would induce millions into a life of addiction which, according to Rosenthal, is a virtual state of bondage. Charles Krauthammer, an editor for the *New Republic*, summarized the argument when he wrote, "In order to undercut the black market, legalization must radically reduce the price of drugs. And the price of drugs is the surest predictor of use. Drugs are like any other commodity, the lower the price, the higher the consumption."[21] Ultimately, prohibitionists say, the drug problem would become much worse if legalization were effective. Moreover, even though alcohol and tobacco are legalized, their legal status does not support legalizing another harmful substance.

James A. Inciardi, director of the Division of Criminal Justice at the University of Delaware and a leading opponent of legalization, suggests that the very mechanism legalizers rely on to reduce the harms of drug use will exacerbate them. One of the most "powerful aspects of American tradition," Inciardi notes, is "the ability of an entrepreneurial market system to create, expand, and maintain high levels of demand."[22]

Inciardi notes that a very small proportion of the total population are current users of drugs (12 percent for marijuana and 3 percent for cocaine). Rather than taking this as evidence that there are cultural restraints on drug use, Inciardi sees these low levels of drug consumption as an indication of how much the market for currently illicit drugs could be expanded. Since over 50 million people smoke and and over 100 million use alcohol, the belief that drug use would remain at currently low levels is "naive." "Moreover," he continues, "it considerably underestimates the advertising industry's ability to create a context of use that appears integral to a meaningful, successful, liberated life."[23]

The prohibitionists assume, of course, that the primary determinant of drug use is their legal status or the price. In essence, they buy the strict economic argument that price and quantity demanded are inversely related. Indeed, even decriminalizers agree that lower prices will probably increase overall consumption. The point of disagreement revolves around the magnitude. Decriminalizers believe that other factors intervene irrespective of legal status and even price.

Data does not exist capable of deciding this issue once and for all. The evidence presented in this book, however, strongly suggests that the costs of addiction will increase only modestly. If the number of regular cocaine users doubled to 2 to 3 million, the number of deaths resulting from overdose or poor quality would, in all likelihood, remain substantially less than the deaths resulting from drug prohibition. In addition, the effects of cocaine use would still be minimal compared to problems associated with the legal drugs, alcohol, tobacco, and even caffeine. Tobacco alone contributes to the deaths of almost 400,000 people each year. The doubling of the number of cocaine "addicts" (regular users) would require a doubling of the number of users from 10 to 12 million. Moreover, almost none of the evidence on drug use or abuse indicates that reducing the price of any drug, or relegating it to legal status, would double its consumption or the number of users.

In the case of cocaine, the chances of doubling consumption is even less likely since the drug's effects are better known each year. In fact, Lloyd Johnston, an internationally recognized expert on drug use trends, notes that the reason the rate of crack use increased among high school seniors and young adults during the 1980s (to 6 percent in 1987) while marijuana use declined is attributed to differences in the perceived harmfulness of the drug. "Only in '87 did we see for the first time a downturn [in cocaine use], a fairly sharp one for a single year," observes Johnston in an interview in *The Detroit News.*

> I think it's related to a couple of things. One was the deaths of Len Bias and Don Rogers, which certainly got the attention of the country and young people, and I think challenged a cherished belief, which was that you could fool around with cocaine and not run any risk. The other thing was that cocaine really came into media attention. It got a tremendous amount of media attention in mid-to-late 1986.[24]

Johnston describes how the same trend is evident in marijuana use and even crack use. "Certainly we have an epidemic with crack—and it's a serious and important one," he continues. "But I think it could be much worse. The very rapid diffusion of information about the dangers of crack really but a lid on the thing."[25]

Historically, consumers have reacted to information about drugs in dramatic ways. David F. Musto, a historian of drug laws, notes that the Pure Food and Drug Act of 1906 substantially altered the consumption of patent medicines when they were required to list narcotics as ingredients. Within a few years after the Act was passed, "it was estimated that patent medicines containing such drugs dropped in sale by about a third."[26] More recently, consumers have moved steadily toward less potent legal drugs such as light beer, wine coolers, and low-tar cigarettes.

Potential increases in drug use must also be compared to the costs of prohibition. A death resulting from an overdose may have substantially different consequences than a death resulting from a drug-related drive-by shooting. For example, if the government sends a soldier to war and he dies, few claim that the government is a murderer. If, on the other hand, the government kills civilians for reasons unrelated to national security or protecting its citizens, the action is considered murder and the perpetrators tried in criminal proceedings. The standard for evaluating death varies with the circumstances.

Similarly, an addict who dies from an overdose of drugs should not be compared to the gunning down of a nine-year old child as a consequence of a drug market turf battle. The first case, while tragic, is at least controllable by the addict. The addict can choose when he or she will take drugs and from whom the drugs will be bought. To the extent that the drug overdose is due to imperfect information (e.g., there may be no way to test for drug quality), the death may also be a result of a prohibitionist policy that undermines competition aimed at ensuring quality products are placed on the market.

The latter death, however, is a symbol of how the rules of the game have changed and reflects the full force of the current prohibitionist policy. Prohibition engenders violent solutions to solving disputes. The result is a genuine breakdown of law and order and the significant discounting of human life. The death of a nine-year-old child is symptomatic of a shift in how individuals are relating to each other. Even if the child's death is a mistake, it becomes an accepted part of the trade and the risks of living in a drug neighborhood.

In the end, the legalization opponent is not willing to take the risk that the number of addicts will increase. "True, there is a large segment of people who won't find drugs attractive," economist Peter Reuter observes, "but who wants to take the risk of seeing whether the number of those who want drugs is 500% greater than now, rather than only 50% greater."[27] Two other scholars, John Kaplan and Mark Kleiman, reach similar conclusions in their studies of heroin and marijuana policy. Yet, as this book has emphasized, drug users are not the only victims of the drug trade.

Feeding the Criminal Element

A second argument advanced by decriminalization opponents is that legalizing the distribution of drugs would actually feed criminals and drug cartels. "What seems at least as likely," writes *Washington Post* columnist William Raspberry, "is the development of drug cartels with an interest both in increasing the number of drug users and in maintaining prices at levels that would ensure their profitability."[28] Existing organizations have proven extremely efficient in distributing drugs to consumers and they will likely continue. If drugs are decriminalized, the argument continues, the same people selling drugs now will be selling them later.

The drug cartels and the institutionalized violence seem an indelible characteristic of the drug market. Comprehensive decriminalization will not eliminate the criminals. After all, alcohol prohibition did not create the Mafia. Similarly, the Mafia remains even after Prohibition ended.

Strong empirical and theoretical reasons exist suggesting that this is an unlikely consequence.[29] First, the argument assumes that the behavior tolerated and encouraged in the illegal drug market would persist in a legal drug market. This argument also ignores the importance of public policy in defining the environment, or rules of the game, for economic market activity. Although Prohibition did not create the Mafia, it provided the environment conducive to its growth and the consolidation of a large underworld of violence, corruption and arbitrary personal power. Similarly, as the previous chapters have detailed, prohibition has provided the incentive and fuel for the growth and consolidation of violent drug cartels. The characteristics of the illegal drug market suggest that it is an inferior system of distribution and production. A decriminalized drug environment would radically alter the character of drug markets. The ability to solve disputes peacefully through the court system would substantially reduce violence in the drug markets. Liquor stores are rarely fortresses. Alcohol is rarely bought or sold in open-air markets on street corners or in school yards.

More important, drug-distribution systems that operate as legitimate businesses would grow and become even more efficient, competing for business by offering better service and better quality products. Accountability exists in illicit drug markets only at the end of a gun (or assault weapon). In legitimate economic markets, accountability is more efficiently implemented through the profit and loss system. Stable and permanent locations are essential to ensure a stable and peaceful clientele and has proven time and time again to be superior to street peddling.

Society Cannot Condone Drug Use

Perhaps the most common argument invoked against decriminalization centers on morality and socially acceptable behavior. Drugs are bad and therefore society should not condone drug use. Anything short of comprehensive prohibition would send the "wrong signals" to children and adults concerning drug use. Government is viewed as a direct representative of the collective will of society.

This argument assumes that citizens take their queues concerning right and wrong from government policy or the legal system. If this were true, the fundamental principles or representative government have been turned on their head. While laws are reflections of culture, democratic governments are established to protect the rights of their citizens. Often times, these rights conflict with broader social concerns. The law, for example, protects the right of the Ku Klux Klan to hold public rallies and demonstrations. This is not interpreted as public support for the goals, objectives and beliefs of the Klan.

In contemporary democratic societies, moral values are not imposed by the state. More important, democratic governments are responsible for protecting individual rights rather than the collective rights of specific interest groups. While the government enforces the law, it cannot pass judgement on the correctness of the law.

A compelling argument can also be made that prohibition has supported the behavior prohibitionists want to discourage. Richard Cowan has noted that prohibition has created "accidental perversities" in drug consumption.[30] By making drug distribution a risky and expensive undertaking, the unintended consequences of government control have been to encourage the production, marketing and consumption of more potent drugs that can be distributed more easily.

Intensified interdiction efforts encouraged drug traffickers to switch from marijuana, which is bulky and easily detectable, to cocaine, which can be transported in small quantities. The reduction in imported marijuana has resulted in domestic cultivation of more potent strains. Similarly, the army's crackdown on marijuana in Vietnam led to a heroin epidemic. More recently, crack was developed (a technical innovation) as a potent, but cheap alternative to cocaine capable of being marketed in poor sections of America's inner cities. In principle, every naturally grown drug could be substituted for by more potent designer drugs capable of being developed in the crudest chemistry labs. Thus, while consumers are opting for less potent legal drugs, public policy is encouraging the development and distribution of more potent illicit drugs.

Experiences with Drug Tolerance

To some extent, the experiences of other countries may be helpful in disentangling the issues in the continuing debate over drug legalization, decriminalization, and prohibition. A regime of drug legalization does not exist among the current industrialized countries. Most pursue policies of strict prohibition. Thus, good information enabling a comparison of different drug control strategies is unavailable. Nevertheless, some examples of more tolerant attitudes toward drug use exist and, combined with the information provided earlier, some tentative observations may be made to help assess the likely consequences of a demand-oriented, rather than supply-oriented, drug strategy.

Some states have "experimented" with a very limited form of decriminalization of marijuana. After the publication of the National Commission on Marijuana and Drug Abuse in the early 1970s, a substantial political movement emerged favoring the decriminalization of marijuana use. Several states relaxed laws concerning the possession of small amounts of the drug, beginning with Oregon in 1973. President Carter even came out in favor of decriminalizing the possession of one ounce of marijuana. None of the states decriminalizing marijuana experienced significant changes in patterns of drug use or abuse.[31] In fact, data from 1982 show that in Alaska, which decriminalized marijuana on state constitutional grounds in 1975, daily marijuana use was lower than the national average.[32]

More meaningful comparisons may be gleaned from an analysis of more extensive experimental drug policies in Britain and the Netherlands. The Netherlands has pursued a policy of tolerance toward drug use since the 1960s. The Dutch have not legalized drug use and drug trafficking. In fact, the Dutch target drug trafficking in their drug enforcement efforts and 60 percent of all new prison cells built in 1990 will house violators of drug laws.[33] The official policy of the Netherlands is to pursue a "balanced" strategy that combines law enforcement strategies with treatment and education.

An important element of the Dutch strategy is to allow discretion by police in the enforcement of drug laws. This is particularly true for the enforcement of marijuana laws since the drug is considered less "dangerous" than cocaine, heroin, or other illicit substances. According to the Dutch Ministry of Welfare, Health and Cultural Affairs, marijuana use has stabilized in recent years even though it is effectively decriminalized. While cocaine use has increased, Dutch authorities do not believe the increase is "alarming" and in keeping with broader trends evident in other countries that pursue a narrower prohibitionist strategy.

Marijuana can be sold in small amounts with little risk of arrest or imprisonment. Stores and shops display signs indicating that marijuana is sold on the premises. Despite this policy of radical tolerance (by U.S. law enforcement standards), *marijuana use rates remain lower in the Netherlands* than in the United States or other European Nations.[34] A study conducted by the Amsterdam-based Foundation for the Scientific Study of Alcohol and Drug Abuse among 1,306 residents of Amsterdam found that marijuana use was 10 percent lower among fifteen to twenty-four year olds in the Netherlands compared to a similar group in the United States.[35] In summarizing the Dutch experience with drug tolerance, Arnold Trebach argues that "the youth of the Netherlands have not been harmed by one of the most tolerant drug policies of any country in the world."[36]

The experience of Britain with heroin is often cited as a case where a decriminalization strategy has failed. Physicians can prescribe almost any drug for long-term care of the organically ill in England, although prescriptions and dosages are monitored by the government. Britain attempted to solve its heroin problem by allowing physicians to prescribe heroin for addicts in an effort to reduce their dependency (eventually). Critics often note rising use rates as testimony that a medical approach to heroin addiction will not work. Yet, Britain has *never* embarked on a policy of widespread decriminalization and has continually enforced drug laws directed at trafficking as well as possession. Heroin use has increased in Britain, but at the same time that drug laws and enforcement efforts have become tougher.[37]

Unfortunately, these brief and limited examples of drug tolerance and marijuana decriminalization provide little help in assessing the efficacy of a broader decriminalization strategy. Yet, the fact that drug use did not increase substantially as a result of the more tolerant attitudes bears some significance for those favoring broad-based decriminalization or drug legalization. Even if drug use increased significantly, this pattern would not necessarily result in a substantial increase in the addict population.

Conclusion

A substantial philosophical schism exists between decriminalizers and prohibitionists that significantly undermines the prospects for developing a "third way." Decriminalization and prohibition advocates operate from different sets of principles. On the one hand, those proposing decriminalization emphasize individual accountability and responsibility. The role of public policy centers on the protectionist state where personal rights and freedoms are defended.

On the other side, prohibition advocates emphasize the importance of collectivism. "Society" has an obligation to impose certain standards on individual behavior even when the behavior is voluntary and rational. Prohibitionists, unlike many decriminalizers, view the state as a unified expression of a collective will that supersedes voluntary and peaceful actions of individual citizens.

Prohibition proponents have criticized decriminalization advocates for not proposing specific policy recommendations. This criticism, however, is a red herring. A detailed policy recommendation presumes that a consensus exists that America's drug policy should be reconstituted on the principles of decriminalization. Any recommended strategy will not satisfy prohibition proponents because they remain unconvinced that decriminalization is a legitimate or viable policy option.

The War on Drugs has created observable effects, many of them negative. Drug prohibition has not limited the accessibility of drugs for most potential users. On the contrary, drug accessibility has increased over the years. Yet, drug prohibition has resulted in huge drug profits that have facilitated the emergence of violent drug cartels. More peaceful, small-time traffickers have been excluded from legitimate economic markets, retreating to the violence of black-market operations. The black-market trade is an artifact of the legal system.

In the process, the War on Drugs is undermining the values that are essential components of the institutions favorable to economic development. By encouraging and sustaining an environment that reinforces violence and the arbitrary decisions of people instead of abstract principles embodied in the legal system, the respect for law and private property is weakened. Without these institutions, urban communities will continue to stagnate economically, further entrenching the underground economy as the foundation of the inner-city economic and social system.

Decriminalization will eliminate most (but not all) of the law enforcement problem that has emerged. It will also move public policy more in line with the principles necessary to promote economic and community development. As earlier chapters have attempted to outline, the "drug problem" today is largely a crime problem, manifesting itself in overcrowded jails, attenuation of civil liberties, and the expansion of the power of law enforcement agencies at the expense of freedom.

Decriminalization is offered as a first step toward refocusing drug policy on the human dimension. From a social perspective, the "drug problem" should encompass social controls over drug abuse and the consequences of addiction. Prohibiting any use of illicit drugs ignores the complexities of drug use and addiction. Decriminalization admits that not all drug use, like not all alcohol use, is drug abuse.

The argument for decriminalization rests on an understanding that America's current "drug problem" is not a "drug addiction" or a "drug abuse" problem. The harms associated with drug use and abuse revolve around the violence and apparent chaos in the inner cities, which, in turn, is an unintended consequence of public policy. Decriminalization would allow policymakers and policy analysts to focus on the consequences of drug use. The current regime concerns itself almost exclusively with the legal dimensions.

Broadly speaking, the decriminalization argument acknowledges that economics figures prominently in any solution to the drug problem. The foot soldiers of the drug industry are taken from the ranks of the unemployed with few realistic options in the legitimate economy. In addition, as long as a demand for illicit drugs exists, profits will persist. Eventually, as long as the industry remains underground, the effects will become violent and destructive. Only by acknowledging the limits of public policy in a free society and the fundamentally economic character of the drug problem in the United States can the problem be addressed substantively. Ultimately, decriminalization of heroin, cocaine, and marijuana provides the most realistic and progressive alternative.

Notes

1. For a popular review of the pros and cons of legalization, see George J. Church, "Thinking the Unthinkable," *Time*, 20 May 1988, pp. 12-19.
2. Ethan A. Nadelmann, "Drug Prohibition in the United States: Costs, Consequences, and Alternatives," *Science* 245, no. 4921 (1 September 1989): 939.
3. For a brief discussion of Szasz's perspective and a thoroughly libertarian argument, see Thomas Szasz, "The War Against Drugs," *Journal of Drug Issues* 12, no. 2 (Winter 1982): 115-22; and the path-breaking work *Ceremonial Chemistry: The Ritual Persecution of Drugs, Addicts, and Pushers*, rev. ed. (Holmes Beach, Fl.: Learning Publications, 1985).
4. Michael C. Monson, "The Dirty Little Secret Behind Our Drug Laws," *Reason*, November 1980, p. 52.
5. Steven Wisotsky, *Beyond the War on Drugs: Overcoming a Failed Public Policy* (Buffalo, NY: Prometheus Books, 1990).
6. Milton Friedman, "An Open Letter to Bill Bennett," *Wall Street Journal*, 7 September 1989, reprinted in *The Crisis in Drug Prohibition*, ed. David Boaz, (Washington, D.C.: Cato Institute, 1990), 114-16.
7. William S. Maddox and Stuart A. Lilie, *Beyond Liberal and Conservative: Reassessing the Political Spectrum* (Washington, D.C.: Cato Institute, 1984). These results included broad classifications of libertarians. If voters were considered "conservative" on economic issues and "liberal" on social issues, they were classified as libertarians.
8. Mervin Field, "Trends in American Politics," in *Left, Right, and Babyboom: America's New Politics*, ed. David Boaz (Washington, D.C.: Cato Institute, 1986), 15-21.
9. William F. Buckley, Jr., "Legalize Dope," *Washington Post*, 1 April 1985, sec. A, p. 11.
10. Richard C. Cowan, "How the Narcs Created Crack," *National Review* 38, no. 23 (December 1986): 28-29.
11. David Boaz, "Let's Quit the Drug War," *New York Times*, 17 March 1988.
12. Reported in Tom Bowman, "Drug Summit's Emphasis Misplaced, Schmoke Says," (Baltimore, Md.) *Sun*, 3 June 1989.
13. Arnold S. Trebach, *The Great Drug War: And Radical Proposals That Could Make America Safe Again* (New York: Macmillan, 1987). Trebach does not believe in the legalization of all drugs. Publicly, he favors the legalization of marijuana although he thinks it should be taxed heavily and the proceeds used to fund drug treatment (see pp. 368-69).
14. Bowman, "Drug Summit."
15. Kurt Schmoke, "Drugs: A Problem of Health and Economics," *Washington Post*, 15 May 1988; reprinted in Boaz, *The Crisis in Drug Prohibition*, 9-12.
16. William Bennett's remarks occurred after federal judge Robert Sweet in New York announced he was in favor of legalization in December 1989.
17. This claim was made by Representative Schroader during a debate on drug legalization sponsored by *Firing Line*.
18. See John Kaplan, *The Hardest Drug: Heroin and Public Policy* (Chicago: University of Chicago Press, 1983); Mark A.R. Kleiman, *Marijuana: Costs of Abuse, Costs of Control* (New York: Greenwood Press, 1989).

19. Quoted in "Bennett: Legalized Drug Idea 'Stupid,'" *USA Today*, 18 December 1989, sec. A, p. 3.
20. A.M. Rosenthal, "Legalize Drugs: A Good Case for Slavery," *Dayton Daily News*, 7 January 1990, sec. B, p. 7. Reprinted from the *New York Times*.
21. Charles Krauthammer, "Mistakes of the Legalizers," *Washington Post*, 13 April 1990, sec. A, p. 25.
22. James A. Inciardi, "The Case Against Legalization," in *The Drug Legalization Debate*, ed. James A. Inciardi (Newbury Park, Calif.: Sage Publications, 1991), 56.
23. Ibid., 57.
24. Lloyd Johnston, "I Think We're Playing A Game We Can't Win," in *Drugs: Old Problem New Options* (Detroit, Mich.: The Detroit News, 1988), 11-12.
25. Ibid., 13. See also Gina Kolata, "Old and Weak: Crack Users' Image Falls," *New York Times*, 23 July 1990, sec. A, p. 14.
26. David F. Musto, *The American Disease: Origins of Narcotic Control*, exp. ed. (New York: Oxford University Press, 1987), 22.
27. Quoted in Alan L. Otten, "Experts in the Field Of Narcotics Debate Ways to Curb Abuse," *Wall Street Journal* 29 November 1984, p. 20.
28. William Raspberry, "Don't Legalize Drugs," *Washington Post*, 26 May 1989.
29. Inciardi, however, has argued that violence will escalate with legalization. While the violence associated with the drug trade might decrease, violence associated with the pharmocological affects of drug use would increase. Although the present author believes Inciardi's point is important, his conclusion that "in all likelihood *any declines in systemic violence would be accompanied by corresponding increases in psychopharmacologic violence*" (emphasis in original) seems much too strong given the evidence he presents. See Inciardi, "The Case *Against* Legalization," 58-59.
30. Cowan, "How the Narcs Created Crack," 28.
31. A review of this episode in American political history can be found in Musto, *The American Disease*, 262-269.
32. Trebach, *Great Drug War*, 103.
33. "Fact Sheet on the Netherleands: Drug Policy" (Ministry of Welfare, Health and Cultural Affairs, The Netherlands, 1989), 3.
34. Douglas McVay, "Marijuana Legalization: The Time is Now," in Inciardi, *The Drug Legalization Debate*, 157. See also L. Erik Calonius, "The Drug Trade: Controversy Surrounds the Ways the Dutch Treat Heroin Addicts," *Wall Street Journal*, 5 December 1984, pp. 1, 17.
35. Reported in Trebach, *Great Drug War*, 105.
36. Ibid., 105. For a dissenting opinion, see Jeffrey Eisenach and Andrew Cowin, "Fighting Drugs in Four Countries: Lessons for America?" *Backgrounder No. 790* (Washington, D.C.: Heritage Foundation, 24 September 1990).
37. Trebach, *Great Drug War*, 305. The experience of Britain with respect to the efficacy of prescribing heroin to addicts moves beyond the scope of this book. For those interested in the subject, one of the most extensive analyses of the British experience is contained in Arnold S. Trebach, *The Heroin Solution* (New Haven, Conn.: Yale University Press, 1982), 171-225.

PART IV

CONCLUSION

9

Decriminalization, the Drug Economy, and the Future of American Cities

The War on Drugs has taken center stage in most major American cities during the 1980s and promises to continue well into the 1990s. Television crews routinely enter into the bowels of our inner cities, tracking down the "drug problem" for mass media consumption. Despite billions of dollars poured into this war, little progress is evident: drug-related crime is increasing, the number of users has not decline significantly, new innovations (e.g., crack and ecstasy) are introduced, and more crack babies appear on the nation's television sets.

While many have discussed the role government can take in the national assault on the market for illicit drugs, few have analyzed its role in creating and sustaining the social ills associated with the industry. Even fewer have focused on the consequences of the drug industry as a major component of modern urban economies. This book has attempted to focus concretely on the implications of current drug policy and the drug industry for economic development.

Rather than alleviate the consequences of drug abuse, current policy has encouraged the spread of drug-related crime. Current policy has made drug use a criminal problem rather than a health problem. By focusing on a supply-side enforcement strategy that maintains extraordinarily high profit margins for drug traffickers, the negative attributes of the underworld now pervade the economic and social systems of American cities. The results of this inquiry have led to a seemingly

243

radical, although rational, policy recommendation: illicit drugs should be decriminalized.

Public Policy and Urban Development

The modern city has undergone radical economic and social transformations during the post-World War II era. The startlingly rapid out-migration of employment and population during the 1950s and 1960s left previously vibrant central cities empty and stagnant. Employment opportunities declined for low-skilled, poorly educated workers as manufacturing firms moved out, or were replaced by high-technology companies requiring a more skilled work force. Within a few decades, diverse urban neighborhoods became impoverished centers inhabited by those who could not afford to move to the suburbs.

The inability of many cities to revitalize the low-income areas of their cities facilitated the emergence and development of a vast underground drug economy. Ironically, many of the very characteristics that make central cities the administrative and service hub of their region facilitate the drug trade (which is largely a marketing and distribution industry). Major cities provide a natural staging area for the drug industry through their location as major ports of entry and their transportation links to major regional markets. Many cities have population densities high enough to effectively hide substantial underground economies. The structural transformation of urban economies has left a reserve of underemployed youth more than willing to seize any potentially lucrative economic activity. Once the full breadth of underground economic activity is considered, cities have proven remarkably adaptive in responding to economic crises.

Property Rights and Public Policy

Public policy on local and national levels has inadvertently encouraged the growth of underground economic activity by changing the rules of the game in the legitimate economy. The adherence to basic rules of behavior began to weaken as the right of private individuals—homeowners, tenants, and businessmen—to use and control their property has eroded. The power of policymakers and bureaucracies to control economic life in the city has expanded dramatically as zoning and eminent domain were used to pursue abstract political goals. Private property became subject to the whims of policymakers as local governments increasingly used their authority to pursue objectives irrespective of the rights of those affected by the decision. Private property rights are acknowledged only to the extent the use of property conforms to the wishes and desires of the ruling public officials.

The use of government power to restrict private property rights has become even more prevalent in the modern city as local policymakers have attempted to stimulate economic development. These trends have destabilized the central city as an investment center. The result has been increasing regulation in urban economic development, which, in turn, has stimulated the growth of underground economies. Ironically, in the pursuit of economic development, local public policy has weakened the institutional foundations necessary to sustain long-term economic development.

These changes parallel similar property-rights infringements evident in the War on Drugs. Public policy in the war has sought to weaken the rights of the individual relative to the authority of the state. The Bill of Rights is applied in criminal cases with the "drug exception" in which suspects are routinely subjected to search and property seizures that violate the spirit (and sometimes the letter) of constitutional restraints on law enforcement.

Sentences are becoming longer and the ability of law enforcement agencies to use arbitrary force to coerce citizens is increasing. In some cases, such as property seizures, being a suspect in a drug case permits law enforcement authorities to set aside constitutional protections of due process and the right to privacy.

Property Rights and the Drug Trade

The destabilizing influence of public policy in the legitimate economy and criminal justice system has been compounded by the rise of the drug economy. Disturbing parallels exist between the rules governing individual behavior in the legal and illegal economic sectors. In the legal sector, success often depends on the willingness of public officials to sanction or underwrite private business activities.

Similarly, drug trafficking is characterized by rules that emphasize arbitrary political will over abstract laws. The illicit drug industry is founded on personal power and personal law, with violence a routine and accepted enforcement mechanism. Contracts are difficult to enforce since peaceful means for resolving disputes are unavailable. The rule that ensures survival in the illicit drug industry is "might makes right." The gang that is capable of marshaling the largest army of enforcers will prevail in the street wars of the drug trade. The abrogation of law and order (crime) makes inner cities even more inhospitable as potential investment areas.

Property Rights and Economic Development

The effect of public policy and the emerging influence of the drug trade has been to weaken the institutional foundations necessary to sustain economic growth and development. Businesses will invest in an enterprise (or location) only if they feel their interests will be protected long enough to earn a profit. The more unstable the property-rights structure of a city, the less likely it is that it will be able to sustain economic growth. By encouraging the breakdown of law and order in the legitimate economy, the underground economy, and the criminal justice system, public policy is systematically undermining the very social structure that enables economic growth and development to occur at all. To the extent urban policy encourages the abrogation of these property rights, economic development remains tenuous.

The values that are an inherent part of the drug trade work against the long-term interests of the traffickers as well. Without the ability to negotiate and enforce contracts peaceably, agreements break down and must eventually be settled through force and flagrant coercion. Success in the drug industry is fleeting since, at any time, an entrepreneurial trafficker's organization can be toppled by a well-orchestrated attack by law enforcement authorities or rival dealers. In fact, many trafficking organizations are short-term ventures, lasting only a few years and ending in the death, injury, or incarceration of their leaders.

Clearly, the effects of the drug trade move far beyond the illicit drug industry. As drug trafficking undermines the institutional foundations for economic growth in the drug industry, the effects spill over into neighborhoods and legitimate businesses as well. A neighborhood racked by drug-related violence will face difficulty attracting or retaining legitimate enterprises. Further, the neighborhoods will be inhabited by either those that want to be near the trade or those that cannot afford to move out.

Public policy perpetuates these effects by ensuring that the drug trade remains lucrative and profitable. By further excluding drug traffickers from the judicial system (which could peacefully resolve contract disputes), public policy encourages the violence. Clearly, the peculiarly violent nature of the drug trade is a direct result of its legal status. To the extent that it involves underground economic activity with a guiding set of rules that enhance or destroy the institutional foundations for development, the "drug problem" is an economic development problem as well as a public health problem.

Drug Policy as a Crime Policy

One of the most prominent features of drug trafficking, aside from its characteristic violence, is the number of inner-city minority youth employed in the industry. In some cities, as many as one in four young adult males traffic in drugs on at least a part-time basis. The economic incentives to sell drugs are substantial, often quadrupling earnings available in the legitimate economy.

Drug Dealing and Employment

These earnings, which translate into extraordinarily high per hour wage rates for many low-level traffickers, distort the incentives facing young adults. The perceptions of high wages prompt many (but by no means all) to maximize short-term income gains in drug trafficking and discount the nonpecuniary benefits of working in the legitimate economy.

Although most dealers leave their relatively lucrative career by their mid to late twenties, they have lost several years of valuable work experience in the legitimate economy. These lost years seriously truncate their training and employment career in the legitimate economy.

Ignored in much of the discussion of the drug trade, however, is the fact that older, more experienced traffickers require higher compensation to continue selling drugs. Most often, low- and mid-level dealers leave their trade by their late twenties and settle into legitimate jobs. Even in the lucrative drug trade, the risks of jail, injury, and death,—the inevitable consequences of prolonged exposure to the industry—cannot be overcome by money alone.

The War on Drugs has placed the most emphasis on the supply side of the drug industry: arresting traffickers and reducing drugs at their source. The effect has been to create a crime tariff that reflects the risks of working in an illegal industry. In fact, the income gains experienced by drug traffickers almost perfectly offsets the supernormal risks to injury, death, and incarceration that form such a visible and debilitating part of the industry. As many drug traffickers mature, they begin requiring higher returns for the risks they undertake in selling drugs.

The supply-side strategy spearheaded on the federal level and implemented largely on the local level has greatly facilitated the development of an industry capable of employing thousands of underemployed inner-city youth. The low-skilled blue-collar manufacturing jobs have been replaced by white-collar sales jobs in the illicit drug industry. The requirements of success for low-level dealers are a healthy respect for your supervisors, the willingness to protect your market at "all costs," enthusiasm for the job, perseverance and intelligence. Formal education is unnecessary. Skills such as quality control, inventory management, and employee supervision are taught on the job. Productivity is determined by sales volume under the watchful eye of a higher-level distributor.

Public policy must concentrate on ways that the energy and entrepreneurial skills of these young adults can be brought back into the legitimate economy. Framing drug policy in the rhetoric of drug abuse ignores the far more damaging consequences of sustaining a vibrant drug trade. The focus of drug policy should be on how public policy affects the incentives and choices faced by the young adult with few employment opportunities and little hope for a future in the high-technology legal economy.

Public Policy and Drug Use

Moreover, despite the persistent efforts of federal, state, and local narcotics enforcement units, government narcotics agencies have done little to reduce the accessibility of illicit drugs. One of the great untold stories of the drug war may revolve around the unwillingness of teenagers and young adults to use them. Despite the fact that almost 90 percent of all high school seniors report that marijuana is easy to get, less than 50 percent report ever using it. Despite the fact that well over half of all seniors report that cocaine is easy to get, 12 percent report ever having used it. Despite the fact over 30 percent of all high school seniors say they could obtain heroin if they wanted it, significantly less than 2 percent ever do. Of the over 30 million Americans who have ever used marijuana, cocaine, or heroin, less than 2 or 3 million are regular users or addicts in the medical sense. These statistics hardly paint a portrait of a society unable to control drug use through its exposure to the products.

Only a policy that effectively eliminates (or greatly reduces) the extraordinary profits of the drug trade will be capable of moderating the wage distortions clearly evident in many major American cities with large local drug industries. By eliminating the supply-side scourge now encompassing the drug industry, a substantive demand-side policy strategy can be developed with a focus on reducing the demand for drugs and increasing the legitimate economic opportunities for underemployed inner-city youth.

Decriminalization as an Essential Component
of any Long-Term Solution

American drug policy should be realigned according to the potential harms of drug abuse and the economic development needs of American cities. As long as drug policy ignores the demand side of the drug-use equation, little headway will ever be made in the battle to reduce drug addiction and abuse. Drug policy, through most of U.S. history, has been supply-side oriented, implicitly assuming that eradication of the source would miraculously reduce the demand for illicit drugs. The reality has been the persistence of a drug industry feeding on the demand for illicit psychoactive substances. As law enforcement efforts become more concentrated, the drug industry becomes more violent, profitable, and debilitating.

Decriminalization is a strategic shift to a demand-side strategy that concentrates on education and treatment. Decriminalizing drug use and trafficking will greatly increase our ability to cope with the human dimensions of drug abuse. Moreover, by shifting to a demand-side strategy, that uses comprehensive decriminalization as a cornerstone, urban policy can concentrate more fruitfully on the problem of urban economic growth and development.

In sum, a decriminalization strategy has several advantages over the prohibitionist ideology currently in place. First, decriminalization will refocus the debate on the health consequences of drug use. The standard for an effective drug policy should be its impact on drug abuse (including addiction). Policy, in this context, should focus on the abuse of substances rather than their ingestion per se. In the case of addiction, public policy should focus on developing a system that most effectively delivers the services to those who need it to help themselves. Current policy registers success by arrest rates and trends in drug-related crime (e.g., murders).

Public policy should also be designed to protect the rights and liberties of uninvolved third parties. An important derivative benefit of decriminalization would be the reduction of the fastest growing segment of the criminal population. By eliminating arrests for possession, use, and sale of drugs, the criminal justice system can focus its efforts on crimes against persons and property.

Second, local policymakers will be forced to address economic development issues for poor inner-city and minority residents. The current emphasis on drug trafficking and drug use detracts from a discussion of the economic development problems of these inner-city neighborhoods. Unfortunately, many of these neighborhoods are now sustained by underground economic activity of which drug trafficking is often the largest component. Constrained employment opportunities and poor education systems undermine the long-term chances of their citizens. As long as drug trafficking remains illegal and a steady demand for illicit drugs continues, the drug trade will persist as the most lucrative employment opportunity in the inner city.

Third, decriminalization will restore respect for law and public policy. The values, rules, and customs that have formed the institutional foundation for economic development and progress since the eighteenth century have been assaulted systematically in both the legitimate and illegal economic sectors. The prospects for a long-term solution to the problems of the inner city are unlikely to emerge without a fundamental restructuring of the property-rights structure of the city. Decriminalization would be a first step toward establishing a consistent and stable system of rights and responsibilities capable of sustaining economic development in the long run by reversing the systematic assault on civil liberties and property rights by governments on all levels.

Conclusion

The limits of a decriminalization strategy should be acknowledged. Decriminalization will not eliminate America's historical affinity for psychoactive substances.

Decriminalization alone will not eliminate drug abuse and addiction. The benefits of a decriminalization strategy lie in its ability to substantially reduce the socially destructive unintended consequences of prohibition.

Decriminalization will place drug policy on a more realistic and solid footing. If the harms of drug abuse revolve around the effects on the physical and mental capacities of citizens, public policy should be designed to address those issues directly. Current policy feigns concern for the health effects of drug use, concentrating its efforts on law enforcement and criminal punishment. This strategy has severely handicapped the contemporary city and the consequences move far the beyond number of addicts or street level traffickers put in jail.

America's inner cities can no longer afford to adhere to the prohibitionist ideology that underlies current drug policy. As long as demand for these drugs persists, and official policy takes an aggressive supply-side drug control strategy, public policy will be an unwitting partner in the destruction of the economic and social fabric of urban America. The United States must acknowledge the consequences of a failed public policy. Only a move toward comprehensive decriminalization can restore the efficacy of public policy and move policymakers toward solving the complex economic development problems of cities.

Index

253